Marketing Strategy for Museums

Marketing Strategy for Museums is a practical guide to developing and delivering marketing that supports museums' missions and goals. Explaining how museums can be strategic and proactive in their approach, it also shows how to make effective decisions with limited resources.

Presenting examples from a range of museums around the world, the author positions marketing as a vital function that aims to build mutually beneficial relationships between museums and their audiences – both existing and new – and ensure museums are relevant and viable. Breaking down key marketing models, Lister shows how they can be applied to museums in a meaningful way. She also lays out a step-by-step framework for developing a museum's marketing strategy and for creating marketing campaigns, which can be scaled up or down. Readers will also be encouraged to reflect on topics such as sustainable marketing, ethical marketing, and accessible and inclusive marketing.

Marketing Strategy for Museums provides an accessible guide that seeks to demystify marketing and boost the confidence of those responsible for planning and delivering marketing in museums. It is aimed at people working in museums of all types and sizes and will also be relevant to students of museum and heritage studies.

Christina Lister is a marketing consultant with over 20 years of experience working in marketing, audience development, and PR in a range of agency, in-house, and consultancy roles. Her experience has included international marketing for a global skincare brand as well as PR and communications for a range of leisure, public sector, tourism, and not-for-profit organisations. Over the past 15 years, Christina has specialised in developing marketing strategies, facilitating workshops, running training, and providing mentoring for cultural and heritage organisations including museums, libraries, archives, festivals, arts centres, and theatres. She has worked extensively with larger museums and sector support organisations such as the Museum of London, the Arts Marketing Association, and the Association of Independent Museums, as well as many smaller and independent museums including Jane Austen's House and the Museum of Cambridge. She is a strategic thinker with an insight-driven approach, and her work has won a range of marketing and PR awards. She is passionate about championing audiences, and passionate about the impact that effective and meaningful marketing and audience development can have.

Routledge Guides to Practice in Museums, Galleries and Heritage

This series provides essential practical guides for those working in museums, galleries, and a variety of other heritage professions around the globe.

Including authored and edited volumes, the series will help to enhance practitioners' and students' professional knowledge and will also encourage sharing of best practices between different countries, as well as between different types and sizes of organisations.

Titles published in the series include:

Museums and Interactive Virtual Learning
Allyson Mitchell, Tami Moehring, and Janet Zanetis

The Sustainable Museum
How Museums Contribute to the Great Transformation
Christopher J. Garthe

Museums and Well-being
Rose Cull and Daniel Cull

A Practical Guide to Costumed Interpretation
Jacqueline Lee

Viewing Art with Babies
First Encounter
Kathy Danko-McGhee

Marketing Strategy for Museums
A Practical Guide
Christina Lister

For more information about this series, please visit: https://www.routledge.com/Routledge-Guides-to-Practice-in-Museums-Galleries-and-Heritage/book-series/RGPMGH

Marketing Strategy for Museums
A Practical Guide

Christina Lister

LONDON AND NEW YORK

First published 2024
by Routledge
4 Park Square, Milton Park, Abingdon, Oxon OX14 4RN

and by Routledge
605 Third Avenue, New York, NY 10158

Routledge is an imprint of the Taylor & Francis Group, an informa business

© 2024 Christina Lister

The right of Christina Lister to be identified as author of this work has been asserted in accordance with sections 77 and 78 of the Copyright, Designs and Patents Act 1988.

All rights reserved. No part of this book may be reprinted or reproduced or utilised in any form or by any electronic, mechanical, or other means, now known or hereafter invented, including photocopying and recording, or in any information storage or retrieval system, without permission in writing from the publishers.

Trademark notice: Product or corporate names may be trademarks or registered trademarks, and are used only for identification and explanation without intent to infringe.

British Library Cataloguing-in-Publication Data
A catalogue record for this book is available from the British Library

Library of Congress Cataloging-in-Publication Data
Names: Lister, Christina, author.
Title: Marketing strategy for museums : a practical guide / Christina Lister.
Description: Abingdon, Oxon ; New York, NY : Routledge, 2024. | Series: Routledge guides to practice in museums, galleries and heritage | Includes bibliographical references and index.
Identifiers: LCCN 2023029510 (print) | LCCN 2023029511 (ebook) | ISBN 9781032313177 (hbk) | ISBN 9781032313153 (pbk) | ISBN 9781003309147 (ebk)
Subjects: LCSH: Museums--Marketing.
Classification: LCC AM121 .L57 2024 (print) | LCC AM121 (ebook) | DDC 069.068/8--dc23/eng/20230706
LC record available at https://lccn.loc.gov/2023029510
LC ebook record available at https://lccn.loc.gov/2023029511

ISBN: 978-1-032-31317-7 (hbk)
ISBN: 978-1-032-31315-3 (pbk)
ISBN: 978-1-003-30914-7 (ebk)

DOI: 10.4324/9781003309147

Typeset in Times New Roman
by MPS Limited, Dehradun

For E and O. Everything, always.

Contents

List of figures and tables   ix
Acknowledgements   x

Introduction   1

PART I
Marketing as a bridge   5

  1 Museums   7
  2 Marketing   18
  3 Audiences   29

PART II
Marketing strategy in practice   43

  4 Managing and implementing marketing   45
  5 Developing a museum marketing strategy   52
5a Situational analysis: Where are we now?   57
5b Goals and objectives: Where are we going?   69
5c Target audiences: Whom do we want to reach?   75
5d Strategy and approach: How will we get there?   86
5e Tactics and action plan: What are we going to do to get there?   98
5f Resources: What will it cost?   106

5g Monitoring and evaluation: How will we know if we've
   got there?   113
6 Planning and delivering a marketing campaign   125

PART III
Deeper dives   135

7 Branding   137
8 Pricing   146
9 Communication channels   159
10 Messaging   169
11 Accessible and inclusive marketing   177
12 Ethical marketing   190

Bibliography   *206*
Index   *213*

Figures and Tables

Figures

2.1	An illustration highlighting the more visible and behind-the-scenes elements of marketing	19
5b.1	An example audience journey	71
5d.1	An example product life cycle	89
5d.2	An example positioning map	96
6.1	A billboard from the Natural History Museum's "Come to life" campaign	132
6.2	Posters from the Natural History Museum's "Come to life" campaign	132
7.1	The logo of the Museum of East Anglian Life	142
7.2	The logo of the Food Museum	143

Tables

1.1	How the Natural History Museum's mission and vision statements have changed between 2009 and 2023	14
5a.1	Comparing a museum's offer with competitors	64
5a.2	An example STEEPLE analysis	66
5a.3	An example SWOT analysis	67
5b.1	Examples of goals, objectives, and KPIs	73
5c.1	Factors affecting the choice of target audiences	77
5d.1	An example TOWS analysis	87
5d.2	An example product/audience grid	88
5d.3	An example Ansoff Matrix	91
5d.4	An example Dual Bottom Line Matrix	93
5g.1	Example outputs and outcomes	115
6.1	The stages, channels, and KPIs of an example sales funnel	129
9.1	A template example audience journey grid	164

Acknowledgements

A huge thank you to the following people for generously contributing to this book, answering initial research questions, which shaped its direction; sharing their reflections and experience; and giving permission for me to quote or reference their work or words. The book is infinitely stronger as a result, and I will always be thankful for your support and input.

Garrett Ammon, Pete Austin, Alison Bowyer, Georgina Brooke, Robin Cantrill-Fenwick, Heather Carey, Millie Carroll, Matthew Cock, Jenny Cousins, Merelina Davies, Joshua Davies, Annie Davis, Gini Dietrich, Colleen Dilenschneider, Bernard Donoghue, Russell Dornan, Annie Duffield, Lizzie Dunford, Jonathan Durnin, Jamie Everitt, Bethany C. Gotschall, Amelia Harvell, Jacqueline Haxton, Emily Hicks, Cath Hume, Selen İşyar, Shaina Jagtiani, Elinor James, Simon Kemp, Geraldine Kendall Adams, Adam Koszary, Rachel Kuhn, Anna Lundberg, Simon Manchipp, Oliver Mantell, Katherine McAlpine, Batul Raaj Mehta, Supriya Menon, Margaret Middleton, Steve Mills, Kelly Molson, Professor Christine Moorman, Mike Murawski, Lina Olsson, Richard Orr, Francesca Pellegrino, Jennifer Raw, Lindsey Roffe, Outi Salonlahti, Sari Salovaara, Steve Slack, Jon Sleigh, Matt Smith, Shane Smith, Jen Staves, Chris Unitt, Ivan Wadeson, Professor Ben Walmsley, and Dr. Alexandra Woodall.

A special shout-out to Marge Ainsley and Rebecca Morris-Buck, whose extensive feedback and words of encouragement have meant so much to me.

Thanks also to the following organisations, which have kindly allowed me to feature their research, work, or images in the book:

The Arts Marketing Association, The Association of Independent Museums, The Association of Leading Visitor Attractions, The Audience Agency, The Centre for Cultural Value, Collins Learning, Culture for All Service Finland, The Creative Industries Policy And Evidence Centre, Baker Richards, Decision House, Durnin Research, The Food Museum, Good-Loop, HubSpot, IMPACTS Experience (an offshoot of IMPACTS Research & Development), Imperial War Museums, Ipsos, Jane Austen's House, Kepios, Kids in Museums, Know Your Own Bone, Morris Hargreaves McIntyre, The Museum of Art & Photography, The Museum of Cambridge, Museums Aren't Neutral, The Museums Association, One Further, The Postal Museum, Rahmi

M. Koç Museum, Rubber Cheese, SHARE Museums East, SomeOne, Vocal Eyes, We Are Social.

Thank you to NinaBrownDesign for the graphic on the book cover, the latest of our many collaborations. Thank you to Heidi Lowther and Manas Roy at Routledge, and Kate Pool at the Society of Authors for your input and expertise. And finally, a big thank you to colleagues, clients, and fellow consultants whom I have learnt so much from. What a treat it is to work alongside you and a joy to do this work.

Introduction

Marketing and museums have many similarities. They are multilayered and complex, serving different stakeholders and purposes. They have uncomfortable elements in parts of their histories. They make significant contributions to the economy. They are dynamic and evolve proactively, as well as reactively out of necessity as society and their environment changes. They can provoke strong responses – both have their devotees and critics – but they also face ambivalence and misunderstanding. Combine the two marketing and museums, and we have the basis of what I hope will be an interesting and valuable book.

The aims of this book

This book is a practical guide to developing and delivering museum marketing. It aims to demystify marketing and advocate for its fundamental role in museum practice, supporting a museum's overall purpose and organisational goals, and building mutually beneficial relationships between museums and their audiences. The book explores how museums can position and market themselves successfully to stand out in a crowded marketplace and how they can identify, reach, and connect with audiences. It breaks down key marketing models, showing how they can be applied to museums in an accessible and meaningful way, alongside examples from a broad range of museums.

I hope this book will support museums to become more strategic and proactive in their marketing and ultimately, as a result, more relevant and sustainable. I hope it will boost the confidence of those responsible for planning and delivering marketing activities, enabling them to make effective decisions on how to use limited resources. And I hope it will help people enjoy the process. This book answers questions I am frequently asked as a consultant and trainer, including:

- How can marketing most effectively support our museum's overall mission?
- How do we write a marketing strategy?
- What's the best way of planning a marketing campaign?
- How do we decide which audiences to target?

DOI: 10.4324/9781003309147-1

- How can I advocate for the role of marketing within our museum to senior managers and trustees?
- How do we decide which communication channels to use?
- How can we ensure that our marketing is in line with our museum's values?

This book is not a magic wand that will deliver effortless wins overnight, and since technology and communication platforms evolve so quickly, this book is also not the best place to provide a detailed breakdown of how to use them – the latest guidance and best practice can be found online. Instead, the book proposes principles, ideas, frameworks, and practical inspiring examples, which I hope will encourage museums to reflect and develop marketing more strategically, cohesively, and ethically, to support their relevance and viability in the long term.

Who is this book for?
I've written this book for anyone working in, studying, or simply interested in learning more about museum marketing and the role it plays within and for museums. This includes staff, trustees, and volunteers, with varying levels of involvement in, experience of, and responsibility for marketing. Whilst marketing budgets, skills, and capacity vary enormously between museums, the processes and principles set out in the book have broad relevance and tailored to different museums' needs. The book's mix of content may introduce you to some topics and boost your existing knowledge of others; it may develop or reframe your thinking around marketing; and it could provide broader perspectives and ideas.

Using this book
This book is intended as a digestible reference guide that can frequently be dipped into, as well as a book that can be read from cover to cover. I'd love for this book to act as your companion, guiding you as you undertake or study museum marketing; as a source of encouragement, inspiring you with a broad range of case studies from museums across the globe; as a prompt, opening your eyes to different marketing tools and models you can apply; and as accountability, providing you with cues to keep questioning, exploring, experimenting, and refining what you do.

This is not an encyclopaedic guide to museum marketing, but my thoughts, experiences, and perspectives to contribute to the conversation. Whilst there's not a one-size-fits-all solution, principles and frameworks presented can be scaled up or down depending on the scope, budget, and resources you have available. Although the book focuses on museums, much of its content is also applicable to other heritage and cultural organisations, such as galleries and heritage sites.

I present some core marketing models that are relevant and valuable to museums, as well as approaches and exercises that I have developed and used over the years. I take a holistic and strategic view of marketing, far beyond how marketing has often been pigeonholed as a tactical – not strategic – activity within museums, synonymous with publicity. There may also be elements of the book that you feel veer into audience development, income generation, visitor experience, or other fields, depending on your view of those functions and how marketing sits alongside them within your museum.

Part I features three core chapters that provide context – on museums, marketing, and audiences, which the rest of the book builds on. These chapters help define and anchor these terms, touching on their evolution and how they interrelate.

Part II looks at marketing strategy in practice: managing and implementing marketing in a museum and what marketing functions can look like; a step-by-step process on how to develop a marketing strategy, with individual chapters on each step; and a chapter on developing marketing campaigns, with examples throughout and several key marketing models explained.

Part III covers a more in-depth look at some of the topics featured in Parts I and II, allowing a deeper dive into these fundamental areas. They cover branding, pricing, communication channels, messaging, accessible and inclusive marketing, and ethical marketing. These standalone chapters can be read in any order depending on your interests and priorities.

By providing workshop ideas and questions throughout, I hope the book will encourage critical thinking and reflection. At the end of each chapter or theme, I suggest a few texts for readers who would like to delve into the subject in more detail. Beyond that, chapter reference lists and the bibliography at the end of the book contain a wealth of additional sources to explore, including many that are free to access.

This book draws on my 20 years of experience working in marketing, PR, and audience development across in-house, agency, and consultancy roles, including 15 years in the museums, heritage, and culture sectors. Spending the last 10 years as a consultant has given me an interesting perspective as a part-outsider and part-cross-pollinator, training representatives from hundreds of organisations, discovering the similarities and nuances of the challenges and opportunities they face, and absorbing and sharing lessons from them.

Most of the research I draw on – in particular around the history of museums and on audiences – is from Europe and the USA for brevity and because of the volume of available data that I could access freely and in English. But I have included examples and case studies from a range of museums (in terms of subjects, ownership, governance, location, budgets) from across the world. Whilst you will undoubtedly have heard of some of them, it was important to me to ensure that examples didn't just come from the usual suspects and household names. So many other museums are also doing excellent marketing, with insights that deserve to be shared. A huge and heartfelt thank you to everyone who took the time to share their experiences and work so generously with me, whether as part of background research or for inclusion in the book. Our conversations were a highlight of my research, and these contributions have unquestionably enriched both my practice and this book.

Part I
Marketing as a bridge

1 Museums

Introduction

Museum is an umbrella term that covers a huge variety of organisations, with vastly different funding sources and levels, governance, purposes, locations, facilities, programming, audiences, and more. They may be founded or run by national, regional, or local governments or universities; be independent, run by a charitable trust, or privately owned; and there are differences in the proportion of each type of museum in different countries across the world. Subject matters cover a rich spectrum – to give just a few examples to show the breadth, museums may:

- Have national collections such as the National Museum of Slovenia.
- Cover local areas or regions such as the Museum of Brisbane, Australia.
- Share the story of one person like Museo Frida Kahlo, Mexico.
- Be narrative-based, such as the Apartheid Museum in South Africa.
- Be community-centred, as is, for example, Santa Cruz Museum of Art & History, USA.
- Operate as multisite organisations like Tate (Tate Modern and Tate Britain in London, Tate Liverpool and Tate St Ives in the UK).
- Be quirky or on a specialist subject like The Museum of Miniature Books, Azerbaijan.
- Be outdoor museums such as the Estonian Open Air Museum.
- Be set by historic sites like the Petra Museum in Jordan.
- Be activist museums such as The Vagina Museum, UK.

More recent incarnations include digital-only museums such as Sweden's Internet Museum, and the Museum of Broken Relationships, a global crowd-sourced project that started as a temporary travelling exhibition and now also has permanent homes in Zagreb, Croatia, and Los Angeles, USA.

At one end of the spectrum, national museums often have enormous name recognition, multimillion-pound funding, hundreds of staff members, millions of visitors, and feature in top 10 lists of countries' visitor attractions. They have hero star objects, stage high-profile sold-out blockbuster exhibitions, provide

DOI: 10.4324/9781003309147-3

access to extensive and professional digital collections, sell huge ranges of merchandise, and have several catering outfits. At the other end of the spectrum, there are small, lesser-known museums run by passionate and knowledgeable volunteers, operating on tiny budgets, open only a few hours a week and closed during their winter season. They need *more* visitors as opposed to needing to consider crowd-control measures. And of course, there are countless museums that lie somewhere in between.

Whilst all museums are unique, many face similar challenges, such as attracting funding; balancing their many roles; increasing visitor numbers; broadening access; staying (or becoming) relevant; making decisions on repatriation and restitution; making choices about contemporary collecting; and satisfying and communicating with a huge range of stakeholders such as staff, volunteers, trustees, donors, visitors, funding bodies, national government, local government, local business organisations, tourist boards, and media.

This chapter begins with perceptions and definitions of museums, touching on their history and evolving purpose. It also looks at museum products, examines mission and vision statements, and finishes by summarising the implications of these discussions for museum marketing.

Perceptions of museums

There can be a difference between how people *in* the sector view and value museums compared with those *outside* of it – whether they are politicians, philanthropists, schoolchildren, the local community, or tourists. For example, members of the public are unlikely to know as much about the differences between an accredited and a non-accredited museum. Many of the issues that occupy the sector – and we tie ourselves in knots over – never reach public consciousness (with some exceptions, such as high-profile repatriation debates and sponsorship controversies). Some people may be ambivalent towards museums while for others, visiting is a regular and positive experience.

Trust in museums by members of the public tends to be very high: the 2021 Museums and Trust survey by the American Alliance of Museums found that museums ranked second only to friends and family on trust, making them more trustworthy than researchers and scientists, nongovernmental organisations (NGOs) generally, local and national news organisations, the government, corporations and business, and social media (2021, p. 9). The top three reasons cited are that museums are fact-based, present real/authentic/original objects, and are research-oriented (2021, p. 12). Similarly, a 2021 poll on trust in professions in Britain found that museum curators were joint fourth out of a list of 30 professions (behind nurses, librarians, and doctors), with 86% of respondents saying they would trust museum curators to tell the truth (Ipsos, 2021).

However, it's important to recognise that to others, the word *museum* can also provoke strong adverse feelings for a multitude of reasons. That could be because of a previous negative visit that now defines how they view all museums (perhaps lack of an accessible toilet or their child being told off), or a museum displaying sacred and ceremonial objects from their community of origin, despite repeated pleas from the community not to. And for the many people who never or rarely enter a museum, where do they get their references around museums from? Walking past an imposing building? Seeing simplified (or outdated) depictions of museums or curators in films and TV programmes? Even in searches for a graphic icon to represent a museum on common computer software, you'll typically find traditional images – such as a neo-classical building with pillars and steps, glass cabinets, or a rope screening off an area – which do not do justice to the breadth of work that museums do today.

Defining a museum

On the surface, "museum" is one of those words I imagine most people will use and never give much thought to. Dictionaries keep to straightforward and traditional definitions of museums, centred around preserving, studying, and displaying objects in a building. For example, the Collins Dictionary says a museum "is a building where a large number of interesting and valuable objects, such as works of art or historical items, are kept, studied, and displayed to the public" (no date).

Museums have existed throughout our lives, and we might walk, drive, or cycle past them; visit them with our school; see them in the news or promoted on posters at a bus stop or on the underground; see them in popular culture – the Paddington film (The Natural History Museum, London), as the backdrop for celebrities at the Met Gala (The Metropolitan Museum of Art), or in a music video by Beyoncé and Jay-Z (The Louvre). Scratch a bit deeper, however, and you have opened a can of worms. I want to give an overview of some of the issues that arise when trying to pin down a definition and purpose of museums, and why these matter to marketing. 'Museum' is not a protected word, so there is nothing stopping organisations from calling themselves that. And there is nothing forcing them to sign up to a code of conduct or accreditation scheme (although there are incentives such as being able to tap into some funding streams). The range of names used can also be confusing – how is a museum different from a gallery, and an art gallery different from an art museum? And not only can museums mean different things to different audiences and potential audiences, but also *within* the museums sector there isn't always agreement on what a museum is or should be.

Today the demands, goals, and expectations of museums are enormous, varied, and sometimes conflicting. From preserving collections to minimising their impact on the climate; from being educational to being entertaining; from increasing visitors to improving the visitor experience; and from growing income to opening up access. Museums are complex, heterogeneous entities, and their purpose has evolved. The time taken to develop a new definition of museums by ICOM (the International Council of Museums) between 2019 and 2022 – and the surrounding controversy – highlights this.

10 *Marketing as a bridge*

The discussion is not just about semantics – many national governments use ICOM's definition to determine their own definitions of museums and, therefore, which organisations are eligible for funding, so there can be significant implications of changes to the wording.

Lehmannová sets out ICOM's earlier iterations of its definition of museums including the first from 1946: "The word 'museum' includes all collections, open to the public, of artistic, technical, scientific, historical or archaeological material, including zoos and botanical gardens, but excluding libraries, except in so far as they maintain permanent exhibition rooms" (2020, pp. 2–3). When the time came to revise the definition in 2019 (following revisions in 1974 and 2007), ICOM received 269 proposals from members (ICOM, 2019). Its resulting proposal was put to members, and a heated debate with a split between more progressive and traditional wings ensued. The vote was postponed, and after a long period of further consultation, the following definition was approved at the ICOM General Conference in 2022 by 92% of the participants: "A museum is a not-for-profit, permanent institution in the service of society that researches, collects, conserves, interprets and exhibits tangible and intangible heritage. Open to the public, accessible and inclusive, museums foster diversity and sustainability. They operate and communicate ethically, professionally and with the participation of communities, offering varied experiences for education, enjoyment, reflection and knowledge sharing" (ICOM, 2022). This is more encompassing and progressive than previous definitions, although for some stakeholders it didn't go far enough.

The evolution of museums

The purpose of museums has evolved substantially since their inception. This chapter can't cover a comprehensive or global history of the development of museums, but there are some elements I include because of their relevance to marketing and the context they provide. Many of the challenges that museums are confronting today can be traced back to their origins. Early iterations of museums began as private collections of art or natural objects owned by the wealthy elite, housed in palaces and large private homes. Many collectors were passionate about their collections, and learning from them but displaying them in cabinets of curiosities or 'Wunderkammern' was also about status and showing off, with exclusive and restricted access. The Enlightenment period saw the development of universal museums and the idea of museums as a public space, as places for self-improvement and education. However, early public museums were still exclusive. After opening in 1759, visitors initially had to apply for tickets to enter the British Museum during limited opening hours, which meant that "entry was restricted to well-connected visitors who were given personal tours of the collections by the museum's Trustees and curators" (British Museum, no date).

How some of these objects were collected, structured, and displayed was problematic and racist, for example, objects that were looted or financed from enslaved labour. Many museums in Western Europe and the USA in particular are now confronting this legacy. The Ashmolean in Oxford opened as Britain's first public museum and the world's first university museum in 1683, and its website acknowledges, "the uncomfortable truth is that much of the collection was inevitably selected and obtained as a result of colonial power" (no date). Similarly, Manchester Museum's website states, "The museum was born of civic spirit, curiosity and ambition at the height of British colonial rule, and how we acknowledge, interrogate and address this complex history is critical and urgent work" (no date).

Museums gradually began opening up more. They became more professional and entrepreneurial, broadening their sources of income to include a range of earned income beyond public funding or endowments. National and international bodies – such as the UK's Museums Association (1889) and ICOM (1946) were formed and today provide a range of opportunities for the professionalisation of museum practice, including training, networking, codes of ethics, and advocacy. Museums have faced more scrutiny from funders and the public, becoming increasingly accountable and transparent in their evaluation and reporting.

Over time, museum audiences have ranged from exclusive patrons to curious visitors; passionate culture fans to indifferent browsers; informed consumers; engaged participants and co-producers; protestors and activists. In recent decades an expanded focus on inclusion, access, and participation has developed, which can range from authentic and effective, to well intentioned but misplaced, to tokenistic and counterproductive. Many museums have developed more community-centric approaches, enabling deeper audience engagement, and audiences to be involved in co-curation and participatory projects. Rather than just view objects passively, audiences can listen, touch, interact, question, and respond, as well as instigate, create, and curate projects in many museums. However, some practitioners still prefer a hierarchical approach to knowledge, valuing curatorial and academic expertise above community knowledge, lived experience, and involvement.

Many museums have broken down barriers to engagement, are dismantling their institutional power, and are undertaking more socially engaged practice and social justice work. The Museums Association's "Museums Change Lives" campaign seeks to highlight how museums are affecting people and communities (no date) and the *Creative Health: The Arts for Health and Wellbeing* report documented that 600 of the UK's 2,500 museums had programmes targeting health and well-being and advocated for the powerful contribution the arts can make to both (All-Party Parliamentary Group on Arts, Health and Wellbeing, 2017, p. 1).

Museums operate against a backdrop of ever-changing variables and challenges, including political change, the climate crisis, pandemics, war, natural disasters, and economic downturns. They are facing an evolving range of competitors for audiences' income, visitors, and attention. Despite decades of effort by some museums, other museums still have a long way to go to be welcoming to and representative of their communities. Many are starting to confront their impact on the environment, with some setting targets around their carbon emissions, but this work is still in its infancy for most.

In recent years Black Lives Matter protests calling for racial justice in the United States and beyond prompted renewed and intensified scrutiny over institutional racism within museums and a lack of diversity and representation within museum staff. Deep debates and media headlines have been generated around key issues such as decolonisation, repatriation, and restitution. Decades of public funding cuts have forced more commercial income generation, which has sometimes prompted ethical issues. There have been protests against exhibition sponsorship by fossil fuel companies and around the toxic philanthropy of accepting large donations from controversial donors (explored more in Chapter 12).

Many museums also form part of tourism campaigns promoting cities, regions, and countries. They can be used to bolster regional or national identity and pride. The museums sector makes substantial contributions to regional and national economies and employment. They have become more market oriented, identifying the needs and desires of audiences, and developing offerings that satisfy them. They operate and compete in the Experience Economy where organisations need to go beyond providing commodities, goods, and services, to providing audiences with memorable experiences (Pine and Gilmore, 2020). Some detractors criticise the so-called edutainment and Disneyfication of museums, which they see as dumbing down. For others, this is a long overdue necessity to ensure that museums remain relevant, accessible, and valuable to their communities and society today.

While some museums are struggling to fund adequate object preservation, building repair, and security, new museums in landmark buildings are being built; for example, the Grand Egyptian Museum is due to open in Giza, Egypt, in late 2023 as the world's largest archaeological museum dedicated to a single civilization (2023). National and international franchises of big-name museums have opened, with ambitious capital projects cementing these museums' roles in driving tourism and economic regeneration, changing the position or perceptions of a country or area, and being a manifestation of soft power. The "Bilbao effect" now describes the positive impact of the Guggenheim in Bilbao which helped to put the Spanish city on the international map and transformed its tourism economy.

Museum products

Throughout this book, I talk about museum products. It's a term that may not resonate with everyone, but I use it as a catch-all word for brevity. 'Products' are what a museum can offer audiences and stakeholders to satisfy their needs or wants. They can be a physical product, a digital product, a service, an event, experience, or programme. They can be charged for, or free. Today, museums offer a broad range of products and services, including temporary exhibitions, guided tours, trails, hands-on activities, lectures, workshops, performances, evening events, sleepovers; outreach and community programmes; schools and home education programmes; research opportunities and study rooms; conservation and research consultancy; artistic and creative residencies; access to their digital collections and image licensing; virtual events; books; friends and membership schemes; cafés, restaurants, and gift shops; venue hire for weddings, business events, awards ceremonies, and much more.

Different audiences value and want to access different products, just as their overall motivations, barriers, and visiting or engagement behaviours vary. For example, a museum café is a secondary product for some audiences, complementing or facilitating the experience and consumption of the main product. For others, the café is the primary product and reason for going; and others will never set foot in it.

Museums also offer more than simply a product or transactional service – they offer something intangible and experiential. The range of experiences and resulting emotions is vast. Audiences can have a moment of quiet contemplation and reflection, finally get to marvel at a famous artwork, connect with their own cultural heritage, discover something new, be moved, be inspired, have a go at a creative activity, understand a different perspective, have a giggle with friends, and so much more.

Mission and vision statements

Let's turn to the articulation of a museum's purpose, through its mission and/or vision statement. A museum's *mission* is its reason for existing or its purpose, its focus, and what it wants to achieve. It is a foundation and guides a strategic direction and decisions on priorities and actions. A museum's *vision* is its desired end-state, what the world or future will look like once the museum achieves its mission in the long term. For example, the charity Oxfam's vision is: "We believe in a kinder and radically better world, where everyone has the power to thrive not just survive," and its mission: "To achieve this, we must overcome poverty by fighting the injustices and inequalities that fuel it" (2020, p. 4).

A range of factors may influence a museum's mission, including:

- Its history, such as its founding mission.
- Big funders and donors.
- The law, expectations, or requirements from sector bodies or accreditation guidance.
- Staff, trustees, and volunteers – their priorities and ambitions for the museum.
- Broader trends in society, business, the museum sector.
- The museum's audiences, who they are, their needs and preferences.
- The museum's strengths and what makes it unique and distinctive.

- Practical factors, such as the museum's resources in terms of what mission it could realistically achieve, and how often the mission is revised.

A museum's mission and vision will often stay the same for years or even decades, whilst the organisational strategy to achieve them changes in the meantime. However, they, too, will also evolve, reflecting how priorities, society, and what is valued change over time. In recent decades, there's been a shift in thinking about museum mission and vision, moving towards something more outward-looking, often with societal impact; rather than an ambition of simply being the best or biggest, or an operational or functional explanation of preserving objects and safeguarding collections. The mission has developed from being *about something* to being *for someone or something*. One example to highlight this trend is from London's Natural History Museum in Table 1.1.

There is a huge variety of museums and, therefore, a huge breadth of mission and vision statements as demonstrated by this snapshot, drawn from some of the museums named earlier:

- The mission of the Apartheid Museum in South Africa is: "To remind us of the importance of fighting against racism, discrimination and prejudice" (no date).
- Santa Cruz Museum of Art and History: "Our mission is to bring people together through art and local history to explore our diverse cultures" (no date).
- Tate: "Our mission is to increase the public's enjoyment and understanding of British art from the sixteenth century to the present day and of international modern and contemporary art" (no date).

So, are mission and vision statements needed? Critics say a mission statement is meaningless and isn't referred to after it has been created; that it is expensive

Table 1.1 How the Natural History Museum's mission and vision statements have changed between 2009 and 2023

Natural History Museum	Mission statement	Vision statement
2009 (2009, p. 6)	"To maintain and develop our collections, and use them to promote the discovery, understanding, responsible use and enjoyment of the natural world".	"To advance our knowledge of the natural world, inspiring better care of our planet".
2023 (2023)	"Our mission is to create advocates for the planet".	"Our vision is of a future where both people and planet thrive".

and time-consuming to develop; and will never satisfy all stakeholders. I would argue that a *good* mission/vision statement really anchors the museum and helps internal teams to set goals, prioritise activities and budget spend, and is worth developing. When there are so many competing demands on a museum, a solid mission statement can help avoid mission drift, where the museum moves away from its core purpose and tries to be all things to all people. A development process involving genuine consultation with the museum's stakeholders that builds consensus is powerful. A good mission or vision statement also signals what the museum is all about to external stakeholders such as funders; the local community; potential staff and volunteers; and potential sponsors. It often forms part of a museum's governing documents, and in the USA, a mission statement is one of five designated Core Documents required as a prerequisite for museums seeking accreditation for the first time (American Alliance of Museums, no date). And finally, mission/vision statements are also a valuable starting point for developing a marketing strategy. I think valuable mission and vision statements are clear and comprehensible; relevant and meaningful; distinctive; concise and focused; motivational internally; and transparent and publicly available.

Implications for marketing

Museums have had and continue to have a wide variety of purposes, including displaying wealth; conserving and preserving; education and learning; encouraging debate; and stimulating cultural tourism and regenerating areas. They evolve and adapt over time. This chapter has also touched on some of the differing definitions and perceptions of museums; the legacy of their (at times problematic) history; and the many and complex challenges and demands they face today. Some museums are confronting these challenges sensitively and courageously, whilst others are slower to respond. It's not just the awareness and reputation of an individual museum that plays a role in how audiences view it. Public debates and controversies in the museum sector as a whole also have an impact on how potential audiences view museums more broadly. And since the way that museum sector staff and volunteers view museums may differ enormously to how different members of the public view museums, we need to put ourselves in our audiences' shoes.

There are different audiences for different elements of a museum's offering and programming. Potential audiences' barriers to engagement can be complex and run deep, and no amount of clever marketing slogans will be enough to overcome some of these on their own. Getting the product right is arguably one of the most fundamental aspects of marketing, even though it often extends well beyond the marketing person or team's responsibility. Positioning a museum is therefore not as straightforward as it might appear, and finding and connecting with audiences must go beyond a one-size-fits-all approach.

Museum leaders are constantly making active or subconscious choices that reflect their values and practical realities; for example, what they display and how they interpret this, and whom they hire and promote. This applies to museum marketers too. Which audience groups do marketers focus budgets and effort on? Where do they spend their advertising budgets? Who benefits from pricing concessions? What makes an acceptable sponsor? How can museum marketing continue to get results whilst minimising its environmental impact? How can marketing be more inclusive and accessible? These questions will be tackled throughout this book.

Questions to consider
- How would you define the word "museum"?
- How do the origins and evolution of museums affect how museums are perceived today, and how does this vary between different countries, cultures, and communities?
- What do you think makes a good mission/vision statement?

Further reading

American Alliance of Museums (2018) *Developing a Mission Statement*. Available at: https://www.aam-us.org/wp-content/uploads/2018/01/developing-a-mission-statement-final.pdf.

Mason, R., Robinson, A., and Coffield, E. (2018). *Museum and Gallery Studies. The Basics*. Oxon: Routledge.

Simon, N. (2016) *The Art of Relevance*. Santa Cruz: Museum 2.0.

References

All-Party Parliamentary Group on Arts, Health and Wellbeing (2017) *Creative Health: The Arts for Health and Wellbeing*. Available at: https://www.culturehealthandwellbeing.org.uk/appg-inquiry/Publications/Creative_Health_The_Short_Report.pdf (Accessed: 24 September 2022).

American Alliance of Museums (2021) *Museums and Trust. Spring 2021*. Available at: https://www.aam-us.org/wp-content/uploads/2021/09/Museums-and-Trust-2021.pdf (Accessed: 24 September 2022).

American Alliance of Museums (no date) *Core Documents Verification*. Available at: https://www.aam-us.org/programs/accreditation-excellence-programs/core-documents-verification/ (Accessed: 24 September 2022).

The Apartheid Museum (no date) *The New Constitution*. Available at: https://www.apartheidmuseum.org/exhibitions/the-new-constitution (Accessed: 24 September 2022).

The Ashmolean (no date) *History of the Ashmolean*. Available at: https://www.ashmolean.org/history-ashmolean (Accessed: 24 September 2022).

The British Museum (no date) *History*. Available at: https://www.britishmuseum.org/about-us/british-museum-story/history (Accessed: 24 September 2022).

Collins Dictionary (no date) *Definition of 'Museum'*. Available at: https://www.collinsdictionary.com/dictionary/english/museum (Accessed: 23 September 2022).

Grand Egyptian Museum (2023) *Grand Egyptian Museum Profile*. [Instagram] Available at: https://www.instagram.com/grandegyptianmuseum/?hl=en (Accessed: 2 May 2023).

ICOM, International Council of Museums (2019) *Creating the New Museum Definition: Over 250 Proposals to Check Out!* Available at: https://icom.museum/en/news/the-museum-definition-the-backbone-of-icom/ (Accessed: 16 September 2022).

ICOM, International Council of Museums (2022) *ICOM Approves a New Museum Definition.* Available at: https://icom.museum/en/news/icom-approves-a-new-museum-definition/ (Accessed: 16 September 2022).

Ipsos (2021) *Ipsos Veracity Index: Trust in the Police Drops for the Second Year in a Row.* Available at: https://www.ipsos.com/en-uk/ipsos-mori-veracity-index-trust-police-drops-second-year-row (Accessed: 24 September 2022).

Lehmannová, M. (2020) *224 years of Defining the Museum.* Available at: https://icom.museum/wp-content/uploads/2020/12/2020_ICOM-Czech-Republic_224-years-of-defining-the-museum.pdf. (Accessed: 16 September 2022).

Manchester Museum (no date) *Future of Collections.* Available at: https://www.museum.manchester.ac.uk/making-the-museum/futureofcollections/ (Accessed: 21 February 2023).

The Museums Association (no date) *Museums Change Lives.* Available at: https://www.museumsassociation.org/campaigns/museums-change-lives/ (Accessed: 21 February 2023).

Natural History Museum (2009) *Natural History Museum Annual Report and Accounts 2008-9.* Available at: https://assets.publishing.service.gov.uk/government/uploads/system/uploads/attachment_data/file/248146/0907.pdf (Accessed: 19 September 2022).

Natural History Museum (2023) *Our Vision and Strategy.* Available at: https://www.nhm.ac.uk/about-us/our-vision-strategy.html (Accessed: 15 April 2023).

Oxfam (2020) *For a Radically Better World.* Available at https://www.oxfam.org.uk/documents/241/Oxfam_GB_Strategy_Document__FINAL.pdf (Accessed: 19 September 2022).

Pine, B. J. and Gilmore, J. H. (2020) *The Experience Economy.* Boston: Harvard Business Review Press.

Santa Cruz Museum of Art and History (no date) *About the MAH.* Available at: https://www.santacruzmah.org/about (Accessed: 24 September 2022).

Tate (no date) *Governance.* Available at: https://www.tate.org.uk/about-us/governance (Accessed: 24 September 2022).

2 Marketing

Introduction

Marketing is one of those terms that everyone has heard of but may find hard to define succinctly and definitively. Just as "museum" can mean different things to different people and organisations, so too can "marketing". When potential clients approach me asking for marketing support, this often ends up meaning a huge variety of things. Marketing is often a maligned and misunderstood topic within the museum sector and beyond. It can feel elusive, and it is forever changing. For some museum practitioners, it is a jarring term because of its origins in business and perceived emphasis on profit. Therefore, it can translate as just being about income and numbers of visitors through the door, simple and commercial metrics. "Marketing" is sometimes used interchangeably with "publicity" or "promotion" and viewed as something to be tacked on at the end of a process or project once plans for a new exhibition or programme have been drawn up. And if that exhibition's or programme's numbers are deemed disappointing, marketing is often an easy scapegoat.

This chapter sets out common criticisms of marketing and then looks at definitions of marketing, proposing *a* guide – rather than *the* guide – to defining museum marketing. It provides a light-touch overview of the development of marketing and museum marketing and considers museum marketing today. It finishes with a look at "good" marketing and sets out three core premises central to my approach to marketing and this book.

Common criticisms of marketing

Marketing – in any industry – is not without its critics, and common criticisms include:

- It is an unnecessary waste of an organisation's money.
- It is manipulative, stimulating consumer demand and changing consumer behaviour.
- It promotes consumption of resources and is not environmentally sustainable.

Figure 2.1 An illustration highlighting the more visible and behind-the-scenes elements of marketing.

- Attempts to make marketing more ethical are simply performative and cynical attempts to stay relevant with consumers and, ultimately, profitable.

When it comes to museums, criticisms of marketing have tended to focus on the tension between profit-driven marketing and the broader social and educational goals of museums; that marketing reduces the interaction between audiences and museums to a simple transaction; and that it is focused only on growth, of income and audiences. For some, there has been an uneasiness around the commodification of our history and heritage, and the so-called Disneyfication of the visitor experience.

Marketing terminology can be alienating or seem irrelevant in the context of museums. It can be viewed as gimmicky, peppered with meaningless corporate buzzwords and approaches that some consider crass, such as "segmentation labels" (covered in Chapter 5c). Unscrupulous marketing operators and practice have also negatively affected the reputation of marketing over the years. Like "museum", "marketer" is not a protected term, so there's nothing stopping anyone from calling themselves that. Some criticisms relate to outdated views of marketing or a lack of understanding of what strategic marketing is or how it can be done well within the museums sector. Not everyone appreciates that there is more to it than throwing up a couple of social media posts and pumping out a press release. If you imagine an iceberg, the visible tip represents what people immediately tend to associate with marketing – visual and often tactical elements. But under the water, there is a much bigger part of the iceberg that, though not visible, comprises core and crucial strategic elements of marketing (see Figure 2.1).

Defining marketing

There is no concise, universally agreed-upon definition of marketing (whether between sector bodies, academics, people who work in marketing, or across museums). This is part of the challenge for museum marketers, making advocating for marketing internally harder. Dictionaries tend to include the early meaning of marketing (the buying or selling at a market) and a simple definition, focusing on tactics such as promotion, selling, and advertising. Turning to professional marketing bodies, the UK's Chartered Institute of Marketing defines marketing as: "The management process responsible for identifying, anticipating and satisfying customer requirements profitably" (2015). You can substitute "audiences" for "customer" to make this more relevant to museums. In terms of "profitably", museums need to be pragmatic and bring in income, but this is not typically their fundamental mission or driver in the way it is for most for-profit organisations.

The American Marketing Association says: "Marketing is the activity, set of institutions, and processes for creating, communicating, delivering, and exchanging offerings that have value for customers, clients, partners and society at large" (2017). This clearly shows that marketing is about more than communication. The fact that this definition doesn't mention profitability or income and the inclusion of "partners and society at large" reflects marketing's relevance and application beyond for-profit organisations, and the increasing importance of the societal impacts of marketing.

Arts marketing and museum marketing

Arts marketing and museum marketing are arguably not as straightforward as marketing for profit-making businesses – cultural organisations and museums can have a vast range of missions and goals, and audience and stakeholder needs to meet. Marketing is given varying levels of priority and resources in different museums, and where marketing sits as a function (figuratively and literally) can also vary, such as sitting alongside, underneath, or above audience development and engagement, income generation, visitor operations, or commercial services. This makes creating a definitive definition of arts or museum marketing challenging.

Considering a series of definitions of arts and museum marketing (such as those proposed by Diggle, 1994, p. 25; Hill et al., 2018, p. 2; Kotler, Kotler and Kotler, 2008, p. 22; and McLean, 2002, p. 47), there are some differences between the definitions, but also commonalities. The main unifiers across the definitions are that marketing:

- Is a management or strategic process.
- Is an exchange process between the museum and its audiences.
- Does not place income as central, or where it *is* mentioned as a goal, it is explicitly not at the expense of the organisation's mission.
- Supports the museum's mission and/or goals.
- And identifies, understands, and provides something of value to audiences.

For me, museum marketing is essentially a bridge between museums and their audiences. Marketers are champions of both. It is easy to view museums as being about objects, and marketing about products. But that is only partly the case. They are both about people, stories, and storytelling. Marketing is a strategic process that supports the museum's overall mission and organisational goals, identifying and understanding audiences and their needs; building connections and relationships with them; catering to and communicating with them in ways that are of value and relevant to both sides. Museums benefit from audiences' attention, interest, money, time, and support. In return, audiences also benefit; for example, they will learn something, have fun, or feel inspired. There is substantial overlap between marketing and audience development, which is explored in Chapter 3.

The development of marketing

Marketing has evolved organically as society has evolved, influencing and reacting to trends and contemporary thinking along the way. Its development has also been punctuated by seismic events such as the two world wars and accelerated by technological advancements that have provided a stream of new opportunities and challenges. It has long been subject to government policy and regulation, from the 19th-century advertisement duty on newspaper adverts in the UK, to laws around trademarks, competition, free trade, and more recently, social media.

Marketing originated in the 6th and 5th centuries BCE, in the ancient world, probably in Athens, with a standardised, recognisable, and accepted coinage (Shaw, 2019, p. 38) and spread along trade routes into India and China (ibid., p. 33). In the medieval period, developments included trade fairs and guilds, which had a monopoly of their product or service in a particular area and aimed to uphold a certain quality. Over time, the invention of the printing press enabled pamphlets, posters, and flyers to be produced quickly, cheaply, consistently, and in large numbers.

The expansion of transport in the 18th and 19th centuries, including the development of canals and railways, meant there was a bigger market available for many goods. Much of modern marketing can be traced back to the Industrial Revolution when new machinery and working practices facilitated the mass production of manufactured goods and packaging. Competition increased and businesses had to consider how to stand out in a more crowded marketplace and whom they were trying to reach, finding customers for their products. Shop signs, window displays, and street posters were staples. The 1800s also saw further development of distribution methods and point of sales, with the establishment of department stores and mail order catalogues. Brands and trademarks have been used for centuries as markers to identify property (such as cattle) and as signs of quality, but an expansion of trademark law in the 1800s supported their development; as companies could protect their names, products, and logos, they were incentivised to invest more in them.

As literacy rates increased and newspapers grew in number and circulation, newspapers and their adverts could reach and be read by more people.

Marketing, and in particular advertising, took off as functions and fields, with a growth of advertising agencies and the first university courses taught on marketing subjects in 1902–3 at the Universities of Michigan and California in the USA, and Birmingham in the UK (Witkowski and Jones, 2016, p. 399). Marketing became increasingly sophisticated, associating products with emotions and not just selling their functionality. Marketing techniques expanded beyond products and were used to sell social and political ideas, and market and consumer research began to be used more extensively. Marketing continued to professionalise and what is now the UK's Chartered Institute of Marketing was founded in 1911 as The Sales Managers' Association (no date) and the *Journal of Marketing* was founded in 1936, followed by the American Marketing Association in 1937 (American Marketing Association, no date).

During the Great Depression of 1929–39, consumer demand fell, and businesses had to think smarter to appeal to a more limited market, differentiating themselves from the competition. The interwar years brought the widespread embrace of radio and cinema, providing mass communication channels to reach consumers and enabling creative ways of telling stories. During the two world wars of the 20th century, governments created powerful propaganda campaigns to boost their war efforts and appeal to a range of emotions, such as fear, patriotism, nostalgia, and a sense of duty.

The explosion of consumerism post-WWII provided new opportunities for marketing. Purchasing and owning goods was appealing to the growing middle-class population with disposable income, and TVs became another way of reaching consumers directly in their homes. In the second half of the 20th century, marketing as a discipline and profession really took off. There was a golden era of advertising, depicted in the lives of advertising executives and agencies of the 1960s in the 21st century TV series *Mad Men*. The well-known 4Ps marketing mix model (Product, Place, Price, Promotion) was first proposed in its modern form in 1960 by E. Jerome McCarthy and subsequently popularised by Philip Kotler, a well-known marketing thinker and writer.

For companies and sales to grow, it wasn't always enough to determine and satisfy consumer demand, so companies also understood the benefit of creating demand in the first place. This leads to some criticisms of marketing, in that it creates needs that aren't otherwise there, seducing people to spend their money on unnecessary items. This is a concern that remains valid today, especially in light of the unsustainable depletion of Earth's finite resources. Globalisation and the growth of multinational companies went hand in hand, supported by substantial investment in marketing, in particular in FMCG companies (Fast Moving Consumer Goods, which sell quickly and frequently in large volumes at low cost, such as shampoo and soft drinks). Marketing directors became board directors, and marketing techniques spread beyond goods to apply more extensively to services, charities, government, political parties, and people (celebrities, politicians, and social media influencers).

As well as legislation, there are voluntary codes of conduct from professional marketing bodies to guide marketers to ensure they operate lawfully, professionally, and ethically. What is considered ethical and best practice has evolved over time; for example, restrictions around tobacco advertising and advertising directly to children. There has been a growth of socially responsible marketing, social marketing, and brand activism, where companies work to promote or effect social, economic, political, or environmental change. Furthermore, consumers increasingly expect companies to take a stand on political, social, economic, and environmental issues. This can be a minefield for companies to navigate since not all consumers, employees, shareholders, and stakeholders share the same values.

The Internet has meant that everything is just a click away for consumers and organisations. Competition is high, as are consumers' expectations. Consumers are deluged with choice and advertising messages daily across many platforms including an ever-expanding list of social media platforms. And organisations can be deluged with data to dissect, interpret, and act on. Marketers are increasingly focused on building communities and loyalty around their products and services, and turning transactions into relationships. Technology has facilitated opportunities for more personalisation and customisation of communication with consumers, as well as of products and services themselves.

The development of museum marketing

Marketing and attracting hordes of visitors were not a core feature of early museums – the focus was more about preservation, research, and a display of wealth as the previous chapter set out. Broadly speaking, modern marketing practices were introduced relatively late to museums, and in some cases reluctantly, out of necessity because of reductions in government funding. This drove more of a market orientation, with museums looking to alternative and additional sources of income and self-sufficiency. Marketing also supported the sector's evolution from the traditional curatorial primacy to be more audience-focused, alongside a growth of visitor studies and audience research.

Rentschler suggests that museum marketing has been academically conceptualised as falling into three main periods. During the foundation period of 1975–1983, articles on museum marketing focused on educating visitors, raising staff awareness of the benefits of visitor studies, and on occasion explaining the economic impact of the arts on society (2007, p. 15). The professionalisation period of 1988–1993 saw museums becoming more democratised, with marketing departments added to museums and funders demanding greater accountability. The entrepreneurial period of 1994–present (when published in 2007), saw evidence of collaborative marketing models, a new view of visitors, and the diversification of revenue sources in museums, as well as a big rise in the proportion of articles in industry journals that discuss marketing as strategy rather than tactics (2007, pp. 15–6). There was also a growth in the number of museum marketing directors during this time; for example, the Association of Art Museum Directors' annual salary survey showed that 17% of its American member museums had a Director of Marketing in 1989, and 50% by 1999 (as quoted by the Smithsonian Institution, 2001, p. 3).

Building on this and reflecting on my experiences of museum marketing in practice, I would suggest that another two phases have developed since then. First, a phase from around 2010–19 which I suggest was the social or data phase. Museum marketing became more audience-centric, with greater access to and more sophisticated use of data and analytics, enabling better segmentation and tailoring of approaches to different audiences, and more direct communication with audiences through an expansion of e-newsletters and social media usage. Since around 2020, I feel we are in a fifth period, which could perhaps be called the re-evaluation or reflection phase. As a result of the so-called permacrisis global turmoil that includes the Covid-19 pandemic; the racial reckoning prompted by the murder of George Floyd at the hands of police in the USA (see Douglas, Chrisafis, and Mohdin, 2021); war in Ukraine; economic crises; and the climate crisis, museums and museum marketing are not dealing with business as usual, but rather they need to adapt and fundamentally consider their purpose in – and impact on – society and the environment. Ethical considerations are starting to be much more acknowledged, such as where to advertise, how to make marketing more inclusive and accessible, and which sponsorship is acceptable.

Museum marketing today

The old adage and assumption "Build it and they will come" has never been more misleading than it is today. There is increased competition for museum audiences' attention, time, and money from other cultural and heritage organisations, attractions, and leisure activities; an ever-growing range of digital experiences and distractions at our fingertips in our hyperconnected world; and other personal and work commitments and pressures for our audiences. There is talk of the "attention economy" in terms of the scarcity of our attention in an information-rich world (a term coined by Herbert A. Simon). Museums need to know how to position themselves successfully to stand out in a crowded marketplace. They need to be in tune with audiences' needs and wants; be relevant; be able to build relationships with existing audiences; attract and engage new audiences, staff, volunteers, and partners; and generate income. Marketing is crucial to all of this.

However, some tensions persist within the museums sector around the purpose and impact of marketing. I have come across people so passionate about their museum that they almost feel offended that they should have to proactively undertake marketing – they think the museum's existence should be enough to draw huge crowds. Others feel that visitors are an unwelcome distraction (albeit perhaps a necessary evil) from caring for the museum's collections. Many people still view marketing as a tactical function, seeing it as promotion and publicity.

On the flipside, there are certainly many museums that understand the importance of marketing and, as a result, invest in it through dedicated and professional staff and training, by allocating time and/or budgets for delivery. ICOM (the International Council of Museums) has an International Committee for Marketing and Public Relations (ICOM MPR), and the UK's Museums + Heritage Awards have a Marketing and Communications Campaign of the Year category. Many national museums are internationally renowned, protect their brands, invest in understanding their audiences and communicating with them, have substantial marketing teams with their own expertise, and deliver award-winning campaigns. But it is not fair to say that big museums "get it" and small museums don't. The biggest difference is that the smaller and often volunteer-run museums don't have access to the same resources (teams and specialists, time, and budgets) and head start (name and brand awareness, star objects, high-profile blockbuster exhibitions, and so on).

There is much that the museum sector can learn from other sectors that may be more dynamic, innovative, and risk-taking when it comes to marketing. Approaches from the tourism sector and not-for-profit fundraising campaigns can provide valuable lessons. With the growth of museum activism, there can also be a lot to learn from social marketing, which is marketing that aims to effect positive social change, increase awareness of something, and change the public's behaviours. However, some of the challenges faced by museums also require a more museum-specific approach. Museum budgets are increasingly squeezed whilst the roles and demands they face continue to expand. At the same time, other funding sources are not unproblematic substitutes – the sustainability and longevity of the blockbuster exhibition model is under question, as are sources of sponsorship and philanthropy. In addition, many museums are grappling with a huge range of ongoing challenges such as the climate crisis and issues around decolonisation and restitution.

Looking ahead

There is still work to be done to ensure that the contribution that good marketing can make to support museums is more universally acknowledged. Looking forward, museum marketing will need to continue to evolve, adapting as museums and society evolve. That pace of change is more turbocharged today than in previous decades: a Hubspot survey of over 1,200 global marketers at the end of 2022 found that 78% agreed with the statement that "Marketing has changed more in the past three years than in the past 50" (Iskiev, 2022). Museum marketing practitioners and researchers will need to play an active role in the re-imagining of the future of museums, in particular in terms of alternatives for the relentless pursuit of audience growth. I believe that values, ethics, sustainability, accessibility, and inclusivity will continue to grow in importance. As budgets dwindle, targeted marketing and marketing evaluation will be nonnegotiable, and partnerships will be invaluable.

As museums, technology, and society are changing, so, too, are the skills and experience required of museum marketing staff. For example, less of a focus on creating printed leaflets, and more emphasis on video production and online community management. Marketing teams must constantly upskill and ensure they recruit appropriately to meet the circumstances of today and the future. However, the constant advancements in technology, best practice, and the enormous amount of data at our fingertips can be overwhelming and intimidating. Directly linking outcomes to actions and seeing a return on investment is not always straightforward. Coupled with the fact that marketing evaluation is often not given the resources it deserves, this means that the value of marketing isn't always appreciated in a museum. Therefore, there's often an internal lobbying job to be done to advocate for marketing as a fundamental necessity and less of a dark art.

New platforms and technology will develop and offer new opportunities and challenges. There are no guarantees that today's social media platforms will be here in five years' time, so investing in museums' own platforms and channels will help ensure they are less vulnerable to external changes. AI, artificial intelligence, is already used in marketing – for example, for the personalisation and targeting of ads and for media monitoring analysis and reporting. But the capabilities of AI and the spotlight on it have recently exploded, for example, around the potential of generative AI for content creation, as well as intense accompanying ethical debates around the intrinsic bias of AI, consumer consent, cultural sensitivities, privacy, and more. As in many other sectors, the expansion of AI is likely to lead to some marketing activities and positions being redundant, so the question for museums is what remit will the marketing team have in 10–20 years' time, what skills will be needed, and what value can they add? Will the authenticity of museum marketing be valued in the same way that the authenticity of museums' objects and experiences are?

As an experiment, I asked artificial intelligence chatbot ChatGPT the question, "What is the future of museum marketing?" Within seconds I had a response of 232 words that included six trends likely to shape the future of museum marketing – personalisation, virtual reality, augmented reality, social media, sustainability, and collaborations – and ended with the quote "Overall, the future of museum marketing is likely to be shaped by technology, data, and a desire to create more engaging and interactive experiences for visitors" (2023). Everything it said was relevant and plausible (albeit generic), and responses will keep getting better.

"Good" marketing

What does "good" marketing look like? It's a subjective term but at its simplest, it is successful and effective marketing that meets its goals. More than that, perhaps it is a philosophy, an approach, that is an intrinsic part of a museum's culture, that is outward-looking and audience-centric. It needs to be integrated with and embraced by the whole organisation. It doesn't require huge budgets, but it does need a consistent investment of time. For me, good marketing is all about connecting with audiences, listening to them, and understanding them. People who undertake marketing for museums should be audience champions, have curiosity, be empathetic, and use research and data to make decisions. I also think a healthy dose of pragmatism is needed and that some experimentation is valuable.

Furthermore, good marketing is lawful and ethical, adhering to legislation and appropriate codes of conduct, ethics, and accreditation guidance. It should be honest, transparent, accessible, and inclusive, and grounded in a museum's mission and values. However, no matter how "good" your marketing is, marketing is not a panacea for all challenges that museums face. Satisfying audience and organisational goals cannot be considered a success – and is tolerated less and less by the public – if it comes as a result of practices that have an unmitigated negative impact on the environment, that involve an exploitation of labour, or that perpetuate exclusive gatekeeping.

To conclude this chapter, I set out three core premises that are central to my approach to marketing and this book:

1 Far from detracting from a museum's core purpose, I believe that good marketing supports and adds value to it.
2 Audiences' attention, money, time, and trust are precious and finite, so you need to earn and value them, not demand them or take them for granted.
3 Museum marketing must continue to proactively develop more sustainable, inclusive, accessible, and ethical approaches.

Questions to consider

- How would you define marketing?
- How is marketing viewed in the museum sector more broadly and/or in your museum?
- What do you think museum marketing will look like in 10–20 years' time?

Further reading

Ekström, K. M. (ed.) (2020). *Museum Marketization. Cultural Institutions in the Neoliberal Era*. Oxon: Routledge.
Ewen, S. (1996) *PR! A Social History of Spin*. New York: Basic Books.
Jones, D. G. B. and Tadajewski, M. (eds.) (2019) *The Routledge Companion to Marketing History*. Oxon: Routledge.

References

American Marketing Association (2017) *Definitions of Marketing*. Available at: https://www.ama.org/the-definition-of-marketing-what-is-marketing/ (Accessed: 5 May 2022).
American Marketing Association (no date) *Academic Journals*. Available at: https://www.ama.org/ama-academic-journals/ (Accessed: 23 September 2022).
Chartered Institute of Marketing (no date) *Our History*. Available at: https://www.cim.co.uk/about-cim/our-history/ (Accessed: 22 February 2023).

Chartered Institute of Marketing (2015) *7Ps. A Brief Summary of Marketing and How it Works.* Available at: https://www.cim.co.uk/media/4772/7ps.pdf (Accessed: 5 May 2022).

Chat GPT (2023) *Welcome to ChatGPT.* Available at: https://chat.openai.com/ (Accessed: 28 February 2023).

Diggle, K. (1994) *Arts Marketing.* London: Rhinegold Publishing Limited.

Douglas, D., Chrisafis, A., and Mohdin, A. (2021) *One Year On, How George Floyd's Murder has Changed the World.* Available at: https://www.theguardian.com/us-news/2021/may/22/george-floyd-murder-change-across-world-blm (Accessed: 23 February 2023).

Hill, L., O'Sullivan, C., O'Sullivan, T., and Whitehead, B. (2018) *Creative Arts Marketing.* Oxon: Routledge.

Iskiev, M. (2022) *The HubSpot Blog's 2023 Marketing Strategy & Trends Report: Data from 1,200+ Global Marketers.* Available at: https://blog.hubspot.com/marketing/hubspot-blog-marketing-industry-trends-report (Accessed: 3 May 2023).

Kotler, N. G. Kotler, P. & Kotler, W. I. (2008). *Museum Marketing & Strategy: Designing Missions, Building Audiences, Generating Revenue and Resources.* San Francisco: Jossey-Bass.

McLean, F. (2002) *Marketing the Museum.* London: Routledge.

Rentschler, R. (2007) 'Museum Marketing: No Longer a Dirty Word' in R. Rentschler & A. Hede (eds.) *Museum Marketing: Competing in the Global Marketplace*, pp. 12–20. Burlington: Routledge.

Shaw, E. H. (2019) 'Ancient and Medieval Marketing' in D. G. B. Jones & M. Tadajewski (eds.) *The Routledge Companion to Marketing History*, pp. 23–40. Oxon: Routledge.

Smithsonian Institution (2001) *Audience Building: Marketing Art Museums.* Available at: https://www.si.edu/content/opanda/docs/rpts2001/01.10.marketingart.final.pdf (Accessed: 18 April 2023).

Witkowski, T. H. and Jones, D. G. B. (2016) 'Historical Research in Marketing: Literature, Knowledge, and Disciplinary Status', *Information & Culture*, Vol. 51 (3), pp. 399–418. Available at: 10.7560/IC51305 (Accessed: 22 February 2023).

3 Audiences

Introduction

I've always been fascinated by marketing because ultimately, it's about people, their interests, values, and behaviours. What drives someone to visit one museum but not another, spend money on an activity, donate to a particular cause, appreciate a certain object, volunteer their time for an organisation but not another? And how can museums tap into this?

Audiences are individuals, and their perceptions and attitudes towards museums and how they interact with them (if at all) depend on a vast range of factors, from past experiences and interactions with museums; their values and their cultural upbringing; where they live and what they have on their doorstep; their interests; their families, social circles, and the norms of that group; what they come across in media and social media; their disposable income. Equally, museums aren't a homogenous group with the same set of core and potential audiences, and there are distinctions between countries and cultures. This chapter can't cover all the nuances relating to each but emphasises the importance of each museum understanding its own audiences. It summarises typical core and traditional museum-visiting audiences and underrepresented audiences, common motivations, and barriers to engagement, as well as Covid-19 pandemic and post-pandemic audiences.

Defining audiences and audience development

Audiences

I refer to "audiences" throughout the book as an all-encompassing term for anyone who interacts or engages with museums. They may be visitors to a physical museum, an attendee at an outreach event, members, a workshop participant, a user of a research service, a listener to a lecture, someone who engages with a museum digitally, donors, someone who buys something in the gift shop or enjoys a drink in the museum café. They can be potential, future, current, or lapsed audiences for the museum.

"Audiences" is not a universally loved or perfect term. Derived from performance arts, it can sound passive – audiences traditionally listen, watch, and receive information more than they participate and engage, and museums are more participatory than ever before. But it is a useful catch-all and a commonly used term and, importantly, goes beyond in-person visitors, which is too limiting a focus for museum marketing. This book considers a broader range of groups throughout, such as digital audiences and people who take part in outreach events, who may never set a foot in a museum building.

A few alternative terms are users, customers, clients, and community. With "users", there's a synergy with User Experience (UX), how a user experiences or interacts with a product or service, and User Experience Design. These are concepts often applied to creating websites and apps. However, I'm not sure that "users" quite captures the relationship between museum and audience. "Customers" and "clients" arguably feel too commercial for many museums and are not directly applicable to museums that are free. Whilst a customer-focused orientation can be beneficial regardless of whether there is money that changes hands, "customers" or "clients" are perhaps terms more suited to describing people who use the museum shop or café, and individuals and organisations that hire the venue or use museum consultancy services.

"Community" is another rather nebulous term used in many different circumstances, such as talking about a museum's local community or online community. For the purposes of marketing, I would argue that a museum's "community" is a smaller subset of very engaged people *within* the wider audience group who have a long-term and deeper relationship with a museum. For example, repeat visitors, volunteers, donors, or people who are very active with the museum's social media. They have a stronger affinity with the museum and hopefully also feel they *belong* to that community. It can be a community of place, interest, or shared values. Entirely replacing "audience" with "community" is perhaps an aspirational statement of how a museum *wants* to view and value their audiences, rather than a term that describes them all.

Audience development and marketing

"Audience development" is a sustained and deliberate effort to develop existing audiences, and build relationships with new ones, increasing and diversifying a museum's audiences. It is about understanding and meeting the needs of existing and potential audiences, recognising that different audiences have different interests, habits, behaviours, preferences, resources, likes, and dislikes. They are often funded by shorter-term project grants, but should be a longer-term commitment, integrated and supported across the museum. There is often pressure to find and entice new audiences, but this book also emphasises the importance of repeat audiences and deepening relationships with existing audiences. Inspiring a new one-time visit can absolutely be a success. But constantly chasing new visitors is hard, is time-consuming, can be expensive, and isn't always sustainable. A common old rule of thumb in the marketing industry was that it costs five to seven times more to acquire a new customer than it does to retain an existing customer. This figure is not necessarily universally applicable, but the principle that building deeper and longer-term relationships with audiences is beneficial certainly applies to museums. In some cases – especially with international tourists – trying to encourage some audiences back can be more expensive and less effective.

There is a lack of consensus around where arts marketing stops and audience development starts. Wadeson's presentation to the Arts Marketing Association's conference back in 2003 proposed a series of concentric circles each representing arts marketing and audience development, with options for how they fitted together – overlapping each other or one within the other. He concluded that the terms are essentially two sides of the same coin, virtually overlapping, both trying to meet the same aims: "arts marketing and audience development *both seek to create and retain audiences*" (2003, p. 77, emphasis added), and I would agree.

Anecdotally I'd suggest that many museum practitioners are more comfortable with audience development as a concept than marketing because of the problems I set out with marketing in Chapter 2, and since audience development can seem more closely aligned with museums' core educational purpose. Even though audience development and (arts) marketing have many similarities, on a practical level, they can end up separated in museums, with more distinct and smaller remits as a result. Marketing often ends up more concerned with the *quantity* of audiences, income generation, and bringing people into contact with the museum in the first place. Whilst audience development often ends up concentrating more on the *quality* or depth of engagement, working with underrepresented and marginalised groups, and less about driving income. In some museums, there are marketing and audience development officers or managers whose responsibilities straddle both. But in other museums, the two functions can be quite separate, with marketing sitting more closely (literally and physically) with income-generation teams, and audience development sitting closer to education, learning, and outreach teams. Although this book is called *Marketing Strategy for Museums*, it includes content that some may class as audience development in order to take a holistic and strategic approach.

Why undertake audience development?

At their core, museums serve society and the public, but more than that, as ICOM's most recent definition of a museum says, museums are "open to the public, accessible and inclusive [...] They operate [...] with the participation of communities" (ICOM, 2022) – it's about more than simply opening your doors to the public. There is also a moral obligation for museums with public funding to ensure everyone has the chance to benefit from and enjoy museums, and equity of access to cultural resources. The United Nations' 1948 Universal Declaration of Human Rights, Article 27, states: "Everyone has the right freely to participate in the cultural life of the community, to enjoy the arts" (United Nations, no date).

Furthermore, museums need public support from those who are paying to support them, whether through taxes, lotteries, donations, or other mechanisms. When national or local governments consider cutting grants and subsidies to museums, it is important that museums can prove their value and that their audiences and stakeholders also feel invested enough to advocate on their behalf. If your/a museum is threatened with closure or disappears, who would miss it? And who would speak up about it? Thinking purely from a business sustainability point of view, museums usually need a constant stream of audiences (new and repeats) to drive attendance income, whether directly through ticket sales and donations, or through secondary spend such as in cafés and shops. Museums also need to avoid an overreliance on one audience group, which can leave them vulnerable if that audience group – or its interest in the museum – shrinks.

Aside from the moral and financial reasons, I'd also argue that taking an audience-centric approach can genuinely improve a museum in a whole host of additional ways, from creating enhancements to the museum to improving staff and volunteer motivation. Ultimately, it helps museums stay relevant. And finally, even if a museum doesn't want to do it, it is often a requirement of accreditation schemes, an expectation from many funders, and valued by many donors and sponsors.

Core or traditional museum audiences

Different museums have different core audiences, depending on a range of factors including location, size, subject matter, facilities, accessibility, products and programmes, policies, values, price, and reviews. For example, a free, national museum in a capital city is likely to have a big audience of international tourists; a local history museum that has an active programme of family activities and affordable family membership scheme is likely to have a substantial repeat local family audience; and a special interest museum is likely to attract a lot of enthusiasts from further afield. Within audience groups there will be seasonal peaks and troughs – families with school age children typically visit at weekends and in school holidays, especially on wetter and colder days.

However, historically there are audiences that have consistently tended to visit and engage with museums more than others, and whilst some museums have upended these patterns, in many museums and to some extent across the sector, audience breakdowns have remained stubbornly the same. There is not space here to summarise each country's core audiences, so I pull out some data from England, the European Union, and the United States as examples. In many cases, core museum audiences are universal, except for visitors' ethnicities, which vary across the globe.

Early modern museums were exclusively for the wealthy and educated. Today, there is no educational pre-requisite for visiting a museum, however, research shows that people with a high level of education tend to be over-represented as museum visitors (Mason et al, 2018, pp. 87–8; Bounia et al, 2012, pp. 71–5; Dilenschneider, 2019a). Another key predictor of whether people will visit museums is whether they were taken as a child and whether this was a positive experience (Mason et al, 2018, p. 89).

In England, the Taking Part survey (a regular household survey to establish reliable national estimates of engagement with arts and culture since 2005) has shown consistent patterns of museum attendance. The 2019/20 survey showed:

- People with higher managerial, administrative and professional occupations were more likely to have visited a museum/gallery in 2019/20 than those with routine and manual occupations (66% compared to 36%).
- People living in the *least* deprived areas were more likely to have visited a museum/gallery than people living in the *most* deprived areas (59% compared to 34%).
- Respondents who were working were more likely to have visited a museum/gallery than those who were not working (56% compared to 45%).
- Black respondents were less likely to have visited a museum or gallery (28%) compared to Asian respondents (46%), people with a mixed ethnic background (63%), white respondents (53%), and other respondents (42%)[1].
- People aged 25–74 years old were more likely to have visited a museum/gallery (54–55%) than 16–24 year olds (45%) and people aged 75 years old and above (36%) (Taking Part, 2020).

A report by the European Union charts similar findings around core and underrepresented museum audiences in EU countries (2012, pp. 17–23). Likewise, Dilenschneider's analysis of data from IMPACTS Experience's National Awareness, Attitudes and Usage Study of over 100,000 adults in the USA (2019a) shows the top shared attributes amongst people in the USA who have visited any type of cultural organisation in the last two years are: white non-Hispanic, graduated college, have a high income, are super-connected (broadband access at home, work and mobile) and a homeowner.

Common motivations for visiting or engaging with museums

Closely tied to *who* visits and engages with museums is *how* and *why* – alone, with a partner, family or friends, or in an organised group; for fun, to study, to catch up with a friend. Audiences may have several different motivations for visiting, and the same person may have different motivations, with different visiting patterns at different museums. Whilst audience demographic information is useful in identifying who audiences – and therefore underrepresented audiences – are, they are not necessarily direct predictors of motivations to visit museums.

The Audience Agency's Museum Report – with data from 39,000 audience surveys from 105 museums across England – found that social and learning based motivations are the main drivers for museum attendance. Learning is the most consistent motivation across all age groups, with the proportion of respondents giving learning as their reason for attending increasing with the respondent's cultural engagement level, whilst the proportion citing social decreases with the respondent's cultural engagement level (2018, p. 8). In a visitor survey project I worked on a few years ago with 13 museums in England, the visitor responses about why they visited varied substantially from museum to museum. For example, the most popular reason for visiting the two transport museums and a technology museum was an interest in the museum's topic; whereas for a free local authority museum it was to take children or family; and for a local village museum it was to find out more about the area.

There can be distinctions in motivations for visiting different types of museums, countries, and cultures. In research for national museums in nine European countries, visitors were given six multiple choice options to answer the question "Why did you come to the museum today?": Education/learning was the most popular response for visitors in the German Historical Museum, the National Historical Museum of Athens, the National Museum of Estonia, and the Museum of the History of Catalonia, whereas entertainment/pleasure was the priority in the Rijksmuseum in the Netherlands, the National Museum of Scotland, Nordiska Museet in Sweden, the National Museum of Ireland and the Open-Air Museum of Latvia (Bounia et al, 2012, pp. 79–81). Researchers indicated that differences between the cultural and educational policies of each country influenced the relationship between visitors and the museums, contrasting Scotland's emphasis on making museums a place of enjoyment for visitors, with Greece's emphasis on museums as institutions for the protection of heritage and collaborators with schools (ibid., p. 17).

I have analysed a lot of visitor surveys, and seen may different classification of visitors and motivations. Whilst the category names differ, they broadly cover the same variations of themes:

- Education, learning and discovery (from informal learning with children, to professional research).
- Entertainment and enjoyment.
- Social activity and interactions.
- Experience-driven, status, and FOMO (fear of missing out).
- Self-fulfilment such as reflecting and reminiscing.
- To take others (such as school groups).

This will be built on in Chapter 5c in discussions on segmentation. What is clear – and crucial for marketers to remember – is that not all audiences have the same motivations, and not all audiences are primarily motivated by certain objects or exhibitions, or even the museum itself. Whilst arts, heritage and culture are very important, enriching, and enjoyable for many people, a visit to a particular museum is for most people something they can live without, rather than a necessity.

Underrepresented and marginalised audiences

How the sector refers to people who don't visit museums has evolved as our thinking around audiences has evolved. "Hard-to-reach audiences" was a term I came across a lot in the 2000s and early 2010s, although already by 2014 it was seen as a problematic – I delivered a presentation that year where on one slide I wrote Underrepresented not hard-to-reach audiences". Whilst I still occasionally come across it today, it is recognised that "hard-to-reach" unjustly puts the blame and responsibility on audiences for not engaging or making it harder for arts organisations to reach them. In fact, most barriers are created by the museum, by structural or systemic factors, and it is the responsibility of museums to remove or minimise those barriers. Alternatives now often used include "underserved audiences", "Underrepresented audiences", or "marginalised communities", recognising that the onus is on museums to do the heavy lifting.

There have always been people who never or rarely visit museums, whether out of choice or because they are excluded from museums for a multitude of barriers and reasons. England's Taking Part survey showed that 52% of respondents hadn't attended a museum or gallery in the past year (2020). There are commonalities in terms of underrepresented audiences across the museums sector, for example audiences who have long-term physical or mental health conditions or illnesses. However, there are also nuances and differences between countries, cultures, and different museums. For example, younger children are more likely to be a higher proportion of visitors in interactive science museums than art museums.

Common barriers to reaching and engaging audiences

Barriers to engagement or visiting museums are complex, individual, and can change over time. Many will also be specific to a museum – for example a rural museum may not be accessible by public transport; another museum is only open on weekdays; another museum may have poor reviews. The European Union's Work Plan for Culture 2011–14 grouped barriers as falling into four categories: physical, financial, geographical, and cultural (2012, pp. 39–55). I have expanded on them below, adding sensory access and social barriers, and further examples for each:

- **Physical and sensory access barriers**: for example, a lack of wheelchair and pushchair access; insufficient interpretation that is accessible to D/deaf, blind, or partially sighted people; a lack of pre-visit information about facilities.
- **Financial barriers:** entrance fees; the price of a special exhibition; public transportation costs to get there or car parking charges; not being allowed

to take in a picnic or own drinks into venues; needing a sizeable mobile data allowance or Wi-Fi to download and access digital interpretation.
- **Geographical barriers:** living in rural areas and further away from museums; having poor internet or mobile data signal restricting digital access to museums.
- **Cultural and social barriers:** more intangible barriers such as interests, priorities, linguistic barriers, museums not reflecting or welcoming the certain audiences, a previous negative visit.

In England's Taking Part research 2019/20, the five most common reasons reported by respondents for not visiting a museum or gallery were (2020):

- I'm not interested – 41%.
- I don't have time – 38%.
- I have a health problem or disability – 13%.
- They are difficult to get to – 8%.
- They are too expensive – 7%.

Whilst many people are time-poor or not interested in the subject matter of many museums, there is also likely to be a proportion of people who don't value the museum's offer enough to invest their time, effort, and money in a visit. Dilenschneider's analysis in the USA (2019b) shows that the top three barriers for people who say they are not interested in visiting cultural organisations are:

- Preferred alternative leisure activity (such as a sporting event or movie).
- Attitude affinity perceptions ("not for people like me"), often relating to issues of diversity, equity, and inclusion.
- Negative precedent experience.

And research about inactive visitors who have an interest or potential interest in attending cultural organisations, but haven't visited in the last two years or more, found the top three reasons were:

- Preferred alternative leisure activity.
- Access challenges ("hard to get there" and "hard to plan").
- Have already visited ("nothing new to see or do") (Dilenschneider 2019c).

A literature review on hurdles to the participation of children, families, and young people in museums for Kids in Museums found that hurdles included:

- Practical barriers such as the lack of public transport and its cost, the cost of participation, poor communication, and marketing.
- Social and attitudinal barriers including low income, lower educational qualifications, emotional barriers such as a fear of being judged or feeling out of place.

- Pressures on schools such as budget cuts, curriculum changes with less of a focus on arts, making it hard for museums to create and sustain relationships with schools.
- Limited consultation with young people to understand their needs and interests.
- Poor collaboration and co-production with community groups (Whitaker, 2018, pp. 2, 8–10).

Price can be a barrier for some audiences but isn't necessarily the universal barrier that it is often assumed to be – in fact, many studies have shown that making museums free can increase the number of repeat visitors, but it does not automatically increase the diversity of visitors (see Chapter 8). It is also worth noting that the lack of diversity amongst some museum audiences is mirrored with a lack of diversity in many museums' staff, trustees, and volunteers. Many museums aren't representative of their communities or audiences. For example, data from Arts Council England on museums that it designates as National Portfolio Organisations shows only 6% of the museum workforce are Black, Asian, or Ethnically Diverse, compared to 17% of England's working age population (2022, pp. 7–8).

Reaching and engaging new audiences

It's important to understand the multitude of reasons why someone might not engage with any museum or your museum, since different reasons require different approaches. This book focuses on barriers that marketing can overcome. But realistically, marketing is only one part of a bigger set of solutions, that in some cases may require substantial transformation within museums, uncomfortable conversations and decisions, a realigning of power, and involving every department. Some people working or volunteering in museums are so incredibly knowledgeable and passionate about their collections and museums as whole that they can find it hard to step into someone else's shoes and understand why they may not want or choose to visit a museum, let alone their museum. There can be an assumption that a lack of awareness of the museum is the only hurdle to museum attendance and after a few more leaflets and social media posts new audiences will flock in.

If low public awareness of a museum and its offer is the only problem, a good marketing campaign is likely to be an effective answer. But if the barriers run deeper, a marketing campaign could be a waste of time and money and could even do more harm than good if it's seen as hypocritical or tokenistic. Being audience-centric takes more than a hollow slogan. A very easy first step that won't cost a thing is for museum teams to remember the mantra "We are not our audiences", as there can be a tendency for some museum staff and volunteers to assume that everyone behaves and thinks like them. Just because a trustee reads reviews in a certain newspaper doesn't mean that all audiences do; and just because a volunteer finds an exhibition interesting doesn't mean everyone will. Engaging new audiences may include consulting audiences and underserved audiences and really listening to them; involving and valuing them; reflecting and representing them; welcoming them, catering to them; and working with them. It's likely to take time and effort but doesn't always have to involve big budgets. Authenticity, intention, respect, and commitment are key.

Leisure activity exercise

A simple warm-up exercise I use in workshops to counter this, involves showing photos of different leisure activities such as watching snooker on TV; going to a live boxing match; watching a contemporary dance performance; going rock climbing; taking part in a life drawing class; eating in a Michelin star restaurant; visiting a local park. I ask people to consider which activities they:

1 Do regularly and/or feel comfortable doing.
2 Have tried but don't do regularly.
3 Have never done but *would* try and.
4 Have never done and would *never* do.

Then I invite them to reflect and share their answers and reasons (if they want to) as a group or in smaller groups. Often reasons people give for 1) are that it's an activity they always did with their family growing up or they have the facility on their doorstep; whilst for 4) it's just not something that interests them, they place a value on or feel comfortable doing – perhaps they hate the idea of watching boxing, don't feel they have the skills for or feel intimidated by a life drawing class, or find a Michelin restaurant pretentious and overpriced. There is a lot that can be explored from responses there. But often where the real magic happens is exploring the reasons participants give for placing activities in categories 2) and 3). Why don't they return to something they have tried, or try something they have expressed an interest in? For example, they might keep meaning to but never get round to it, or they haven't got anyone to go with. The next step is to consider how can we apply this to museums and what aspects can marketing do something about?

Pandemic and post-pandemic audiences

The Covid-19 pandemic forced museums across the world to close their doors to visitors, decimating their income. This brought an increased focus on and appreciation of online channels and methods of engaging audiences for museums, with many launching, expanding and experimenting with digital content such as virtual gallery tours, online creative workshops for families, quizzes, and engaging social media content. For example, The Cooper Gallery in Barnsley, England created free online jigsaw puzzles of artworks from their collection with a competitive leaderboard (Barnsley Museums, 2023). Many museums also undertook activities cementing their relationship with, and relevance in, their communities. For example, Ipswich Museum in England provided multi-lingual activity packs to support some of the town's most vulnerable communities, partnering with charity Volunteering Matters to distribute the packs via food banks, factories, and schools (Root, 2020). Many museums provided creative offline engagement methods too, for example the LAM Museum (Lisser Art Museum) in the Netherlands offered "Viewphone", providing people who signed up with a ten-minute phonecall in which one of the museum's employees chose a work of art and talked to them about it (Brown, 2020).

The challenges, benefits and results of digital engagement were varied. On the one hand, digital engagement enabled museums to connect more with a willing audience with no geographic limitations, but on the other hand, it opened up those museums to enormous competition also available at the click of a button. There were also resource implications for creating the digital activities, especially once museums reopened – ICOM found that only 26% of respondents reported that their museums had full-time dedicated staff for their digital activities (2020, p. 9).

As the Culture in Crisis report on the impacts of the Covid-19 pandemic on the UK cultural sector found, digital engagement wasn't the panacea to all of the sector's diversification challenges. The report found that whilst the number of *cultural engagements* increased during the pandemic, the number of *engagers* remained stubbornly static. However, the increase in digital provision did make a difference, in particular for disabled audiences and many older audiences who don't live in large urban centres. The digital offer also has a much younger (and more ethnically diverse) audience (Walmsley et al, 2022, p. 68).

In addition, the pandemic drove several broader trends, which have continued to affect museums, such as a substantial drop in international business and leisure travel, especially to cities, which in 2023, have not returned to pre-pandemic levels. One of the many enduring lessons of the pandemic in terms of audiences, is the importance of museums not being over-reliant on any one audience segment or profile, making them vulnerable to the impact of external events, policies and trends.

Questions to consider
- How would you explain the difference between audience development and marketing?
- Who are your/a museum's core audiences?
- Who are your/a museum's under-represented or marginalised audiences?

Note

1 No further breakdown of ethnicities was available in the data.

Further reading

Dilenschneider, C. (no date). *Colleen Dilenschneider. Know your own bone*. Available at: https://www.colleendilen.com/.
Falk, J. (2016) 'Museum Audiences: A Visitor-Centered Perspective', *Loisir et Société/ Society and Leisure*, 39(3), pp. 357–370. Available at: 10.1080/07053436.2016.1243830.
Simon, N. (2010) *The Participatory Museum*. Santa Cruz: Museum 2.0.

References

Arts Council England (2022) *Equality, Diversity, and Inclusion*. Available at: https://www.artscouncil.org.uk/equality-diversity-and-inclusion-data-report-2020-2021 (Accessed: 27 February 2023).
The Audience Agency (2018) *Museums Audience Report*. Available at: https://www.theaudienceagency.org/resources/museums-audience-report (Accessed: 31 January 2023).
Barnsley Museums (2023) *Barnsley Museums Puzzles*. Available at: https://www.jigsawplanet.com/BarnsleyMuseums (Accessed: 27 February 2023).
Bounia, A., Nikiforidou, A., Nikonanou, N., and Matossian, A. D. (eds.) (2012) *Voices from the Museum: Survey Research in Europe's National Museums*. Linköping: Linköping University Electronic Press. Available at: http://liu.diva-portal.org/smash/record.jsf?pid=diva2%3A563949&dswid=4748 Accessed: (23 February 2023).
Brown, K. (2020) *The Staff of a Tiny Locked-Down Dutch Museum Is Offering to Talk to Anyone Who Wants to Chat About Art. So I Gave Them a Call*. Available at: https://news.artnet.com/art-world/lisser-art-museum-phone-call-1837677 (Accessed: 27 February 2023).
Dilenschneider, C. (2019a) *Active Visitors: Who Currently Attends Cultural Organizations?* Available at: https://www.colleendilen.com/2019/01/23/active-visitors-currently-attends-cultural-organizations-data/ (Accessed: 20 September 2022).
Dilenschneider, C. (2019b) *They're Just Not That Into You: What Cultural Organizations Need to Know About Non-Visitors*. Available at: https://www.colleendilen.com/2019/02/06/theyre-just-not-that-into-you-what-cultural-organizations-need-to-know-about-non-visitors-data/ (Accessed: 20 September 2022).
Dilenschneider, C. (2019c) *Inactive Visitors Are Interested in Attending Cultural Organizations. Why Don't They?* Available at: https://www.colleendilen.com/2019/01/30/inactive-visitors-are-interested-in-attending-cultural-organizations-why-dont-they-data/ (Accessed: 20 September 2022).
European Union (2012) *Work Plan for Culture, 2011–14: A Report on Policies and Good Practices in the Public Arts and in Cultural Institutions to Promote Better Access to and Wider Participation in Culture*. Available at: https://ec.europa.eu/assets/eac/culture/policy/strategic-framework/documents/omc-report-access-to-culture_en.pdf (Accessed: 25 September 2022).
ICOM, International Council of Museums (2020) *Museums, Museum Professionals and COVID-19*. Available at: https://icom.museum/wp-content/uploads/2020/05/Report-Museums-and-COVID-19.pdf (Accessed: 25 September 2022).
ICOM, International Council of Museums (2022) *ICOM Approves a New Museum Definition*. Available at: https://icom.museum/en/news/icom-approves-a-new-museum-definition/ (Accessed: 16 September 2022).
Mason, R., Robinson, A., and Coffield, E. (2018) *Museum and Gallery Studies. The Basics*. Oxon: Routledge.

Root, E. (2020) *Taking Ipswich Museum to our Community*. Available from: https://suffolkmuseums.org/taking-the-museum-to-our-community/ (Accessed: 27 February 2023).

Taking Part (2020) *National statistics. Museums - Taking Part Survey 2019/20*. Available at: https://www.gov.uk/government/statistics/taking-part-201920-museums/museums-taking-part-survey-201920 (Accessed: 20 September 2022).

United Nations (no date)*Universal Declaration of Human Rights*. Available at: https://www.un.org/en/about-us/universal-declaration-of-human-rights (Accessed: 24 September 2022).

Wadeson, I. (2003) *Seminar: Audience Development - Unpacking the Baggage*. Available at: https://www.culturehive.co.uk/wp-content/uploads/2014/01/Audience-Development-Unpacking-the-baggage..Ivan-Wadeson..20031.pdf (Accessed: 24 February 2023).

Walmsley, B., Gilmore, A., O'Brien, D., and Torreggiani, A. (eds.) (2022) *Culture in Crisis*. Available at: https://www.culturehive.co.uk/wp-content/uploads/2022/01/Culture_in_Crisis.pdf (Accessed: 20 September 2022).

Whitaker, S. (2018) *Hurdles to the Participation of Children, Families and Young People in Museums: A Literature Review*. Available at: https://kidsinmuseums.org.uk/wp-content/uploads/2018/12/Hurdles-to-Participation.pdf (Accessed: 24 February 2023).

Part II
Marketing strategy in practice

4 Managing and implementing marketing

Introduction

Marketing is vital for museums, but it is just one integral component of a complex ecosystem of functions within them and needs to work in tandem with other departments. Challenges for those with responsibility for marketing are vast, including a lack of budget and time; a constantly changing environment; staying on top of new communication platforms and algorithm changes; and the need to advocate for the role of marketing internally when it comes to influence and budget-setting. Without doubt, the most common challenges I hear from people with responsibility for museum marketing are a lack of time and budget, regardless of the size of the museum and what country the museum is based in. But these issues are of particular severity for the smallest museums, where a lack of skills or expertise across the full range of marketing specialisms is also often an issue. This can be frustrating and stressful for marketing teams.

Setting up the internal marketing function appropriately and optimised for your museum is a fundamental step to success. But what this looks like will vary greatly from museum to museum. This chapter considers how museums run their marketing, including roles and responsibilities and working with external providers. It suggests what makes a thriving marketing function and how to advocate for marketing internally.

Responsibility for marketing

The marketing function in museums varies enormously depending on factors such as the size and type of museum, budget, culture, and preferences of senior managers or trustees. Large museums tend to have a marketing team that executes marketing activity, led by a head of marketing or similar who is part of the senior management team. Each team member has their own area of responsibility and expertise, such as email marketing, digital content creation, or PR. Some local authority-run or university museums have a marketing team or officer who sits within the broader organisation and has a much wider remit (so their time may also be spent on communication on planning applications or academic research). In smaller and volunteer-run

DOI: 10.4324/9781003309147-7

museums, a trustee may be responsible for all aspects of marketing, or it will be only one element of a paid staff member's many responsibilities.

In some museums, marketing sits with development, fundraising, and income-generation teams; in others, marketing and audience development are closely intertwined. There are also differences in where responsibility for digital content sits. It can fall under the responsibility of marketing; in other cases, under engagement and learning teams, or digital teams. A UK museum workforce survey for Arts Council England found that only 2.8% of the around 2,000 respondents said the *main focus* of their job role was marketing and communications (ranked 10th after roles such as curatorial, education and engagement, and conservation/preservation). However, when asked about other duties on which they spend at least 10% of their time, 7.2% of respondents said marketing and communications (Naylor, McLean, and Griffiths, 2016, pp. 35–6). Many staff and volunteers within the museum who don't form part of the marketing team are likely to still play a valuable role in marketing; for example, helping to define target audiences for events and exhibitions; providing ideas, stories, objects, and photos for digital content; and feeding back observations and feedback from visitors. It is important that there is both a practical mechanism (regular meeting slots, ideas noticeboard, space on the intranet) and organisational culture (supportive leadership and allocated time) that allow and encourage this interaction and input to ensure that marketing doesn't operate in a silo.

The UK's Arts Marketing Association's Benchmarking Survey of over 500 members (across art forms, including theatre, music, and dance) found that the marketing team tends to be approximately 10% of total employees, regardless of the size of organisation (2019). The breakdown just for museum responses shows that even in museums with 0–5 employees or full-time equivalent, 64% have a marketing role, with the number of people working in marketing growing in line with the organisation size. For example, for museums with 21–50 employees, 57% have more than three marketing employees (or full-time equivalents), and for organisations with more than 50 staff, 55% have more than six staff in their marketing function (Arts Marketing Association, 2023).

Examples of marketing functions

Below are two examples highlighting the different ways that museum marketing teams can be structured in museums of different sizes.

The Postal Museum

The Postal Museum in London has a total staff of just under 100. The Head of Marketing and Communications is an Executive Team member responsible for the overall marketing and communications strategy and leads the marketing team, which comprises:

- A Marketing Manager, responsible for campaign management and tactical plans.
- A Digital Engagement Manager, responsible for website development and content planning and delivery.
- A part-time Development Manager, focusing on individual giving and some corporate giving (securing trusts and foundations is devolved across teams).
- A Designer/Web Editor reporting to the Digital Engagement Manager and responsible for in-house design for print and digital, video editing, web analytics, and Google Adwords.
- A Communications Officer reporting to the Marketing Manager, responsible for social media content, community management, press and PR (mostly reactive) and influencer liaison. They are also regularly supported by a PR freelancer for exhibition launches and major campaigns (Duffield, 2023).

The Museum of Cambridge

The Museum of Cambridge, UK, has a full-time equivalent staff of 4.6. Marketing is undertaken by the Development, Communications, and Retail Officer (DCRO) who works 0.8 FTE and reports to the Engagement and Collections Manager. The DCRO has responsibility for supporting and leading on aspects of marketing, fundraising, and retail activity. This involves oversight and coordination of social media, coordinating and supporting project officers with marketing campaigns, and leading on publicity aspects of fundraising campaigns. On a tight budget, combining the marketing role with retail and fundraising responsibilities has enabled consistency and some efficiencies. Museum Director Annie Davis says that the investment in this post has been "transformative in supporting the diversification of our income streams" (2023). Previously, marketing activity was completed by individual project officers, so if a project officer was running a memory café, they would design the leaflet, social media content, and work with stakeholders. There were also social media volunteers who created collections-focused content such as "Guess the object". Project funding meant external strategic expertise could sometimes be brought in and professional graphic design and photography was invested in.

Working with external suppliers

An option to enable specialist skills to be utilised flexibly is paying for support from external suppliers such as freelancers, consultants, agencies, other museums, and sector-support organisations. This can be for one-off projects, on a retained basis, or as an interim solution. Common support includes graphic design, website design, photography and video, livestreams, search engine optimisation, paid search, social media advertising, media buying, crisis communications, strategy development, market research, evaluation, and workshop facilitation to name just a few. Whilst using external providers can save internal teams time, to get the best out of the relationship, time needs to be invested to develop a solid brief and to manage the relationship with prompt feedback. Working with external specialists can also provide valuable training opportunities for internal teams to develop skills and different approaches.

A thriving marketing function

Below are some key markers that will help you build a successful marketing function:

A plan

Having a strategic marketing plan that guides and anchors the direction of the marketing department is necessary for a solid foundation on which to build everything else.

The right marketing team

Aim to build the strongest marketing team possible within available resources, with clear roles and responsibilities. Stay on top of audience, marketing and technology developments, and internal strategic plans to understand what experience and skillsets will be needed in the immediate and longer-term future. An annual or biennial team skills and confidence audit mapped against these plans can identify gaps and training needs. Opportunities to connect with other marketers in the sector and beyond – for example heritage, tourism, leisure, and not-for-profit sectors – are valuable.

Organisational culture

It is important that marketing has buy-in from senior management and trustees and that it is integrated into the museum at a strategic level, with an outward-looking and audience-centric approach, and valuing and trusting marketing staff and volunteers.

Investing in marketing

Flowing directly from organisational culture is the need to invest adequately in marketing. This includes paying appropriately for skilled and experienced staff and investing in training and tools to improve their work. Paying suitable salaries and having a valued benefits package is a prerequisite for being able to attract marketing talent and diversifying marketing teams, bringing in people with different expertise and backgrounds.

Internal communication

Internal communication and liaison with other departments is crucial, especially in bigger organisations. It is important that the marketing team has sufficient notice for advance planning and that other departments are aware of the marketing team's deadlines. Those with responsibility for marketing need to build relationships with other departments, and it can be useful to map internal audiences. With an increase in working from home and flexible working, different mechanisms and a more concerted effort are needed to ensure good internal communication takes place.

Staying agile and working "smart"

Marketing – more than ever – needs to be agile to adapt to a rapidly changing world. For example, staying on top of public sentiment and sector research on how audience behaviour is changing; learning from and sharing best practice with colleagues from other museums; and ensuring sign-off procedures are clear and swift. Most museums are never going to have the types of marketing budgets enjoyed by consumer goods marketers, and there are never enough hours in the day. So, working as "smart" as possible and being clear on priorities is advisable. For example, creating templates; planning content in advance; maximising the use of available analytics; creating and repurposing evergreen content; using chatbots for enquiries. A survey of over 1,200 global marketers by Hubspot found that marketers spend an average of five hours a day on manual, administrative, or operational tasks. Clearly, if even some of these could be automated or streamlined, time could be freed up for other tasks that are more creative, strategic, or impactful (Iskiev, 2022).

Monitoring and evaluation

As Chapter 5g shows, monitoring and evaluating activity is crucial for understanding what is working and what needs to be tweaked to improve delivery. Collecting data is not enough; there needs to be time to digest it, make sense of it, and act on it. An organisational culture where team members feel comfortable sharing their input and not finger-pointing blame is key.

Advocating for marketing internally

There is often strong competition for budgets and influence internally. And with funding cuts that many museums have experienced, there can be a disquieting expectation that marketing teams will continue to deliver the same or even more, for less. Marketing teams need to advocate internally for the importance of marketing; for example:

- Identify the hurdles and what you can do about them. For example, is marketing seen more tactically than strategically by senior leaders or other departments? Who needs to buy in to marketing more? Can you present at a board meeting? Can you involve other departments in a planning workshop?
- Find your allies – are there others in the museum who value marketing? Perhaps one trustee who could be a marketing champion?

50 *Marketing strategy in practice*

- Share what marketing is and its strategic potential with others in the museum but avoid jargon.
- Share marketing evaluation results, focusing on the difference marketing has made to the museum's key goals and priorities (see Chapter 5g).
- Put together a researched wish list of what else marketing could achieve if you had two or three further levels of marketing support (staff, budgets, resources). What difference could these make?
- When talking about marketing budgets, frame this as *investment,* not spend, to help make the link with a return. Your budget should be creating value and giving something back, whether that is financial, reputational, audience growth, diversification, or engagement.

Questions to consider

- How is marketing viewed as a function by other departments in your museum?
- What do you feel makes a thriving marketing function or team?
- How can you advocate for marketing internally?

Further reading

This list covers further reading suggestions for all of the chapters in Part II.

Arts Marketing Association (2023) *Culture Hive Free Online Resource Hub.* Available at: https://www.culturehive.co.uk/

The Audience Agency (2020) *Guide | Audience Development Planning.* Available at: https://www.theaudienceagency.org/resources/guide-to-audience-development-planning

The Chartered Institute of Marketing (2015) *7Ps. A Brief Summary of Marketing and How it Works.* Available at: https://www.cim.co.uk/media/4772/7ps.pdf

Davies, S. M. (2023) *Data Driven Museums, SHARE Museums East.* Available at: https://www.sharemuseumseast.org.uk/wp-content/uploads/2023/02/Data-Driven-Museums-2023-FINAL-1.pdf

Foster, H. (2020) *Evaluation Toolkit for Museums, SHARE Museums East.* Available at: https://www.sharemuseumseast.org.uk/wp-content/uploads/2020/05/SHARE_Evaluation_Toolkit_FINAL_WEB.pdf

Hague, P., Cupman, J., Harrison, M., and Truman, P. (2016) *Market Research in Practice.* 3rd edn. London: Kogan Page.

Hill, L., O'Sullivan, C., O'Sullivan, T., and Whitehead, B. (2018) *Creative Arts Marketing.* 3rd edn. Oxon: Routledge.

Kingsnorth, S. (2019) *Digital Marketing Strategy. An Integrated Approach to Online Marketing.* 2nd ed. London: Kogan Page.

References

Arts Marketing Association (2019) *AMA Benchmarking Survey 2019 – Member Report.* Available at: https://www.a-m-a.co.uk/wp-content/uploads/2021/12/AMA-Benchmarking-Survey-2019-_Member-Report.pdf (member-only resource). (Accessed: 5 January 2023).

Arts Marketing Association (2023) Email to Christina Lister, 9 March.
Davis, A. (2023) Email to Christina Lister, 7 May.
Duffield, A. (2023) (The Postal Museum's Head of Marketing and Communications). Email to Christina Lister, 17 March.
Iskiev, M. (2022) *The HubSpot Blog's 2023 Marketing Strategy & Trends Report: Data from 1,200+ Global Marketers.* Available at: https://blog.hubspot.com/marketing/hubspot-blog-marketing-industry-trends-report (Accessed: 3 May 2023).
Naylor, R., McLean, B., and Griffiths, C. (2016) *Character Matters: Attitudes, Behaviours and Skills in the UK Museum Workforce.* Available at: https://www.artscouncil.org.uk/sites/default/files/download-file/Museums%20Workforce%20ABS%20BOP%20Final%20Report.pdf (Accessed: 8 March 2023).

5 Developing a museum marketing strategy

Introduction

Strategic marketing is an integrated part of the museum's overall strategic management process and supports the museum's mission. This often incorporates marketing at board level, recognises it as an important organisational function alongside others such as finance, operations, and HR. It involves understanding the environment the museum operates in, its competitors, and how the museum is positioned; as well as identifying and understanding its target audiences, the value and offer it provides them, and how it does so. It typically involves taking a longer-term view and attributing dedicated resources to marketing (whether that is budget, staff/volunteer time, or both).

In contrast to *strategic* marketing, *tactical* marketing comprises the actions you undertake and the tools needed to achieve your marketing strategy. Tactical marketing should flow from and support your strategic direction – the strategy comes first, even though it can be tempting to fast-forward straight to the tactics, for example, talking about what to put on a poster *before* being clear on whom you need to reach and why.

A strategic marketing approach is likely to result in a written marketing strategy document. The process for its development is covered in the following chapters 5a–5g. This chapter first sets out reasons to develop a marketing strategy, what makes a good one, and who should be involved in its development. It introduces the framework I use to develop a marketing strategy and finishes with pitfalls to avoid and tips to consider.

Why develop a marketing strategy?

A marketing strategy document is a roadmap, identifying an end goal as well as the journey on how to get there. Setting aside time away from the daily to-do list and working through a series of exercises, collating feedback, digesting research, and setting goals is valuable. The process can help challenge assumptions and "we're doing it this way because that's how we've always done it" thinking, as well as identify gaps and inconsistencies in data and knowledge. It also helps in advocating for marketing resources.

DOI: 10.4324/9781003309147-8

The process is proactive and helps you to prioritise audiences, allocate limited resources, and focus activities. Having clarity around goals and objectives makes decision-making and evaluation easier further down the line, which supports accountability and feeds into improving future activities. This helps to identify value for money and minimise a waste of resources. It also encourages a longer-term perspective, helping the museum to anticipate and prepare for change, and be less vulnerable to challenges.

A marketing strategy can be motivating and help unite internal teams around the outcomes. A written strategy captures and shares insights so that they are not all in one team member's head, notebook, or computer, where they could disappear when that person leaves. It doesn't need to be a tome (in fact, it's likely to be more useable if it's not) – even two pages of bullet points can be very valuable if the thinking has been done and the bullet points cover key elements. And finally, a marketing strategy can also support funding and sponsorship bids, and may be a requirement of them.

What makes a "good" marketing strategy?

A "good" marketing strategy supports the museum's overall goals and mission in a cost-effective way and is referred to (and updated regularly if needed) rather than gathering dust on a physical or digital shelf. I would also suggest that markers of a good marketing strategy include it:

- Is tailored to the museum.
- Is based on data and insights you have gathered.
- Has input and buy-in from a broad range of people and departments.
- Is signed off by leaders.
- Is realistic and feasible to implement.
- Sets out how to monitor and evaluate marketing activities.
- Is adequately resourced in terms of budget and staff/volunteer time.
- Covers an appropriate period.
- Has digestible headlines and/or an executive summary.
- Is understandable.
- Is shared with relevant people, departments, and organisations.
- Is referred to and used.

Writing a marketing strategy doesn't automatically guarantee it will be implemented, so consider how it will be used from the outset. Think about who needs to approve, support, and use it.

Time period

The period that museum marketing strategies cover vary in length, sometimes to tie in with an organisational plan's timeframe or a redevelopment.

Some are written to cover five years to provide consistency on the choice of target audiences, how to position the museum, and headline goals. Two to three years is also common and can be valuable to ensure that the key assumptions and research that feed into the plan are updated more frequently, and that the marketing plan stays relevant and fit for purpose as factors change, such as changes to funding; and in the size, skills, and experience of the internal team. The pace of change of many aspects of the external environment (such as technological developments, political polarisation, economic stability) can be quite dynamic. The tactical sides of the marketing strategy including the action plan are better suited to shorter timeframes such as 12 months or, if the museum's environment is very volatile, even breaking it down to quarterly or six-month action plans. Whilst a goal might still be relevant across a three-year period, shorter-term objectives that flow from that and what you will do to achieve that goal in the next six months may change.

Who is involved in developing a marketing strategy?

It is beneficial to assign responsibility for the process, document, activities, and resulting outcomes. Visualise a sand timer or hourglass: consult and involve a broad range of the internal team (and potentially some external stakeholders) at the start when information-gathering and seeking to understand the museum's environment. As well as marketing and audience development, this could include staff and volunteers involved in front-of-house and visitor services, learning and engagement, events, and exhibitions, curatorial, and conservation. The number of people involved is then likely to shrink as you move through the process and work up recommendations and create the strategy. And then finally, the process will broaden out again as you share the recommendations with colleagues and ensure there is sign-off, buy-in, and support with its delivery. As well as going to senior management and staff or volunteers from different departments, the marketing strategy document may also be shared with the board of trustees, funding bodies, sponsors, and marketing suppliers such as research agencies, website developers, and PR professionals (who may receive redacted versions).

Which areas are covered in your marketing strategy depends on your museum's setup and preferences; for example, is fundraising included or is that in a separate fundraising strategy? Will you include goals and objectives that overlap with audience development (and perhaps also name it as a joint strategy) or have them separately? Combining them can ensure a more cohesive approach that is simpler to follow with just one document. However, separate strategies that reference each other can make more sense for museums that separate out marketing and audience development functions, teams, remits, and goals.

Introducing the marketing strategy framework

The strategic marketing planning process involves working through a series of steps to develop the museum's marketing, setting out a forward-looking plan. The following chapters provide a framework for developing a museum's marketing strategy that I use, with each chapter covering one step in more detail:

a Situational analysis: Where are we now?
b Goals and objectives: Where are we going?
c Target audiences: Whom do we want to reach?
d Strategy and approach: How will we get there?
e Tactics and action plan: What are we going to do to get there?
f Resources: What will it cost?
g Monitoring and evaluation: How will we know if we've got there?

Unless you are developing a new museum or perhaps reopening and repositioning after a big redevelopment, you are unlikely to be starting from scratch with a blank piece of paper. Therefore, you may already have a defined and agreed set of target audiences or marketing goals, in which case you can bypass that content or swap around the order in which you read the chapters.

The matrices and models presented invariably rely on the quality of input, which can be subjective or patchy. They also often assume a level of logical behaviour from audiences, whereas in reality, audiences are complex and don't always behave in such rigid ways. Use the framework as a guide and adapt it to your needs, research, and circumstances – some models and matrices will resonate more with you than others. Many of the recommendations can be scaled up or down, and not everything needs to be done exhaustively, especially for smaller, largely volunteer-run museums.

Key pitfalls

Some key pitfalls to watch out for as you develop your marketing strategy:

- Not enough analysis – missing the first step and diving straight into decision-making.
- Too much analysis – getting bogged down in data and not drawing conclusions from it.
- Jumping straight into tactics, without thinking about your strategic approach.
- Being overambitious with what you can do and achieve on your resources available.
- A lack of buy-in, meaning that the strategy isn't supported and can't be delivered.

Marketing strategy in practice

Top tips

And some tips to reflect on:

- Remember the purpose of the marketing strategy and whom it needs to serve.
- Break the process down, and take a step at a time.
- Tweak the framework and format to work for you and your museum.
- Consider how you can increase the likelihood of your finished strategy being used.
- Value progress over perfection – monitoring and evaluation will help you fine-tune things.
- Enjoy the process as well as the outcome; be curious.

Questions to consider

- What does a "good" marketing strategy look like to you/your museum?
- What do you want to achieve with your marketing strategy?
- Who needs to be involved in its development and in what capacity?

5a Situational analysis
Where are we now?

Introduction

Situational or situation analysis is the first step in creating a marketing strategy. It involves gathering and analysing data to enable you to make evidence-based decisions and to provide a baseline from which to measure progress. You may know a lot instinctively or anecdotally, but don't assume that everyone does, and it is still worth writing things down. It can be tempting to skip or fast-forward this step, but spending time on it helps to avoid making decisions based on assumptions or incomplete information. At the same time, you need to be disciplined so you don't get too weighed down by all the data and never emerge. Be systematic in your approach, as well as realistic and honest. This chapter covers the following themes, with questions at the end of each that you can use as prompts: an internal analysis of your museum and marketing; your audiences; and an external analysis, including a competitor analysis and using a STEEPLE framework. I have set out an extensive list of questions and prompts – you can choose what you include according to what is appropriate for your circumstances. As well as information-gathering, you need to *analyse* that information to identify insights, opportunities, and challenges that will affect or feed into your strategy. The chapter finishes by covering how to draw conclusions – including identifying gaps in information – and then summarise and present them succinctly.

Internal analysis: Your museum

Start with key information about your museum that is relevant to your marketing. Some of the prompts below might be important in larger organisations, in museums with new marketing teams, or for a big project where the funder expects to see a considered marketing strategy but may not be for smaller museums.

Key organisational information

Consider your organisation's history and legal status, and summarise its main collections, venue, and people, especially if the strategy will be shared with external organisations and stakeholders.

DOI: 10.4324/9781003309147-9

Your mission, vision, and values

Set out your museum's key strategic goals and how marketing should support these. Include your museum's mission, vision, and values if they exist and how they can influence marketing.

Income

Summarise key sources of income and funding, and the proportional split between categories that are relevant to your museum, for example: grants, ticketing, events, memberships, donations, sponsorship, retail, venue hire, catering, and so on. Provide breakdowns by audience segments if you have them. Identify any trends from the past few years, such as a fall in group visit income or a rise in venue hire income. Explain any key seasonal variations and patterns, and whether the museum is meeting targets and expectations. Highlight significant income drivers, such as certain event days or a successful fundraising campaign. Include future income projections from the business plan.

Typical questions to answer

- What strategic vision and mission does marketing need to support?
- How should or could the museum's values influence its marketing?
- What are recent income patterns and income projections, and resulting implications for marketing?

Internal analysis: Your marketing

Undertake an audit of your current marketing, strategy, activities, resources, and results.

Your museum's marketing strategy

Reflect on your current marketing strategy (if you have one), how useful it has been, and any lessons you have learned from its development and implementation. For example, were the goals met? Were the resources used as allocated? Why/why not? What did your evaluation tell you (see Chapter 5g for prompts)?

Your museum's positioning

Your museum's positioning is how your audiences perceive you and your offer, in comparison with your competitors. Consider what audience surveys, consultation, and reviews tell you. Is the museum seen as good value for money, expensive, family-friendly, interesting, and so on? How does this compare with how you *want* the museum to be perceived? Are there differences between the desired and actual perceptions that you want to do something about?

Your museum's marketing mix

Undertake an audit of your marketing mix for a relevant timescale, typically 12–24 months to cover seasonal variations. The marketing mix comprises the tools and techniques that an organisation uses to achieve its marketing strategy and objectives. The original four components – Product, Place, Price, and Promotion – were expanded to the 7Ps to include People, Physical Evidence, and Process in 1981 by Booms and Bitner, which is now the version recommended by the UK's Chartered Institute of Marketing (2015). The categories are useful prompts to reflect on.

Your museum's products

Summarise your museum's key products or services – for example, your permanent collections and exhibitions, temporary exhibitions, events, membership, schools programme, your café, your shop, and merchandise. If there have been certain events, exhibitions, and programmes that were particularly successful by the metric(s) the museum values (be that income, attracting a new audience, audience satisfaction, reviews, and so on), include a brief explanation of why.

Your place

"Place" refers to where and when your products or services are available or distributed to your audiences. Your venue, site, and buildings are a starting point, alongside your facilities and opening hours. Whilst your venue's physical location is unlikely to change, you may also undertake outreach activities in your local community, or digital engagement such as talks and workshop online. If you sell tickets or memberships, where can they be purchased? Are the places and distribution methods appropriate to your audiences?

Your pricing

Summarise what products and services you charge for, your charging policy, and data such as the average price achieved per temporary exhibition or event. Review pricing to take account of inflation, cost changes, and comparison against competitors and comparators. To what extent is pricing a barrier to visiting or engaging? For whom? Do your pricing policies support your values and audience goals – who can access discounts and concessionary rates? Include any trends and changes from the last few years. See Chapter 8 for more.

Your promotion

This covers the way your museum communicates with its audiences. Review your marketing evaluation, and make the most of data you have, such as visitor surveys and website and social media analytics. You might want to consider the success of your marketing campaigns, media coverage, best performing content on social media, and best performing content on your website. Set out your current communication channels and activities, and consider which reach and engage your different audiences.

Your people

You can choose to just focus on the marketing team here or take a wider interpretation that includes anyone who encounters audiences and is involved in delivering their museum experience. A helpful front-of-house team member can really make someone's visit, just as a negative interaction can ruin it. Museum staff – and in particular, volunteers in smaller museums – are often one of the main positives in visitor survey comments and online reviews. Identify who comes into contact with audiences, from in-person interactions (front-of-house welcomes, tour guides, café staff, and so on), to telephone and email enquiries, social media communications, and online review responses. Collate and review feedback, and be clear on strengths, what audiences are noticing and valuing, and any issues that may need tackling. In terms of the marketing team, consider its composition, skills, and expertise: Are they relevant for the museum's needs?

Your processes

This involves zooming out and considering the audience visit or engagement as one step of a broader process. How do you manage relationships and interactions with your audience? Do you use CRM (Customer Relationship Management) systems and software to record, organise, report, and analyse these interactions? What tools do you use to better understand your audiences' behaviour and develop more tailored communication? Where are the pain or pinch points, and what can you do about them? There's a lot of digital data you can access that will give you information about the user experience. If you have an online shop or sell memberships and tickets, where does the highest drop-off rate or cart abandonment occur? Can you reduce the friction anywhere? How can you make the audience journey as smooth as possible (see Chapter 5b for more)?

Your physical evidence

The museum's physical (and digital) evidence, which gives your audiences cues and reassurances about what to expect, is particularly important for people who have never visited or engaged before. For example, what does your building and its surroundings say about your museum (are you traditional, contemporary, welcoming, accessible, intimidating)? What do online reviews say about the museum? Consider whether you provide enough information for potential audiences, such as what facilities you have.

Situational analysis: Where are we now?

Your marketing resources

Set out who is responsible for marketing strategy and delivery, the reporting structure, and how the marketing department (whether a team or individual) sits as part of the wider organisation. Summarise key roles, and identify the team's core strengths and skills. Be honest if there are gaps; for example, if there are vacancies or areas the team needs to develop competencies in. You can also include which – if any – marketing services or support is brought in from freelancers, consultants, or agencies, and any key stakeholders such as local or regional tourism partners and a local authority's communications team.

Include a list of key equipment, tools, and subscriptions that the marketing team uses, such as graphic design software, a social media scheduling tool, or subscription to a media-monitoring service. Set out a breakdown of the annual marketing budget and what it is spent on, including research, delivery, and training if relevant. Include insights from any evaluation on budget spent and value, such as return on investment (see Chapter 5g for more).

Typical questions to answer

- What marketing activities and approaches does the museum currently use?
- How do you evaluate the success of your current marketing?
- Have you met your recent marketing goals and objectives? Why/why not?
- Has the allocated marketing budget and time spent been sufficient to deliver on existing goals and objectives?
- What are the lessons learned?

Your audiences

Your audiences straddle the internal and external categories – your audiences themselves are external, but your approach to choosing, reaching, and engaging them comes from within the museum. Set out whom your *target* audiences are (if you have them), the segmentation system you use (if applicable, see Chapter 5c for more) and data on your *actual* audiences – in-person and digital if relevant. Use any information sources available to you, such as:

- Ticketing/booking information, CRM data.
- Visitor surveys.
- Front desk data collection such as postal codes, first-time visitors.
- Membership data.
- Online reviews.
- Website and social media analytics.
- Observation/anecdotal feedback from front-of-house teams or a visitor book.
- Insights from focus groups.
- Data from school bookings.
- Information on venue hirers.

Summarise what you know about your audiences, for example:

Who are your audiences?

- Where do they live?
- What is their demographic breakdown?
- How do they differ across the week/year, events, or exhibitions?
- Who are your digital/online audiences?
- How do they differ from your in-person audiences?

What are the engagement or attendance drivers?

- Why do your audiences visit or engage with your museum?
- How do they find out about you? What communication channels do they use?
- Why do they become members or patrons?

Where and how do they engage with you?

- Where do your audiences engage with you? In-person at the museum or somewhere else? Digitally? Only for particular exhibitions or events? Only your shop or café?
- How do they travel to you?
- What proportion are first-time or repeat visitors/participants? How does this vary for different exhibitions or activities?
- How often do they visit/engage/attend?
- How long do they spend visiting or engaging?
- Whom do they visit the museum with? On their own, with family, children, friends, colleagues, in a group?
- When do they visit? What time of day, day of the week, month of the year?

How satisfied are your audiences?

- How satisfied are your audiences with their visit, engagement, or purchase?
- What are their highlights?
- What would they change?
- If they have paid, do they feel they got value for money?
- Would they recommend your museum to others?
- Do they intend to return or engage again?
- What is your Net Promoter Score (if you use this measure of satisfaction), and how does this compare over time?

You may have a lot of information to distil, so summarising key information in tables and/or visually in graphs and charts is useful. Be careful about jumping headfirst into conclusions if the data is patchy or not very robust. A participant

Situational analysis: Where are we now? 63

in a training session I once ran gave this example as a cautionary tale: their museum really pushed visitor survey completions on big event days as an efficient way to meet their sample size target. One of the areas they wanted to explore was the visitor demand for a café, which they didn't currently have. However, the overreliance on event day feedback meant there were barely any comments about the need for a café since event day visitors enjoyed access to specially brought-in caterers (which visitors to non-event days did not).

Stakeholders

You can also include a list of stakeholders that you work with and/or communicate with, such as funders and tourism partners.

Potential audiences

Once you are clear on who your audiences are, you can start to identify who is *not* visiting, engaging, or participating and see where there is potential for growth or change. Chapter 5c delves into making decisions about which audiences to target and engage.

Typical questions to answer

- Who are your current audiences and what do you know about them?
- Do your current audiences meet your audience targets and museum goals? Why/why not?
- Are there significant patterns from recent years? For example, a stagnation in visitor numbers, a growth of a particular audience segment?
- Does your current segmentation model serve you well (see Chapter 5c)? Is it meaningful to your staff and volunteers? Is it relevant across the museum?
- What (if anything) don't you know about your current audiences that you need to find out?
- Which of your audiences are overrepresented or underrepresented compared with your local community, the national population, or other comparator museums?
- What do you know about potential audiences you want to attract and engage, and what don't you know that you need to find out?

External analysis

Competitor analysis

I have sometimes heard museum representatives say that their museum has no competitors, since there is no other museum with the same collection in their vicinity. Many of them also don't like viewing other museums or cultural or visitor attractions – which may be partners or collaborators – as competition. However, this doesn't mean that museums don't face any competition for their audiences' time, attention, or money, all of which are finite.

64 Marketing strategy in practice

There are two main categories of competitors: direct and indirect. Direct competitors essentially offer the same product as you and in the same market (such as another museum), whilst indirect competitors have a different offering, but one that could still satisfy the same audience needs and goals (such as a cinema for an indoor activity, a library's story time for a toddler activity). Competitors are therefore not just other museums, or even other cultural organisations or not-for-profit organisations; they may also be commercial businesses and free public spaces. Different audiences view competitors differently, and museums' different products also have different sets of competitors.

Let's take a fictitious industrial heritage museum in Canada as an example. I am using generic examples here, but I recommend being specific and naming competitors. There may be some academics, researchers, and enthusiasts so interested in the collections there that they are prepared to travel far and spend a lot of money to reach the museum. But they are likely to be in the minority. Alternatives for them may include other industrial heritage museums, books on industrial heritage, online communities, and online talks by experts. Whereas for families looking to entertain their children, someone in the family might have an interest in industrial heritage or steam engines that motivates their choice of activity, or their main criterion might be to keep their children busy on a rainy afternoon. Alternatives for them can include other local museums, the local library, leisure activities such as a soft play centre or bowling, staying home, or visiting friends or family.

Another way of considering competitors is looking at each of your core products and services. Table 5a.1 shows examples of two products from the industrial heritage museum example and their competitors, alongside what the competitors can offer that the museum in question can't, and what sets the

Table 5a.1 Comparing a museum's offer with competitors

Product or programme	Key competitors	What they offer that the museum does not	What sets the museum apart
Local schools programme	Local arts centre Local art gallery Local theatre Another local/ regional museum	More established programmes Free of charge A dedicated schools' room with picnic tables	Ties to science curriculum Hands-on fun: interactives, experiments Original objects Object handling
Venue hire	A village hall Local hotels Other local museums and galleries The local university	More state-of-the-art conference facilities Better accessibility Bigger capacity Exclusive venue hire	Quirky and interesting building Great photo opportunities Unique social activities such as behind-the-scenes tours

museum apart. This can feed into your positioning, your Unique Selling Points, marketing messaging, and campaigns, covered in subsequent chapters.

If you don't know who your competitors are, ask your audiences and potential audiences. Step into your audiences' shoes and put their likely searches in search engines (such as "family-friendly day out Montreal" or "local history talk Toronto") and see what other organisations and activities come up. Look at the competitors' websites, e-newsletters, other marketing materials, and reviews of them. You can also undertake some mystery shopping online or visit them in-person to fully understand what they offer and whom they appeal to.

A STEEPLE analysis

A STEEPLE analysis is a useful tool to identify and understand external influences on your museum as prompts to consider. It is one of the iterations based on the original ETPS analysis developed by Francis Aguilar in 1967, covering Economic, Technological, Political, and Social factors. It was re-arranged to the snappier PEST and then expanded to various formations over the years, including SLEPT, PESTEL, PESTLE, or STEEPLE, the latter of which I use since the inclusion of Ethical and Environmental are of particular importance today.

External influences can be opportunities, challenges, or both. Seek contributions from a range of individuals, departments, and sources for a comprehensive analysis with different perspectives. Sources you might find useful include sector data and research; tourism data and trends; population data and trends analysis; public sentiment surveys; funders' strategic plans; and the news. For each category, you can consider local, national, and international factors if relevant. There is the potential to end up with a huge list of factors, so the next step is to be disciplined and filter out ideas that may affect your *museum,* but not *marketing* specifically. Ask yourself "So what?" as a prompt.

Another way of whittling down the list is using criteria to grade the factors, for example against likely impact, importance, urgency, reach, or what you can act on. And decide what time period you want to look at. For example, a longer-term trend for many countries is an ageing population, but will your museum notice a difference from that in terms of visitors over the next two years? If not, capture such longer-term trends elsewhere, and focus on the issues that affect the strategy's time period. Table 5a.2 shares an example short STEEPLE analysis, along with implications for marketing.

Typical questions to answer

- Who are your main competitors overall, by audience segment and/or by product or programme?
- What do they offer that you don't?
- How are they marketing themselves? What channels do they use to communicate with their audiences, and what messages do they convey?

Table 5a.2 An example STEEPLE analysis

Category	Examples	Implications for marketing
Social/Socio-cultural	New residential development being built in our town.	Potential for new visitors. Opportunities to build relationships and play a role in fostering a sense of place and community.
Technological	Constant changes to social media platforms and algorithms.	Ensure museum isn't too reliant on social media platforms – cultivate website, e-newsletter, and other platforms we have more control over.
Economic	High inflation currently and predicted for the next 12–18 months.	Take account of this in our upcoming marketing budgets. Review our ticketing, costs, and charges. Consider impact of inflation on audiences.
Environmental	Increased audience consciousness around the climate crisis and expectations of organisations taking action.	Undertake a carbon footprint audit of our marketing; create an action plan of what steps we can take to reduce our environmental impact. Communicate this with audiences.
Political	Change of local government – new political party now has the majority.	Understand their culture policy. Develop relationships with the new local politicians, and invite them for a tour.
Legal	Changes to laws on declaring sponsored content on social media.	Impact on our relationships with social media influencers – need to understand legislation and ensure our influencers comply too.
Ethical	Previous use of gallery sponsorship from fossil fuel companies.	Need to agree on clear sponsorship policy going forward.

- What sets you apart? What do – or can – you offer that audiences value and that competitors don't have?
- Which key external factors will affect your museum's marketing in the next few years?

Identifying gaps

Throughout this process, you might identify gaps in your data or knowledge that are critical for you to plug before you go any further, or deal with as part of your next steps. For example, if you don't know what barriers potential audiences face, or which are the most significant, find out through focus groups, surveys, a stand at a community fair, or conversations with community leaders. When planning research, consider these steps:

1 **Question:** What do you want or need to know? Why? How will you use this insight? What resources are available, and what limitations do you need to work with? What is your deadline?
2 **Capture:** Where/How will you get this information? Who will undertake the research? How can you make this as robust and inclusive as possible?
3 **Analyse:** What does the data tell you? What conclusions can you draw?
4 **Act:** How will you use these insights? What will you do/change? Whom do you need to inform about them?

Recruiting, planning, delivering, and writing up a focus group or online survey is clearly much more time-consuming than a social media poll or having a comment wall or drop box with tokens at the museum. If you have no capacity or budget available to undertake any research, what can you glean from sector research, social listening, public sentiment research, or the news? It might not be tailored to your museum and your audiences, but there will still be valuable insights into audience behaviour and trends you can reflect on. You can also set research objectives as part of your marketing strategy for the coming year, rather than try to plug the gaps at this stage.

Analysing and summarising your information: SWOT analysis

You now need to distil the information you have collected and focus on key implications for your marketing. Keep your research for reference but focus on highlighting the most important points in your marketing strategy document. A SWOT analysis is a classic model that can capture key information with implications and takeaways. Sort your findings into your museum marketing's internal strengths and weaknesses, and external opportunities and threats it may face. A short example is in Table 5a.3.

Table 5a.3 An example SWOT analysis

Strengths	Weaknesses
Our summer events programme is very successful in attracting new audiences.	Our rate of membership renewals has been steadily declining over the past three years.
Our new email marketing platform enables us to create tailored content for different audiences.	Compared to comparator museums, our pre-school audience is low.
Opportunities	**Threats**
A new residential development is being built in our town – potential for new visitors and for us to help foster a sense of place and community.	Competition from other free venues and activities being more appealing to our audiences during the economic downturn.
Our regional tourism development body is creating an off-peak winter tourism campaign.	Overreliance on social media to reach our audiences leaves us vulnerable.

A SWOT analysis is a familiar and simple way of presenting your findings and helps categorise insights. But bear in mind its limitations:

- It is subjective and reliant on the information included (including honesty around weaknesses).
- It can become lengthy and unwieldy.
- It doesn't show the interrelation of points in the different categories and may lead to an oversimplification of complex issues.
- It is a static model; on its own it doesn't help you to develop strategies or prioritise.
- Opportunities and threats can be hard to identify (who had a global pandemic in their SWOT analysis before 2020?).

To mitigate these limitations:

- Involve a range of people in the development of the SWOT analysis.
- Be honest about key assumptions you've made or limitations of the data.
- Shortlist the most important aspects that affect *marketing,* not your *museum* more broadly.
- Prioritise and ask "So what?" for each point, and focus on potential implications.
- Revisit the SWOT analysis annually to update it.
- Use your SWOT analysis as input into the TOWS analysis (set out in Chapter 5d).

Questions to consider
- Who will be responsible for the situational analysis, and who will contribute?
- What data and information do you currently have?
- What conclusions can you draw from your situational analysis, and how will they inform your next steps?

Reference

Chartered Institute of Marketing (2015) 7Ps. *A Brief Summary of Marketing and How it Works.* Available at: https://www.cim.co.uk/media/4772/7ps.pdf (Accessed: 8 April 2023).

5b Goals and objectives
Where are we going?

Introduction

Spending time on setting relevant marketing goals and objectives is worthwhile: it helps you to decide what actions to take, how to prioritise limited resources, and guides your evaluation. You can't do all things and be all things to all people, especially on tight budgets. The purpose of museum marketing is typically to increase audiences, income, and engagement and to help ensure the museum is sustainable in the longer term. But just saying "We want to grow income" is too general to guide your activity. This chapter covers how to be more specific. It defines goals and objectives, and KPIs (key performance indicators) and shares examples of each and how they interrelate. It discusses how to set them and link them to evaluation.

Marketing goals

A marketing goal is a desired result or outcome you want to achieve, often quite broad in scope and relevant in the medium or longer term. It should follow on from your museum's organisational goals, mission, vision, and values and be informed by your situational analysis. Looking back to the three example mission statements toward the end of Chapter 1, we see that they set very different directions for marketing. Marketing goals may aim to create audience awareness, develop knowledge or understanding about something; encourage audiences to form a particular attitude, opinion, or perspective; undertake a desired action or behaviour; or be a combination of them. Examples of marketing goals are to:

- Grow income (from ticket sales, events, venue hire, donations, sponsorship, and so on).
- Grow certain audience segments.
- Increase loyalty and retention, and/or deepen relationships with existing audiences.
- Nurture new audiences.
- Diversify audiences.
- Increase digital engagement.

DOI: 10.4324/9781003309147-10

- Raise awareness of the museum, its programmes, or offers with target audiences.
- Reposition or rebrand a museum.
- Inform audiences about something.
- Launch new products or programmes.
- Develop the museum's marketing capacity or processes.

In the pursuit of new audiences, ensure you don't forget to set goals around your existing ones. For very popular (and sometimes overcrowded) museums, there may also be goals around the redistribution of visitors to quieter times to manage peaks and troughs of visitor demand and potential capacity issues. This can be a form of demarketing, which is when a museum aims to reduce the consumption of a product or service. Many museums that historically never had to consider demarketing did so on reopening after Covid-19 lockdowns to restrict visitor numbers to adhere to social distancing requirements. You might also want to create a goal around green marketing to ensure this stays on your agenda (see Chapter 12 for more on demarketing and green marketing).

Use your situational analysis to inform your goals. For example, using findings from the SWOT analysis at the end of Chapter 5a:

- **A goal to counter a weakness:** To increase our rate of membership renewal (since it has been declining steadily over the past three years).
- **A goal built on a strength to make the most of an opportunity:** To launch a new winter events programme for inclusion in the regional tourism campaign, which will attract new audiences (using lessons from our successful summer event programme).
- **A goal built on a strength to minimise the impact of a threat:** To increase sign-ups to our e-newsletter (to minimise our overreliance on social media channels).

Goals may also end up becoming a strategy, especially if your museum already has its target audiences specified before you set the goals. For example, if you know you want to engage more family audiences, you might set a goal to position the museum as a family-friendly venue. Positioning your venue as a family-friendly venue might also be your strategy. If you want to avoid this overlap between goals and strategies, keep asking yourself *why* you want to do something. Why do you want to position the museum as a family-friendly venue – it's so that you can attract and engage more family audiences, which then becomes your goal.

Audience journey

Another way of coming up with goals is to think about the audience or customer journey, a representation of the average metaphorical journey your audiences might take from becoming aware of your museum, to being interested in it,

Figure 5b.1 An example audience journey.

considering a visit or purchase, undertaking that action, then perhaps also becoming a repeat visitor or supporter and advocating on your behalf (for example, by telling others about it or writing an online review). Your goals and objectives will differ depending on which stages of the audience journey you are focusing on. See Figure 5b.1 for a visual example of a typical audience journey you can adapt, and Chapter 9 on how to undertake an audience journey mapping workshop.

Marketing objectives

Marketing objectives are targets that you work towards, to help you to meet a goal. They are operational, typically actionable, more granular, and cover a shorter time period than goals. They may relate to specific audience segments. They can be targets for outputs or outcomes, outputs being activities and actions delivered, and outcomes relating to what happens as a result of the outputs. For example, "To generate five pieces of media coverage" is output related and "To increase memberships by 10%" is outcome related. Whilst goals are broader, aim for objectives to be SMART, the list below adapted from the original version created by George T. Doran in 1981:

- **Specific:** Details what need to be done, listed as precisely as possible. For example, define "local", "families", "young people", "community".
- **Measurable:** Ensure that your progress or achievement of the objective can be measured, whether quantitatively or qualitatively (see Chapter 5g on evaluation).
- **Achievable:** Your objective should be realistically achievable and accepted as such by the team (whilst still being ambitious).
- **Relevant:** Objectives should be important and worthwhile to the museum, relevant to your mission, and support your organisational and marketing goals.
- **Time-framed:** The time period for achieving the objective is clear and has an end point, such as during a particular quarter or by the end of the year.

Consider these examples and which aspects of the SMART framework they don't meet:

- To increase our membership renewals by 200% next month.
- To engage more younger people digitally.
- To have more website hits than the Tokyo National Museum.

As mentioned in the previous chapter, if you identify gaps in your information and knowledge about audiences, you can set goals and objectives around this. For example, you want to reach more families with pre-schoolers but you're not sure what their main motivators and barriers are. You could therefore set a goal: To understand the needs and barriers of families with pre-schoolers who are not currently visiting us, and a supporting objective: To run two focus groups with parents/carers of pre-schoolers by the end of the first quarter to identify their perceptions of us, needs, and barriers to visiting.

Avoid vanity objectives that sound important but don't have any meaningful relevance or don't directly support your goals. For example, I still come across the occasional desire for coverage in a particular newspaper, for the main reason that the person who requested it reads and values that newspaper, not necessarily because that would reach the museum's target audiences. And of course, every social media manager's dreaded words: "Make us go viral".

Key performance indicators (KPIs)

Key performance indicators (KPIs) are metrics used to measure your performance and whether you are on track to meet your objectives and goals. We are typically deluged with data, especially digitally, so you need to home in on the "key" aspect – what is important and relevant. Examples of common marketing KPIs include website traffic, social media reach, volume of positive media coverage, email click-through rates, referral traffic, brand mentions, hits to a website landing page, and conversion rates.

How to set your objectives and KPIs

It can be difficult to gauge what is an appropriate and achievable objective or KPI. Should you aim for a 5% increase or 10%? Using past data is a useful starting point. If your average year-on-year increase in visitors is 7%, then 5% is not a stretch, but 40% is likely to be too ambitious, unless you have a very different set of circumstances, such as a competitor closing, a significant increase in marketing resources, and a new events programme. Using sector averages and benchmarks can also be helpful when considering what to aim for. For example:

- One of England's regional museum development organisations – SHARE Museums East – found in its Annual Museums Survey report that the increase in social media followers between 2019/20 and 2021/22 was 22% for museums in the East of England, and 33% nationally (2023, p. 22).
- A research report by website agency Rubber Cheese found that visitor attraction websites with e-commerce facilities have an average basket abandonment rate of 70% and a conversion rate of around 5% (Molson, 2022, p. 10).

Table 5b.1 Examples of goals, objectives, and KPIs

Theme	Example of goals	Example of objectives	Example of KPIs
Product/ Programme	To launch a new free programme of winter events to attract new audiences	To have at least 75% of visitors to the winter events programme be first-time visitors	Percentage of new audiences to website's winter events pages
Income/ Financial	To increase income from our venue hire	To increase year-on-year income from venue hire by 15%	The number of venue hire enquiries
Engagement	To increase our membership renewal rate	To increase our membership renewal rate from 50% to 70% by the end of Q4	Open rate and click-through rate of renewal reminder emails
Brand/ Reputational	To increase awareness of our museum with international tourists planning to visit our city	Example proxy objectives/KPIs: To increase international visitors to our website by 20% this year To increase our international social media followers by 10% this year	

Example marketing goals, objectives, and KPIs

Table 5b.1 shows examples of marketing goals, supporting objectives, and KPIs categorised by theme, which can be useful if you have multiple goals. I have simply used percentages in these examples to keep them more universal, but you can include specific financial or numeric targets such as £50,000 income, or 100,000 visitors. Use the time period that your museum normally uses, whether that is financial year or calendar year, and be specific on months, quarters, and years. For brevity, I have also included only one goal, objective, and KPI, but in reality, you are likely to have several objectives and KPIs under each goal.

Evaluation

Make sure you consider monitoring and evaluation at this stage, too, so you are setting goals and objectives that you can actually measure progress against, and you have mechanisms in place to collect the data from the outset. A notoriously difficult goal to evaluate accurately – but one that is often desired – is generating a rise in awareness about a museum. Even if you narrow down the target audiences to a particular audience or community within a defined area, it's still not feasible to ask *all* of them whether they have heard of the museum before and after a campaign and measure the difference. A robust alternative is to commission research with a representative sample of the target audience group such as via an online survey asking a sample of 500–1,000 people a question about name awareness or ad recall before and after a campaign.

But for many museums, this is still likely to be prohibitively expensive or not the best use of a limited budget. So if a goal can't directly be evaluated through manageable SMART objectives, consider proxy measures to provide an *indication* of whether it is likely to have been met (see the awareness goal example in Table 5b.1, where the proxy objectives also overlap with KPIs).

You can also think about macro and micro conversions. A macro conversion is an action an audience member takes that represents your main goal (for example, visit the museum, buy a ticket, fill out a school-visit enquiry form, apply to be a volunteer). A micro conversion is an action that an audience member takes that is likely to be a step *toward* that macro conversion (for example, sign up to receive an e-newsletter, watch a video about school visits, follow the museum on social media). Setting objectives and undertaking evaluation for micro conversions can sometimes be a pragmatic way of evaluating by proxy whether a macro conversion or broader goal has been (or is likely to have been) achieved, piecing them together like a jigsaw puzzle to help tell the whole story.

Questions to consider

- What are the main organisational goals and priorities your museum has that your marketing goals and objectives should support?
- What do you feel makes a good marketing goal or objective?
- What marketing goals, objectives, and KPIs will you set?

References

Molson, K. (2022) *2022 Visitor Attraction Website Report*. Available at: https://www.rubbercheese.com/insights/2022-visitor-attraction-website-report/ (Accessed: 9 December 2022).

SHARE Museums East (2023) *Annual Museums Survey East of England 2021–22*. Available at: https://infogram.com/1pzm59yvjnwm15i25eevn3ldjmi1dpqnxn7 (Accessed: 2 February 2023).

5c Target audiences

Whom do we want to reach?

Introduction

It is tempting to say that you want everyone to come to or engage with your museum. And certainly, the aim may be for anyone and everyone to feel welcome and be able to visit if they want to. But when dealing with limited marketing budget and time, we need to narrow down our focus. And if our marketing communications try to appeal too broadly, we risk them not resonating with anyone. Making decisions about your audiences can be difficult, but it is a fundamental part of your strategic approach. This chapter focuses on how to make decisions about which audiences to reach, attract, and engage; how to segment audiences; and how to present your plans. It covers geographic, demographic, behavioural, and psychographic segmentation and provides explanations, examples, pros, and cons of each.

Choosing your target audiences may not fully be in the hands of the marketing person or team. Your museum may already have strategic commitments on whom to reach and engage. If your museum has a set of audiences to work with, review them with a marketing lens. Are they appropriate? Are they realistic? What is the rationale for choosing them? Will they meet your goals – for example, is the potential big enough to have an impact on your audience growth?

Making decisions about audiences

Your starting point is to understand who your existing audiences are – Chapter 5a set out a series of questions to guide you. Consider whether you have reached a saturation point with those audiences, or whether there is further potential to grow them. For example, is there opportunity to increase the rate and frequency of existing audiences' return visits? Are there more of the same types of audiences you can attract? Or can you identify new audiences to attract? (See also the Ansoff Matrix in Chapter 5d.)

Use the research you undertook in the situational analysis to inform your decisions about audiences. Compare key demographic information of your existing audiences (if you have it) with local, regional, or national population data and available sector benchmarking data to help you identify which audiences are underrepresented in your museum. For example, 9% of a fictitious museum's

DOI: 10.4324/9781003309147-11

audiences in Norwich, UK, are 16–24 years old. This is close to the national figure – 10.6% of the population of England and Wales are 16–24 years old (Office for National Statistics, 2021). However, looking more closely shows that Norwich has a higher-than-average proportion of young people – 17.5% (ibid.), partly as a city with two universities – so there may still be opportunities to grow this audience segment if the museum has or can develop a suitably appealing offer.

Sector benchmarking data is also very valuable to gauge what other museums are doing. In a visitor survey project I worked on with 13 museums a few years ago, one museum's proportion of visitors aged 0–14 years old was 16%, almost half the cohort's average of 31%, motivating the museum to set families as a key target audience. Many countries publish data on their nationally funded museums, which can be a starting point, although they will have more resources and different circumstances than smaller museums. With the huge breadth of products, services, and audiences that museums have, there's rarely one market and market size to consider, and it can be hard to get data on this. Often the most accessible data is on tourism – destination management organisations (such as Visit Britain) also tend to publish quantitative tourism data, with breakdowns from different countries and regions, along with growth trends, which are useful to track and build on. They often talk of market size, which is the total amount of sales, customers, or potential customers in an industry or market over a time period, usually a year. Some museums refer to markets, others prefer audiences.

There are many factors that may affect and influence which audiences you choose to focus on. I have split key factors into four strands in Table 5c.1 covering your museum's strategic ambitions; its identity and brand; pragmatic factors; and the external environment.

Growth versus diversification

You might want to categorise audiences under two umbrella headings – one for audiences with potential for driving *growth* and *income,* and another for audiences where the aim is *diversification* of your audiences. There is not a hierarchy between the two categories – both are important in different ways – but they will require different approaches. Diversifying audiences and reaching underrepresented and marginalised individuals and communities is likely to require more than simply raising awareness that your museum exists. There may be other barriers, such as a lack of access to transport, not feeling comfortable in museum spaces, or a lack of suitable facilities at your museum. Therefore, the remit for this may sit within an audience development and engagement team instead of, or as well as, the marketing team.

Segmentation

Another way of splitting your audiences is simply into existing and new potential audiences, since there are some differences in how you can reach

Table 5c.1 Factors affecting the choice of target audiences

Strand	Your museum's strategic ambitions	Your museum's identity and brand	Pragmatic factors	The external environment
Example factors	The museum's strategic plan. Income and growth goals. Diversification and inclusivity goals	The museum's subject matter, themes, collections. The museum's venue – location and facilities. The museum's reputation and brand	Past experience. Resources (budget, time, skills). Peak and quiet times. Funders' requirements. Partners and stakeholders	The competitive environment. Opportunities identified in your external environment analysis (STEEPLE)
Questions to consider	What do you need to achieve? Which audiences will support your ambitions? Where are the growth opportunities?	Who will your museum interest? Who can realistically reach and access your venue?	Which audiences can you reach and attract within your constraints? Can you develop partnerships to engage new audiences? Which barriers to visiting can you break down?	Which of your audiences are underrepresented compared with the local or national population and comparator museums? What opportunities have you identified in your SWOT?
Example implication	Funding cuts mean you need to prioritise identifying keen audiences who are most likely to visit, return, and spend money in your shop and café.	Your collections tie in well with the national school curriculum, and you can now expand to offer online workshops to schools across the country.	Your weekends are busy but your weekdays quiet, so you identify audiences who can come on weekdays, such as group visits, school groups, retired people.	The new residential development being built on the outskirts of your town offers opportunities to connect with new residents.

them, their pre-existing knowledge and perceptions about the museum and the likely messaging and calls to action you may employ. But it is likely that a more comprehensive grouping of audiences is of value. Segmentation involves breaking down your audiences into groups or segments that have some similarities *within* the groups and differences to *other* groups. The idea is to subdivide a large, heterogeneous group of audiences into several smaller, more homogenous audience groups since not all audiences are or behave the same or have the same motivations or barriers to engaging with your museum. Creating audience segments allows you to develop a more tailored and relevant marketing approach for each. It also means that you can choose where to focus your resources and prioritise groups based on your goals. Segmentation is more pragmatic, feasible, and cheaper than targeting each person individually and more valuable than a broad, one-size-fits-all approach.

I was once asked about the relevance of segmentation for a heritage project in a park in London. The valid point the workshop participant made was that everyone locally uses the park and since the project aimed to engage the *whole* local community, why segment the audience? My response was that segmenting the local community would help the project team both reach and engage people. For example, in thinking about who uses the park and how and when they use the park, compare the times, motivations, and uses for: people walking dogs; people on their way to and from work, using the park as a cut-through; families using the play area; people sitting on benches to eat their lunch in a break from work; runners; people taking part in a bootcamp class; and people going meeting friends and using the café.

Types of segmentation approaches

The four main types of segmentation approaches are: geographic, demographic, behavioural, and psychographic. I explain each below, alongside examples and key advantages and disadvantages of each. The number of pros and cons is not a direct reflection of the segmentation system's value – their weighting will vary from museum to museum.

Geographic segmentation

Geographic segmentation splits audiences depending on where they live. A common way of museums doing this is by categorising visitors as:

- Local (ideally this should be defined, for example, by particular postcodes, local government areas, or within a travel time or distance to the museum).
- Day trippers (who live farther away, but travel to and from the museum in a day).
- Overnight visitors (national or international tourists who stay overnight in the area) can be split by region or country too.

A visitor survey project I worked on with several small to medium-sized UK museums a few years ago showed how results can vary enormously; for example, the proportion of participating museums' international visitors varied from 1% to 30%.

ADVANTAGES

- It is not very onerous for audiences to answer a question on where they live.
- It is low effort and cost for museums to obtain data needed.
- For some museums – such as a local history or community museum – local people and audiences from farther afield may well have different starting points of knowledge and awareness of the museum, as well as interests and motivations.
- The core audience that is most likely to be repeat visitors for many museums is likely to be local.
- There is often a clear seasonal pattern of tourists, which can be useful for planning.
- Your communications can often be tailored and evaluated by location; for example, through targeted digital advertising and choosing certain local newspapers, radio, and TV.
- Some sector tools – such as the Association of Independent Museum's *Economic Value of the Independent Museum Sector Toolkit,* which provides calculations to work out the approximate economic value of your visitors to the local economy – are based on whether your audiences are local, day trippers, or overnight visitors (2019).

DISADVANTAGES

- The categories are broad, and people in each category are unlikely to all behave the same, have the same motivations, or face the barriers to engagement. For example, an international visitor may visit the museum to entertain their children, to undertake professional research, or as part of an organised group.
- Some audiences don't like answering questions on where they live.

Demographic segmentation

Demographic segmentation splits audiences based on *who* they are; for example, based on their age, ethnicity, disability, or educational background. Collecting this data is valuable to understand which audiences are underrepresented in your museum and museums in general.

ADVANTAGES

- If you are aiming to make your museum more inclusive and your audiences more representative of your local community or national population, it is

80 *Marketing strategy in practice*

important to understand and track your progress on demographic factors, even if you don't directly use them to inform your marketing campaigns.
- Population data is usually readily available and allows for easy comparison.
- Life stages can have an influence on audience behaviour. For example, families with school-age children typically visit museums at weekends and in school holidays, whilst retired people often visit in the daytime on weekdays.
- Data is available on media preferences of different generations and the age skews of social media platforms, which can help you if you consider audiences by age.
- Ticketed museums often provide admissions options that match some demographic factors and enable easy evaluation, such as children or family tickets, concessions for retired people, or free tickets for disabled visitors' carers.

DISADVANTAGES

- Identifying some of these demographics can feel intrusive and unwelcome by audiences, and many people in visitor-facing roles feel uncomfortable asking or expecting visitors to answer personal questions such as those about age, ethnicity, gender, and disability.
- To answer a complete set of questions on demographics takes time, which makes it harder to get a representative sample of visitors to answer them.
- Audiences don't necessarily identify in the categories that demographic surveys commonly use, for example: "White Other".
- It is a simplistic generalisation to assume that people share commonalities based on demographic factors alone.

Behavioural segmentation

Behavioural segmentation divides audiences according to their behavioural patterns when interacting with your museum. For example, are your audiences first-timers, regular, sporadic, lapsed, or potential visitors? Which products do they use – everything, just the temporary exhibitions, just the events, just the café? When do they visit – seasonally, weekends, weekdays, school holidays? Do they pre-book or just turn up? An example of behavioural segmentation combines demographic aspects too: research undertaken by Decision House for the UK's Association of Leading Visitor Attractions (ALVA) in June 2021 identified that the groups of people most likely to return to visiting attractions on reopening after Covid-19 pandemic closures were visitors with children, members of attractions, and people aged 16–34 years old. These findings meant that attractions could focus on communicating with the audiences who were more comfortable in returning and receptive to messaging.

ADVANTAGES

- Understanding behaviour can enable more personalised and relevant communications, which are likely to be valued by audiences (for example, e-news about upcoming events to people who have attended events before, an incentive offer for lapsed members to renew their membership by the end of the month).
- It can help you identify your most engaged audiences and nurture them.

DISADVANTAGES

- Audience behaviour doesn't tell you about the *reasons* for that behaviour and what motivated them.
- Audience behaviour can change, both for individual reasons (for example, a loyal repeat visitor moves away) or, more broadly, as societal trends (for example, a drop in visitors in an economic downturn).

Psychographic segmentation

Psychographic segmentation divides audiences according to their personality, values, beliefs, attitudes, interests, and/or lifestyle. For example, why do they visit? What's important to them? Culture Segments, a well-known sector segmentation system developed by Morris Hargreaves McIntyre, is psychographic. Culture Segments was created with data from a large-scale, representative survey of over 5,000 cultural consumers across the UK looking at audiences' needs, values, and preferences. Their eight segments are called: Essence, Expression, Stimulation, Affirmation, Enrichment, Perspective, Release, and Entertainment (Morris Hargreaves McIntyre, no date).

Examples of insights on the Entertainment category are: "Their occasional forays into culture are likely to be for mainstream events or days out. Leisure time is for fun, and this segment is looking for entertainment and escapism – if they do attend, it will be socially motivated [...] Entertainment prefer to stick with the tried and tested, and they view popularity and celebrity casting as endorsements of quality. [...] This segment likes marketing and advertising – it's a useful way to get information. They can tell a lot from marketing – a big, expensive billboard campaign for example is an indicator that something has high production values" (Morris Hargreaves McIntyre, no date).

In contrast, examples of insights on the Stimulation category are: "Stimulation are independent-minded [...] Early adopters, they don't need things to have a proven track record before they get involved: they like to be the one making the discoveries rather than following the crowd. They're not opposed to popular shows or big-name blockbusters, but the real mainstream is probably already passé. [...] Stimulation enjoy marketing as an artform in its own right. If it's clever, beautiful, or tech-y, and hits the right note, they'll share it with everyone. [...] Marketing needs to highlight the hook, the twist, that makes it incredible and different" (ibid.).

By reading these two extracts, you can immediately get indicators of what sort of products, programmes, and marketing messages are likely to resonate with each group. They provide rich cues for your strategy and messaging.

ADVANTAGES

- The segmentation model is linked to motivations and barriers to engagement, which are important in marketing.
- People's personalities, values, and attitudes are arguably less likely to change over time than their behaviours.

DISADVANTAGES

- On its own, psychographic segmentation will not help you to reach audiences that are underrepresented based on demographic factors such as age and ethnicity, since demographics cut across all psychographic segments.
- It is not a segmentation system that most museums can easily create on their own – it is complex to set up from scratch.
- It can be harder to compare your results with other museums unless you use an established scheme.

Choosing a segmentation system

As the advantages and disadvantages of each system above show, there is no perfect system, and what works for one museum won't necessarily work for another. You need to consider whether you want to be able to compare your results with other museums, heritage sites, and cultural organisations (if so, use an established, standardised system); prefer to commission a bespoke system tailored to your museum; or develop something smaller scale on your own. I find that special interest museums often benefit from an enthusiast category; that is, people who are incredibly passionate and knowledgeable about the museum's subject matter and will typically have different needs and behaviours than visitors whose primary motivation is a social day out. It may also be that you use a combination of more than one segmentation approach.

Consider whether your segmentation system will just be for your in-person audiences or also apply to your digital or online audiences. Having one system that covers both allows for comparisons between the two. But the same system may not be as relevant to your digital audiences, and the information you need for classifying online audiences into each segment may be harder to obtain.

Below are suggested criteria to consider when deciding what type of segmentation system to use, to which you can add your own criteria. Your segmentation system should:

- Be of value to your marketing.
- Be applicable to existing and potential audiences.

- Have segments that you can find and target.
- Be affordable and value for money for your museum to set up and run.
- Be feasible to work with using available time.
- Be comprehensible to team members who need to use it.
- Enable evaluation and easy categorisation of audiences into segments.
- Be relevant in the medium to long term so you can compare results year-on-year.

What makes a good segment?

Segments should be:

- **Definable** – you can explain them and who falls into each category.
- **Distinctive** – different from other segments.
- **Meaningful** – they need to be of value to the museum.
- **Measurable** – to evaluate whether you have reached and engaged them.
- **Memorable** – you want teams to be able to understand, recall, and use the segments.
- **Stable** – the segments should not be likely to change substantially in the medium term.
- **Of an appropriate size** – big enough to justify an approach, but not too vast and generic.
- **Of a manageable number** – having 25 segments, for instance, is likely to be unwieldy and unmanageable.

It is important to understand the size and scope of each segment and the resources and approach you need to reach and engage each. There are also some challenges to be aware of, regardless of what system you use. Whilst you want each segment to be distinctive, there may be some overlap between segments or some people who may fit into more than one. People are individuals, and not all people within each segment are the same or will behave the way you might predict or want. Ultimately, segmentation still involves some generalisations and simplifications. Audiences, their motivations, and barriers are a complex and ever-changing web.

Bespoke segmentation example: Jane Austen's House

When I worked with Jane Austen's House a few years ago, we created three simple segments based on audiences' awareness of Jane Austen, alongside a group segment. Austen was a novelist who wrote well-loved books such as *Pride and Prejudice* and *Emma,* which have been turned into many TV series and movies. Jane Austen's House is the cottage in Chawton in the south of England where she lived and wrote her six novels. We created segments based on visitor survey responses to a multiple-choice question about how familiar visitors are with Jane Austen and her work. Audiences in each segment have different motivations for visiting, different starting points for their knowledge and interest in Jane Austen, and therefore also different alternatives for other activities they could choose. The most passionate fans of Jane Austen are clearly most likely to be keen to visit, but equally the largest audience segment with the biggest potential for growth is for audiences who are not so familiar with Austen and her work. For each segment, we defined the category; noted their proportion of current visitors; set a goal; and included where they are based, when they are likely to visit, likely motivational factors and barriers to visiting/engaging; the biggest competitors; key communication channels to reach them; key selling points and messages; and potential partners to work with to reach and engage them. For the fans, the marketing goals centred around retaining the demand, and deepening relationships with these core audiences. For those not so familiar with Austen, the goal was to create and capture a demand, and cultivate, convert, and grow the audience.

Summarising your audiences

Consider how to summarise and present information about your audiences and your approach to segmentation in a useful and meaningful way. For example, it could be a table with key information for each segment such as who they are, their motivations, their barriers, and how you can reach them. Some people and museums find value in creating a set of audience or user personas, fictional characters that represent an archetypal audience member for each segment. They can bring your segmentation system to life and help teams to understand different audience needs and expectations. They can act as useful prompts when thinking about marketing – and be used effectively across the museum, such as when thinking about exhibition design. However, criticisms include that audience personas result in stereotypes and over-simplify complex factors; organisations don't always have sufficient data and insights to create effective personas; and organisations are slow to change them as audiences evolve. A light-touch option is to come up with a few real or likely statements from audiences in each segment to help you focus your marketing messaging. For example:

- "I'm after a free rainy-day activity to entertain my three children of different ages, 3–8 years old".
- "We are on holiday in the area and are looking for things to do".
- "I want somewhere to meet up with an old friend where we can have a wander and a chat over a coffee".

Questions to consider

- What factors influence your museum's choice of target audiences?
- Which of the four types of segmentation system is most relevant to your museum?

- How would your marketing approach differ if you were targeting Entertainment and Stimulation segments from Morris Hargreaves McIntyre's Culture Segments?

References

Association of Independent Museums (2019) *Economic Value of the Independent Museum Sector Toolkit*. Available at: https://aim-museums.co.uk/wp-content/uploads/2019/10/Economic-Impact-Toolkit-2019.pdf (Accessed: 6 February 2023).

The Association of Leading Visitor Attractions (2021) *ALVA Attractions Recovery Tracker Wave*. Available at: https://www.alva.org.uk/documents/ALVA_Attractions_Recovery_Tracker_Wave_9_(17–22_June)_250621_ALVA_v1-2.pdf (Accessed: 3 December 2022).

Morris Hargreaves McIntyre (no date) *Culture Segments*. Available at: https://www.mhminsight.com/culture-segments/ (Accessed: 3 December 2022).

Office for National Statistics (2021) *Population and Household Estimates, England and Wales: Census 2021, Unrounded Data*. Available at: https://www.ons.gov.uk/peoplepopulationandcommunity/populationandmigration/populationestimates/bulletins/populationandhouseholdestimatesenglandandwales/census2021unroundeddata (Accessed: 3 December 2022).

5d Strategy and approach
How will we get there?

Introduction

You now have your starting point, and you have identified key goals that you want to achieve and audiences you want to reach and engage. The next step is working out *how* to get from the former to the latter two, and that involves developing your strategy. The previous chapter covered choosing your target audiences, which is also a core part of that strategy, and this chapter builds on that work. Strategy does not involve a granular list of actions you will deliver; that comes next in the tactical action plan.

In this chapter I've set out a series of models and matrices that can be useful when developing a marketing strategy: the TOWS analysis, a simple product/audience grid, the Product Life Cycle, the Ansoff Matrix, and the Dual Bottom Line Matrix. The chapter finishes by covering positioning strategy and outlines a workshop activity you can undertake to support its development. These models are helpful tools for approaching marketing more strategically, but you don't need to use all of them – consider which are most relevant to your circumstances.

TOWS

The TOWS matrix is the SWOT's lesser-known cousin, developed by Heinz Weihrich in 1982 to help develop strategic options by looking at the relationships between the factors identified in the SWOT analysis. It extends the SWOT analysis and helps temper some of the criticism that it is a static model that doesn't show how the various points raised interrelate. The TOWS framework suggests you consider your strengths, weaknesses, opportunities, and threats in relation to one another to build strategies.

Building on examples from the SWOT analysis in Chapter 5a, Table 5d.1 sets out a simplified example of how to use the TOWS matrix. The example only inputs two of each factor, but in reality, you are likely to start with many more strengths, weaknesses, opportunities, and threats. Pull out key factors, test several combinations, and finish with a longer series of strategic options. The next step is deciding which strategies you want to take forward. Consider evaluating them on criteria such as:

DOI: 10.4324/9781003309147-12

Table 5d.1 An example TOWS analysis

TOWS Analysis	Strengths Our summer events programme is very successful in attracting new audiences (A) Our new email marketing platform enables us to create tailored content for different audiences (B)	Weaknesses Compared with other museums similar to ours, our pre-school audience is low (C) Our rate of membership renewals has been steadily declining over the past three years (D)
Opportunities Our regional tourism development body is creating an off-peak winter tourism campaign (1) New residential development is being built in our town (2)	Make the most of strengths to maximise opportunities: Develop a winter events programme (learning from the summer success) and get involved in the regional winter tourism campaign (A1)	Minimise weaknesses by taking advantage of opportunities: Develop a new pre-school programme with and for the new local community (C2)
Threats Overreliance on social media to reach our audiences leaves us vulnerable (3) Other free venues and activities are more appealing to our audiences during economic downturn (4)	Make the most of strengths to minimise or manage threats: Develop a new email marketing strategy to drive sign-ups and engagement (B3)	Minimise or manage weaknesses and avoid threats: Review our membership scheme, the benefits it offers, and its value for members (D4)

- Which strategy or strategies will best help you achieve your marketing goals?
- Which will be most relevant for your identified audiences?
- How feasible are they to deliver? Do you have the resources, time, and skills?
- How fast will you see results?
- Are there commonalities and approaches that take care of several options?

Product strategies

Getting your product right for your target audiences is absolutely fundamental and should be considered long before you think about what promotion you will do. If the product is not of value or appropriate to your target audiences, no amount of social media posts will entice them to come.

As opposed to many other sectors, decisions on products at a museum are not solely (or sometimes even at all) the responsibility of the marketing team. However, there is a lot of value in the marketing team having input into such decisions in a strategic way, with their data and insights into audiences, competitors, and the external environment. Below, I set out a few different models that can be used to reflect on, identify, and plan different product strategies. I don't suggest you necessarily use all of them, but identify which one or ones resonate with you, your way of working, and what you want to achieve.

- **Product and audience grid:** Provides a snapshot of which products cater to which audiences, and where there are gaps.
- **Product life cycle:** Helps you evaluate whether some products need replacing or refreshing to extend their shelf life and relevance.
- **Ansoff Matrix:** Supports reflections about whether or not you need to develop new products to attract more existing and new audiences.
- **Dual Bottom Line Matrix:** Categorises which products are core to supporting your mission, which are good income generators (or financially sustainable), and which do both or neither.

Product and audience grid

A quick and fairly simple exercise is to plot all of your existing products and services against your target audiences. This can show you at a glance whether there are some audience segments that are well served and whether there are any that you expect to attract without having a suite of products and services that appeal to and are relevant for them. Table 5d.2 shows a simplified

Table 5d.2 An example product/audience grid

Audience segment / Product/Programme	Regional families	International tourists	16–24 year olds	Regional schools
Permanent galleries	X	X		X
Temporary exhibition	X	X		
Guided tours		X		
Craft workshops	X			
Membership scheme	X			
Schools programme				X
Venue hire				

example of what this might look like, highlighting that the current offer does not serve 16–24 year olds, and that there is no identified target audience for venue hire.

Product life cycle

A product life cycle shows the evolution of different stages of a product's "life", from its launch and introduction to audiences, to its withdrawal from the market or from use (for example, the closure of an exhibition, no longer selling a particular piece of merchandise). Originally developed by Raymond Vernon in the 1960s, the product life cycle can be applied to your museum as a whole, using overall visitor numbers, or to a specific product such as an events series. A traditional product life cycle plots sales against time, but you can use audiences instead of sales since not all museum products have a charge. It typically contains the phases Introduction, Growth, Maturity, and Decline (see Figure 5d.1).

Using historical data, you should be able to work out which phase your key products are in. Are numbers rising, and at what rate, or have they stagnated or are falling? Consider whether further growth is likely. You can then reflect on the implications of this for your marketing approach. For example, a heavier marketing effort and budget is likely to be needed in the introduction phase to launch something and generate awareness and early audiences. In the growth phase, some of your communication is likely to be established, and word of mouth should also help get the message out, so you may need less marketing spend and effort.

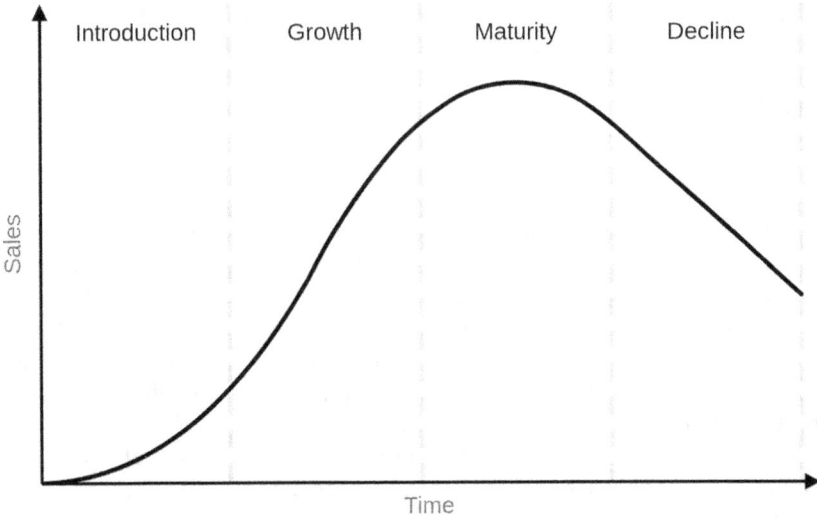

Figure 5d.1 An example product life cycle.

As you approach the maturity phase and growth in sales or audiences start to flatten out, consider whether this flattening of the curve also coincides with you being at capacity for the product. If it does, you might choose to focus marketing effort and spend elsewhere. But if it does not (for example, you have consistently started to sell only 50% of tickets to a talks programme), consider boosting your marketing communication. Are there different audiences you could target in a different way? And do you need to change your tactics, your messaging, or the timings of your product availability to reach more people?

The final stage is the decline phase. It may be that you never reach this phase for some products. But if numbers decline over time, reflect and analyse to understand *why*. Is there more competition now? Is it something that people will do or enjoy more than once? Is audience feedback still positive? Is it still cost-effective (however you define that) to deliver, run, or sell? If so, you might be happy to continue with it as a more niche offering, perhaps with decreased frequency to continue to satisfy a small but loyal audience. However, if it's no longer financially viable, you might prefer to stop providing the product or make some changes. Can you extend the product's lifespan by targeting new audiences or making it available somewhere else? Bear in mind that even if your audience for a product has dwindled, changes or withdrawals may still have a significant negative impact on loyal audiences (however small) and can lead to a backlash or negative PR, so considered communications will be key.

Clearly, the product life cycle graphic will look different for different products. A fabulous blockbuster exhibition that has received a lot of hype before its opening is likely to have a steeper line in the introduction phase. Since its run is likely to be quite short term, it may never reach the maturity phase, let alone the decline phase. In contrast, a museum introducing escape rooms – having never done anything like that before – may find the introduction and growth phases are more prolonged, since the museum doesn't have an established reputation in doing such activities and the potential audiences for it are smaller.

Ansoff Matrix

The Ansoff Matrix builds on work you have done in identifying the audiences you want to reach and engage, and their motivations and barriers. The Ansoff Matrix or Model was developed by Igor Ansoff in 1957, and whilst the original mapped products against markets, I use products against audiences for the cultural and heritage sectors. The matrix sets out audiences (existing and new) against products (existing and new) to help consider different combinations. You can develop ideas for each quadrant that you can consult audiences on, test, and evaluate based on factors such as impact, numbers, costs, benefits, and so on. The model can help to challenge assumptions: some museums assume (and hope) they can keep doing what they are doing and just need to tell more people about it to grow their audiences.

Table 5d.3 An example Ansoff Matrix

Adaptation of the Ansoff Matrix		Your products	
		Existing	New
Your audiences	Existing	**Market penetration** Increase the visit or purchase frequency of *existing* audiences or attract more of the same types of audiences with your *current* products and programmes	**Product development** Increase the visit or purchase frequency of *existing* audiences or attract more of the same types of audiences with *new* products and programmes
	New	**Market extension** Attract *new* audiences with your *current* products and programmes	**Diversification** Attract *new* audiences with a *new* offer that meets their particular interests and needs

Others assume they must dive straight in to creating new programmes to attract new audiences, which might not always be necessary. Table 5d.3 shows an example matrix and the potential types of strategies that could emerge.

Market penetration

Market penetration approaches are likely to require the least amount of effort and budget, since you know your audiences and they already have a relationship with you and interest in your museum. Your existing communication channels and messaging should be effective. However, the growth potential is likely to be smaller, and you aren't meeting any goals of diversifying your audiences. Examples are running your toddler story time session every fortnight rather than every month; and running an email campaign for core audiences promoting your upcoming events programme.

Product development

Product development recognises that there are limited opportunities to grow existing audiences by just continuing to do what you already are doing. So, to attract more of these audiences and/or to increase the frequency of their engagement, you might need to develop new products. Since these audiences are already familiar to you, you are likely to know what they value and can undertake research with them to test new concepts and products relatively easily. Examples are inviting your members to a special behind-the-scenes curator talk and developing a podcast aimed at existing audiences.

Market extension

Market extension and diversification aim to attract and engage new audiences where there is more opportunity for growth and/or to enable the museum to be more representative of its community or minimise its over-reliance on a small pool of existing audiences. Using your existing products requires less investment than developing new ones. However, it may not be enough or relevant for some audiences who face different barriers that aren't broken down by this approach. Examples are running a marketing campaign to change perceptions or raise awareness of your museum with new audience groups; running a special offer for first-time visitors; and developing new relationships with coach tour operators.

Diversification

Consider the expression "Do what you've always done, get what you've always got". To attract new audiences, you might need to change your approach more fundamentally. Since you don't already have established relationships with new audiences, this is likely to be riskier and require more resources. Examples are developing a programme of Friday Lates events with live music aimed at new audiences and creating a co-produced exhibition with community partners.

Dual Bottom Line Matrix

The Dual Bottom Line Matrix is based on the Boston Consulting Group's Growth Share Matrix, which maps market share (company competitiveness) against growth rate (market attractiveness) (Boston Consulting Group, no date). The Dual Bottom Line Matrix (DBLM) by Jeanne Bell and Elizabeth Schaffer is an adaptation that is more relevant to the not-for-profit and museums sectors. This version maps the interplay of financial sustainability, income, or profitability against the mission impact of your products or programmes (Zimmerman and Bell, 2014). Rather than focus on audiences, this model helps you to consider whether your products are supporting your museum's mission and/or its income requirements. List your products, programmes, and activities, and plot them in the matrix according to the extent to which they support your mission and generate income (or are funded).

Different museums have different criteria for mission impact, but here are some example questions you can reflect on when identifying the impact of your products and assign a score to:

- How closely does this product align with our mission and vision?
- Does it meet short-term and/or long-term goals?
- How many people does this product cater for or engage?
- How deep is the engagement or impact?
- What value does it provide audiences, and what demand, or need, is there?
- Is there much competition, or does it fill a gap in the market?

Table 5d.4 An example Dual Bottom Line Matrix

Mission impact	High	"Hearts" A community outreach programme	"Stars" Blockbuster exhibition
	Low	"Question Marks" A trustee's historic pet project	"Cash Cows" Venue hire
		Low	High
		Profitability/Financial sustainability	

Next look at the financial sustainability of each product or programme. You need to consider how this will be relevant to your museum. For example, a straightforward measure of total annual income generated that you score for comparison? Or do you count the average income generated per person? Or if there are no charges, look at how much the programme costs to run (annually or per participant) or the grant funding you have access to.

If you already have new product ideas you are considering (for example, any that you identified in your SWOT or TOWS analysis), you can also include *potential* products (with their potential or likely mission impact and profitability/financial sustainability scores). You can then list your products in each quadrant on the Dual Bottom Line Matrix, similar to the example in Table 5d.4, or you can draw them in circles in accordance with their significance.

"**Stars**" are the ultimate ambition, although it is very unlikely that you will be able to put all of your products in this quadrant. "**Cash Cows**" are the products that generate income, although they don't *directly* support your mission. They serve an important role in generating income and can subsidise other programmes that are high on mission impact but not income. "**Heart**" products really deliver on your mission, but they can cost a lot to fund or not generate income. Ensure you have funding in place to deliver these. "**Question Marks**" products don't score highly on either measure. Some versions of the DBLM suggest you should stop these activities, but I suggest you question their future, but don't automatically write them off. Are there other benefits they achieve that mean they are still valuable? For example, are they high profile and/or innovative so have gained a lot of media interest and might attract sponsorship in the future? But if you are honest and find that such a programme is just one of those programmes you are just doing because you have always done it, is resource-heavy, and has no clear benefits, it is time to retire it.

Having all products in the Star category is unlikely, and having all products in the Question Marks category is undesirable; having a mix of Stars, Hearts, and Questions is common. Consider:

- The likely longevity of the income or funding. Is a project currently a Star or Cash Cow but may move to the Heart quadrant?

- What makes a Star a Star? Can this be replicated anywhere else? Can you seek sponsorship for a Heart programme to move it across?
- How reliant are the products' success on precarious external factors – subject to competition, price elasticity, and so on?

Linking these models together

No one model is all-encompassing, but you can use more than one for deeper insights and combine them in different ways. For example, you can put any new product strategies you identify in your TOWS analysis into the Dual Bottom Line Matrix to help you rate them for likely mission and financial impact. You can also put them into the product/audience grid to help you understand if there are still any of your target audience groups that are not catered for. And finally, revisit the marketing goals you set as another check that any new product strategies would support those goals.

Positioning strategy

Your museum's positioning is how your audiences perceive the museum and its offer (what the museum delivers and the experience and value it can provide audiences) compared with your competitors. And your positioning strategy is how you choose to convey key elements that differentiate your museum and try to influence those perceptions. It needs to be compelling, relevant, distinctive, and consistent. A positioning statement can succinctly summarise how the museum is positioned and fulfils the needs of its target audiences compared with its competitors. It is an internal tool, not an outward-facing strapline.

Your positioning may involve your USPs – Unique Selling Proposition or Point(s) – which make your museum unique or different to other competitors or audiences' alternatives. USPs should be relevant to and valued by audiences, and easily communicated and understood. Your USP(s) may vary from audience to audience: For some, it will be your collection, original objects, or a hero object, whilst for others, it may be a free, indoor safe space for reflection. It may also vary for different exhibitions and programme. There will be more competition for more general positioning such as "family friendly", so consider the balance of a broader, mass market appeal with something more specific.

Museums often focus on learning and the authenticity of their objects and collections. But other organisations also provide interactive and engaging learning experiences, and not all audiences are motivated by original objects. For example, York's Chocolate Story tells the history of the English town's chocolate brands. It is not based around original objects but uses a clever mix of audio-visual and multi-sensory interpretation, including chocolate tasting, which is hard to beat. It is popular and averages 4.5 stars out of five for Tripadvisor and Google reviews. And it charges more than York Castle

Museum (an adult ticket is £17.50 for York's Chocolate Story; compared to £13 online and £16 walk-up price, valid for 12 months, for York Castle Museum).

Positioning workshop exercise

A workshop exercise I find valuable to encourage reflections around positioning involves identifying key adjectives the team associates with the museum:

- Create a long list of wide-ranging adjectives – one per card or paper – for example: family-friendly, credible, formal, familiar, thought-provoking, interactive, inclusive, playful, unconventional, peaceful, accessible.
- Split workshop participants into groups of two to four people, and ask them to place each card in one of three piles: "We are ...", "We are not", ... and "We should/want to be ...".
- Once there is agreement about the cards that fall under each heading, ask the group(s) to take their "We are ..." words and see if they can group them together, picking one adjective from the group (or a new one) as a heading for each group. Aim to end up with four to eight final words.
- These final words can provide a strategic direction for how to position the organisation, its personality, tone of voice, and messaging, and they can be used in positioning maps below. They can also be tested with audiences and potential audiences to see if their perceptions of the museum match how the team views the museum, for example, in surveys, via touchscreens, or drop boxes.
- Consider the responses assigned to "We should/want to be ...", why the museum isn't yet, and what you can do to change this.

Three examples from organisations I have worked with are:

- A museum: Authentic, Inspiring, Stimulating, Playful, Charming, Atmospheric, Warm.
- A science centre: Inspiring, Fun, Inclusive, Collaborative, Trustworthy, and Bold.
- A heritage organisation: Welcoming, Credible, Engaging, Brave, Stimulating, and Contemporary.

Positioning maps

A positioning map visually shows your positioning strategy compared to that of your competitors. It features two axes, each representing key attributes or value provided that are relevant to your museum *and* your audiences. You might look at tangible factors such as price, average dwell-time, average online review scores; or how the organisation is positioned more broadly, such as niche versus

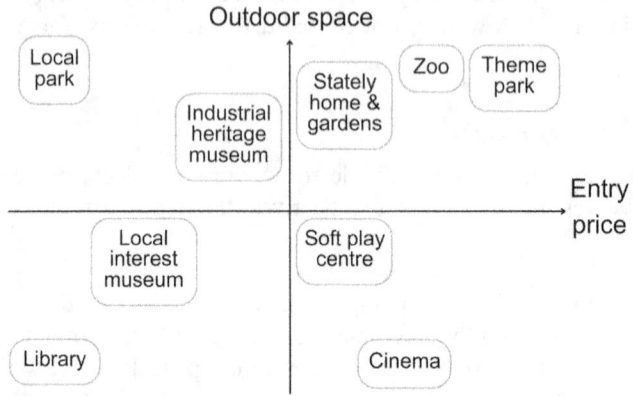

Figure 5d.2 An example positioning map.

mainstream offering, interactive versus passive experience, family-friendly or aimed at adults. You can create a brand positioning map for your museum as a whole, a product positioning map, and/or maps for different audience segments if the competitors and audience priorities vary greatly. Figure 5d.2 shows an example positioning map for family audiences. Look at where your museum sits. If it is a busy quadrant full of competitors, try a map with different variables to see if there are other elements that set your museum apart more that are worth emphasising in your marketing. And reflect back to your situational analysis: does your desired positioning reflect how audiences view your museum, or is there a gap between your aspirations and audience perceptions that you need to tackle? For example, you and your colleagues might consider the museum welcoming, but consultation with potential audiences shows otherwise.

Questions to consider

- Which model or matrix do you think is of most value or relevance to your marketing, and why?
- Can you revisit your SWOT analysis and use the findings to input into a TOWS analysis?
- Which factors would you plot on a positioning map?

References

Ansoff, I. (1957) 'Strategies for Diversification', *Harvard Business Review*, 35(5), pp. 113–124. Available at: https://archive.org/details/strategiesfordiversification ansoff1957hbr/mode/2up (Accessed: 20 April 2023).

Boston Consulting Group (no date) *What Is the Growth Share Matrix?* Available at: https://www.bcg.com/about/overview/our-history/growth-share-matrix (Accessed: 4 December 2022).

York Castle Museum (2023) *Tickets*. Available at: https://www.yorkcastlemuseum.org.uk/your-visit/tickets/ (Accessed: 17 May 2023).

York Chocolate Story (2023) *Opening Times & Prices*. Available at: https://www.yorkschocolatestory.com/plan-your-visit/opening-times-prices/ (Accessed: 17 May 2023).

Zimmerman, S. and Bell, J. (2014) *The Matrix Map: A Powerful Tool for Mission-Focused Nonprofits*. Available at: https://nonprofitquarterly.org/the-matrix-map-a-powerful-tool-for-mission-focused-nonprofits/ (Accessed: 15 April 2023).

5e Tactics and action plan
What are we going to do to get there?

Introduction

This stage is where you develop more detailed plans and actions that you will take to meet your goals and objectives. Whilst some flexibility and pragmatism are needed throughout the year to enable marketing to be nimble and reactive, planning key actions will help you to prioritise and allocate resources. Your tactics are about how you implement your marketing strategy *in practice* and make it a reality, so they should be achievable, not aspirational. They will be influenced by budget limitations, skills and team capacity, past experience, and organisational values.

The level of detail you put in the plan for this stage is up to you. Larger museums with a multitude of programmes and high-profile exhibitions each requiring their own marketing campaign may simply have a line in the annual marketing strategy for each campaign, with separate plans for them to prevent the annual plan from becoming too unwieldy. Other – often smaller – museums might prefer to and manage to have everything in one place. This chapter sets out examples of tactics that flow from your goals and strategies, breaks down the marketing mix with questions to consider for each category, and finishes by discussing how to present your decisions.

How actions flow from goals and strategy

Your actions should be guided by your goals and strategy. Consider these two example goals and strategies from the previous chapters and what actions might look like for each:

Example 1
Goal: To launch a new winter events programme to attract new audiences.
Strategy: Develop a winter events programme and get involved in the regional winter tourism campaign, based on lessons from the successful summer programme.
Example actions:

- Undertake consultation with new audiences we want to reach and engage.
- Find a partner organisation to work with.

DOI: 10.4324/9781003309147-13

- Work with events team to establish the events programme.
- Stage promotional images.
- Work up and submit winter events copy and images to winter tourism campaign team.
- Agree and brief a museum spokesperson for the campaign launch event.
- Draft and issue news releases.
- Create a social media content plan and ad campaign.
- Develop social media and website materials using the campaign strapline, colours, and hashtag.
- Run social media activity around the events.
- Take event photos.
- Gather event feedback.

Example 2

Goal: To increase our rate of membership renewal.
Strategy: Review our membership scheme, the benefits it offers, and value for members.
Example actions:

- Review all existing membership data (numbers and categories; demographics; churn; renewal rate).
- Develop and issue a feedback survey to members and lapsed members.
- Undertake five in-depth interviews with members and five with lapsed members.
- Review membership renewal process, and identify any pain points.
- Analyse key competitors' membership schemes (pricing and levels, benefits, positioning, promotion).
- Write a report with recommendations for the senior management team.

How actions flow from audiences

Who you want to reach will also affect your actions. For example, the Rahmi M. Koç Museum in Istanbul, Turkey, is a private industrial museum. Historically, the museum's main target audiences have been school groups for weekday museum visits, tours, and education packs that support the curriculum, shared through direct communication with schools; and families with young children who visit on weekends and holidays and enjoy interactive elements such as climbing into some of the vehicles, who are reached through social media and traditional media. The museum has recently also been targeting tourists as an audience group and has started to work with tour guides, hotels, and tourism agencies to promote the museum to them (İşyar, 2023).

Picking up the example I mentioned in Chapter 5c, a museum set families as a key target audience, in part after benchmarking showed that their proportion of visitors aged 0–14 years old was around half the project cohort's average. Actions the museum took as a result included strengthening their family offer with activities such as creating children's quizzes; improving their café offer and shop's product ranges; providing family discount vouchers within a 30-minute drivetime of the museum; and commissioning and using a suite of new photography showing families enjoying the museum and it being a hands-on experience. Within two years, family visits were up by 77%.

The marketing mix

Your actions can also be set out by each part of your marketing mix, or you can just use the 4Ps or 7Ps of the marketing mix as prompts to ensure you take a holistic approach to your marketing, rather than just focus on communication and promotion. An alternative approach to the classic 4Ps which some people prefer is the 4Cs which Robert Lauterborn developed in 1990, as a more customer-centric take on the traditional 4Ps: Customer value, wants, and needs instead of Products; Convenience instead of Place; Cost or cost to satisfy instead of Price; and Communication instead of Promotion. Whether you use the 4Ps, 7Ps, 4Cs, a combination, or something else is up to you. What is important is that you think strategically, beyond just promotion, and find a process relevant to your museum and ways of working. I tend use the 4Ps to 7Ps as prompts since they are elements you can control, but as you can see throughout the book, my interpretation of each category is broad and always guided by audience insights.

Product

Having made strategic decisions about the products and services (see the previous chapter), what are the actions that you need to take as a result? For example:

- Do new products, services, programmes, events, and experiences need to be launched?
- If existing products need to be repositioned to attract new audiences or repeat audiences, what actions will you take to do this?

Place

Decide how the location and availability of your products and programmes can best meet your goals and serve your audiences. Where will the products and services be available? At the museum, digitally, in the community, through pop-ups, at partner venues? Would selling exhibition tickets via intermediaries reach new audiences and increase income or just eat into your profit margins? Can your shop products be sold anywhere aside from your museum and its website? For example, The Rijksmuseum in the Netherlands has a gallery space of regularly rotating Dutch art with free access for passengers (often a captive audience looking to fill the time before or between flights) at Amsterdam's Schiphol airport and sells souvenirs from the Rijksmuseum and other Dutch museums in the adjacent shop (Schiphol, 2022). What actions do you need to undertake to support your place or distribution strategy? For example:

- Do you need to research ticketing intermediaries?
- Can you shortlist commercial partners for your shop products?

Pricing

Agree on overarching principles for your pricing. Even if your museum is free to enter, there will be products and services that are charged for, such as refreshments, shop souvenirs, special exhibitions, workshops, membership schemes, and season tickets. You don't have to be the cheapest, but whatever your price point(s), your audiences should feel the pricing is fair and is value for money. For example, who should be able to access concessions and discounts? If you want to increase repeat visits, does your pricing incentivise and reward loyalty through membership, free return within a year, or other discounts? (See Chapter 12 for more on pricing.) Agree on a set of actions. For example:

- If your pricing needs to change due to inflation, a competitor analysis, or audience research, at what level will you set this?
- Do you want to research sector best practice on pricing concessions?
- Are there bundles or packages you can offer to upsell and provide better value for audiences, without significantly affecting the profit margin? For example, a bundle for a ticket and an exhibition catalogue?

Promotion

This is the marketing mix element that most people think of and dive into. Although it is not interchangeable with marketing, it is likely to be a significant part of your plan. It is important to use communication channels that are appropriate for your target audiences and messages that are likely to resonate with them and appeal to them. This includes the language and tone of voice you use and the images you choose. Where possible, tailor your approach to each audience group or segment. Consider:

- **Why** do you want to communicate – inform people and raise awareness, remind audiences, persuade audiences, prompt audiences to act? (Purpose)
- **Whom** do you want to communicate with? (Audience)
- **What** do you want to communicate? Is this different for different audiences? What are the barriers and motivations you can build messaging on? Is there a particular call to action? (Message)
- **How** do you want to communicate it? (Channel)

Communication channels are explored in more detail in Chapter 9 and messaging in Chapter 10.

Content plan

Developing a content plan is worthwhile if you undertake a lot of digital marketing and social media marketing in particular. This can minimise that regular sense of panic when you know you need to post something but don't know what about and can help you to maintain consistency. Identify the purpose of your content – typically content marketing (creating and sharing online content that isn't explicitly trying to sell anything in the short term) is effective at raising awareness; building credibility and trust; creating engagement and interest; earning loyalty; and it can generate leads. Be clear on your target audiences, and consider what they are interested in and what content is popular more broadly. For example:

- Look at or undertake research and consultation with audiences – run simple social media polls, look at your analytics to identify your most popular content.
- Undertake social listening to see what people are saying about your museum and what is trending on social media.
- Research long tail keywords by typing relevant search terms into a search engine and looking at the autocomplete suggestions that come up, as well as the related searches.
- Use tools such as Google Trends, question-and-answer sites such as Quora, or forums like Reddit.
- Look at what other museums or competitors are sharing and what is popular.
- Consult with other people and departments within the museum for their ideas and expertise.

Develop a set of content pillars, a set of themes or topics (typically four to six in number) that are the foundation for content you develop and share, based on your museum's expertise and uniqueness and what audiences' interests are. Themes may be for engagement – such as entertaining and educational content – or more explicitly promotional. Examples are stories about objects and collections; content around products, activities, exhibitions, and events; behind-the-scenes content to share how the museum operates and to get to know its staff and volunteers; how-to guides; visitor feedback; and calendar anniversaries and milestones. Set out the main content formats you will use; for example, short- or long-form video, images, text-based posts, Stories, live videos, infographics, quizzes, user-generated content, blog posts, podcasts. Develop a posting strategy that sets out the communication channels and platforms you will use and how frequently you will use them.

National Museums Scotland is a group of four museums with more than 12.5 million objects in its care – the National Museum of Scotland, the National Museum of Flight, the National Museum of Rural Life, and the National War Museum. The Digital Content team of seven people is responsible for balancing storytelling around this vast and broad range of objects to engage digital audiences globally, alongside sharing operational information around facilities and visiting; promotional activities on events, membership, and exhibitions; and the organisation's research and community work. Russell Dornan, Digital Media Content Manager at National Museums Scotland, explains that the Digital Content team has developed five content principles at the centre of their content plan:

- "**Storytelling**: We tell stories;
- **People**: We place people at the heart of our process;
- **Intent**: We create content that 'radiates intent';
- **Voices**: We call on a plurality of voices; ...
- **Insight**: We are guided by data."

This acts as a framework to make sure content aligns with the organisation's aims and informs decision-making around ideas put forward. There are digital leads for each subject strand – for example, natural sciences, and Scottish history and archaeology – who liaise with curatorial departments to share content ideas with each other. The team uses the tool Notion to plan and schedule content for months ahead, as well as a one-page style guide that covers advice around tone, word count, and accessibility. They also share content highlights and top-level analysis of the impact of the content with the whole museum group. The result is a collaborative and considered process, balancing the needs of audiences with the group's strategic objectives (Dornan, 2022 and 2023).

People

Marketing won't deliver itself but is reliant on a broad range of people who need to contribute to the strategy, be aware of it, and understand it so they can support its delivery. Your audiences may encounter a whole range of different museum team members before, during, and after their visit or engagement. For example, someone who answers telephone enquiries, front-of-house teams, security staff, costumed interpreters, workshop leaders, tour guides, catering and shop staff, gallery invigilators, and so on. Each of those interactions has the potential to elevate the visitor experience or ruin it. It is important that staff and volunteers are well trained, well informed, and valued. A hugely important factor – beyond the scope of just marketing – is that if your museum wants to welcome different communities, the museum should be conscious of ensuring those communities are also represented *within* museum teams.

Within most museums, these aspects may sit under the primary remit of other departments, such as visitor services, human resources, learning, and engagement. However, it is still worth ensuring that marketing feeds into those teams, for example, by sharing visitor reviews (good and bad). A social media policy shared across the museum is also valuable. This should act as a guide to both support and help staff and volunteers handle negative aspects of social media such as trolling, as well as helping balance the need to manage the reputation of the museum, what staff and volunteers' responsibilities are, and the differences between posting in a professional or private capacity. There are also areas that relate specifically to the marketing team to consider:

- Who needs to be involved with the marketing strategy in any capacity – to input, approve, deliver, evaluate?
- Are there any training requirements needed to deliver the marketing strategy?
- What skills and experience might you need in your marketing team in the future, and how can you make the museum's marketing team attractive to top talent?

Processes

Audiences don't just engage with museums suddenly, but rather the interaction is usually part of a series of steps they have taken and processes they have navigated: their audience journey. This might start with being aware of the museum and your offer, reading reviews, calling up with an enquiry, booking online, visiting and engaging, signing up to become a member, visiting again the following year. Each of these steps may not happen or lead to the next if audiences find the steps too cumbersome or time-consuming. A website that is hard to navigate and find basic visit information on or an online shop that has too many steps before checkout is off-putting. Think about how you can optimise your website to improve users' experience and increase conversions. For example, improve your website navigation; reduce the page load time; minimise the number of steps in the online checkout process? Consider the audience journey (introduced in Chapter 5b and explored more in-depth in Chapter 9):

- What are the main touchpoints that your audiences come across, and can you do anything to improve the quality or speed of the interaction?
- How can you make the audience journey as seamless as possible and remove unnecessary friction in your processes?
- Where are the most significant pain points? For example, are membership renewal rates low? How high is your online cart abandonment rate? What is the visitor survey completion rate? And what can you do about this?
- What can you automate to save time and improve the audience experience?

Physical evidence

Physical evidence relates to evidence that audiences can encounter before they visit or engage. For new potential audiences, committing time, effort, and money to something they have never done before can feel risky: Will they enjoy it? Will they feel comfortable? Will they feel it's value for money? Consider what actions you can take to minimise that risk, answer any questions they are likely to have, and reassure as well as entice them. For example:

- What can you do to help audiences experience before they buy, visit, or commit? Are there barriers to engagement around a lack of information or perceptions about your museum you need to overcome?

- How can you make the most of reviews and testimonials?
- Can you collect the most asked questions and create a website page with answers to save audiences and your museum time?
- Can you develop a visual story to help visitors plan a visit to the museum and know what to expect (see Chapter 11)?

Presenting your action plan

There are many ways to bring your information together. You can embed your action plan within the strategy document. Or you might prefer to have it as a standalone document that can easily be updated, with actions ticked off, and the flexibility to shuffle things around if necessary. This could be in a spreadsheet, using project management software, cloud-based whiteboard apps or – if everyone has access to the same room – on a physical wall or board. The important thing is that it can readily be accessed, referred to, and updated. There are also different ways of presenting the actions, for example, by goal or objective, by strategy, by target audience segment, by month, by product/service, and/or by marketing mix. As well as what will be done, include timescales, deadlines, who will be responsible, and the cost. These areas will be explored more in the next chapter.

Questions to consider

- Do you consider the 4Ps or 4Cs to be more useful? Why?
- How will you arrange your actions – as a calendar, by goal or objective, by strategy, by audience segment, by product/service, by marketing mix?
- Where will you house the action plan so that everyone who needs to can easily access it?

References

Dornan, R. (2022) *How We Tell Stories Online at National Museums Scotland*. Available at: https://medium.com/@RussellDornan/how-we-tell-stories-online-at-national-museums-scotland-f573a621d4d7 (Accessed: 11 May 2023).

Dornan, R. (2023) Email to Christina Lister, 19 May.

İşyar, S. (2023) Zoom with Christina Lister, 6 April.

Schiphol (2022) *Dutch Masters*. Available at: https://www.schiphol.nl/en/at-schiphol/discover/facilities/rijksmuseum (Accessed 12 December 2022).

5f Resources
What will it cost?

Introduction

This chapter focuses on the resources you need to allocate to implement your marketing strategy. A big budget is neither likely for most museums nor a necessity, but if you don't invest much time in marketing either, you can't expect any results. Your strategy should include an allocation of your marketing budget – what you anticipate spending within the time period your strategy covers, broken down in a way that works for you, whether by goals and objectives, by audience, campaign, or tactic. This chapter starts by covering timescales and responsibility for marketing, and then shares different ways of setting a marketing budget. It finishes with tips for low-budget marketing and how to make the most of your marketing budget.

Timescales

As long as your SMART objectives are time-framed, they will give you a steer on when your actions need to be undertaken. Consider key deadlines such as big events and launches, and work backward. If you have relevant data from the past, use this to provide indications of when to start activity. For example, how far in advance do audiences typically tend to book? Print media will have longer lead times than digital channels, in particular quarterly or monthly magazines. Ensure you allow sufficient time for sign-off as needed, and take account of staff annual leave and public holidays, which may affect your timescales.

Responsibilities

Unless you are a one-person team responsible for delivering and approving everything, it is important to assign responsibilities. Be clear on:

- Who has overall ownership of the marketing strategy, its delivery, and outcomes (typically the head of marketing or equivalent).
- Who will be responsible for undertaking the actions (this can be one person or several, and can include marketing and audience development staff members, volunteers, freelancers, and agencies).

DOI: 10.4324/9781003309147-14

- Who else needs to contribute ideas, expertise, and experiences (can include other departments).
- Who needs to sign off on and approve actions (often senior management, trustees, sponsors, partners).
- Who (if anyone) needs to be kept in the loop about the strategy and its deliverables.

Setting your marketing budget

There is no right or wrong or universal formula on how much to spend on marketing – it depends on many different factors. However they are set, marketing budgets in museums rarely feel adequate, and teams work incredibly hard to make them stretch as far as possible. There are different methodologies you can use to determine your annual marketing budget either individually or in combination with other departments. Ideally the marketing person or team should be involved in the budget-setting process. But even if a marketing budget is assigned top-down, it can still be useful to test some of the budget-setting methods below for context and to help build a case for more budget in future if this is required. Some common budget-setting methods are the following five ways.

Past experience

Looking back over previous years' marketing spending is useful, especially when linked to evaluation undertaken. Unless there were anomalies such as a big, funded redevelopment and reopening project, basing marketing budgets on previous years' budgets is a good starting point. Clearly, if there are more temporary exhibitions, the introduction of a big new programme, or new events, then additional marketing budget should be set aside unless something else can be dropped or the budget can work smarter.

Percentage of revenue

I am often asked if there is a simple calculation for museums to use to set their marketing budget, and what counts as an adequate budget. The percentage of overall revenue method can provide that calculation, although defining what is "adequate" is a much more nuanced subject, unique to each museum. Revenue also needs defining – does that relate to just commercial revenue or include all grant funding, or in other words, the museum's full budget? Benefits of using this method are that marketing remains proportional – if the museum's revenue increases so, too, does the marketing budget, which is likely to be necessary because of increased output and expectations. However, how do you decide what percentage level is appropriate? Sometimes revenue falls (for example, due to an economic downturn), and it is often then detrimental for marketing spending to fall, too. In addition, not all activity in museums generates revenue, so this figure is not as straightforward as in for-profit companies.

Even if you don't use this calculation to *set* your marketing budget, it is useful to be aware of what your museum's figure is and compare this over time. Perhaps your marketing budget has increased over the past three years, so there is an expectation that it will go further. However, if the museum's programmes and overall revenue have also increased during this time, the proportion spent on marketing may actually have fallen, which is useful context when evaluating its impact.

There is limited data available specifically from the museums sector on this. Therefore, starting with for-profit companies, the 2023 CMO Survey of over 300 marketing leaders at for-profit companies in the USA shows that marketing accounts for an average of 12.3% of overall budgets and 10.9% of company revenues. Marketing budgets as a proportion of budget and revenue tend to be higher in business-to-consumer (B2C) than in business-to-business (B2B) organisations; higher the more e-commerce business an organisation does; and higher for product rather than service businesses (Moorman, 2023, p. 19). Similarly, HubSpot's survey of 1,000 marketers found that B2C product companies allocate the highest marketing budget, at 15.1% of total revenue, compared with 6.5% for B2C services (with B2B products at 7.8% and B2B services at 5.9%). The survey also found that marketing budgets had grown by over 5% between 2011 and 2022 (2022).

In my experience, most UK museums spend less than 5% of their revenue on marketing (and in many cases, much less). ICOM's survey into museums and Covid-19 analysed responses from almost 1,600 museums and museum professionals in 107 countries collected in 2020 (2022, p. 9). It found that the proportion of respondents' overall budgets dedicated to communication and digital activities was split as follows (although what constitutes digital activities may be broader than just a marketing remit):

- Less than 1% of overall budget: 17.8% of respondents.
- 1–5%: 23.8% of respondents.
- 6–10%: 11.0% of respondents.
- 11–15%: 5.4% of respondents.
- More than 15%: 5.4% of respondents.
- Not sure: 35.5% of respondents.

Flat amounts or fixed budgets

This method assigns a flat amount of budget to marketing, which isn't linked or in proportion to revenue. It is typically based on what is deemed affordable, often based on previous years' budgets, and guarantees that pot of money for marketing. However, it can end up as an arbitrary figure – how is the amount agreed and "affordable" judged? I often see this in smaller museums, where they assign a token amount, such as £500 or £1,000, to marketing annually. If this is the case in your museum, you need to work with what you have. Ensuring you evaluate what you do and compare different spends on different channels will help you build evidence to lobby for additional budget should that be needed.

Objective and task budgeting

This method involves setting objectives and identifying actions needed to meet those objectives, then estimating the cost of those actions and totalling them up. This is a logical approach that means your planned actions are all costed and your objectives feasible. However, if this process is done in isolation, it may end up with an unrealistic budget that simply is not available. It can be useful when putting a case together for a marketing budget or allocating marketing for a funded project or redevelopment.

Competitor matching

In some sectors, companies aim to set marketing budgets with reference to their competitors' marketing spending. It can be useful to know how your museum's marketing budget compares with other similar museums, and this can be used as part of internal lobbying for more investment in marketing. However, information can be hard to access, you're not comparing like-for-like, and you may not have any direct competitors, so a comparison isn't very useful.

What to include in your budget

What you include will depend on how your museum's budgets and funding are set up. Below are different ideas to consider, although some might sit under different budget lines. Examples of marketing costs are:

- Advertising costs (online and offline).
- Print and production costs for marketing materials.
- Launch event and private view costs.
- Subscriptions, licences, and costs for tools such as analytics packages, graphic design software, social media management tools.
- Memberships, such as for destination management organisations or trade bodies.
- Freelance, consultancy, and agency support, such as for photography, video, SEO, media buying.
- Staff and volunteer marketing training.
- Marketing staff and volunteer expenses.
- Inflation allowances and annual price increases (especially if the budget covers more than one year).
- A contingency figure for unforeseen opportunities and flexibility.

It can be interesting to consider what you would add as a wish list if your marketing budget increased, or what you would first drop if your budget were cut.

The Cultural Content Survey asked people working with content in 169 arts and cultural organisations how they would spend £10,000 if they were gifted this to spend on online content (One Further, 2022, p. 15). The results were:

- Strategy 20%.
- Photography and/or video 19%.
- Commissioning more content 18%.
- Training 13%.
- Improving SEO 8%.
- Improving existing content 6%.
- Data and reporting 4%.
- Repurposing existing content for different platforms 1%.
- Other 11%.

No- or low-budget marketing

Many micro and small museums – especially those that are independent and volunteer-run – don't have any, or much, budget allocated to marketing. That can clearly be limiting but doesn't mean you should give up hope or drop marketing from the agenda. In fact, a lot can be achieved on no budget or a low budget, providing some time is invested. For example:

- Drill down and focus on what's important to your museum and who your audiences are. Consider what you *can* achieve without budget, and what is hard to achieve without it; existing audiences can usually be reached more easily using free channels, such as your e-newsletter, than new audiences.
- Encourage word of mouth through reviews, selfies, and photo opportunities at the museum; urge people to share your museum or exhibition hashtag on social media; and provide incentives for sharing your content or photos.
- Make the most of your partnerships by sharing and cross-promoting each other's content and events. Your money may go further if you contribute to wider tourism campaigns, rather than trying to do everything on your own.
- Don't take a scattergun approach or spread yourself too thinly. Aim to do one thing well rather than risk doing several things badly.
- Make the most of your own channels, from your website and e-news to spaces in your museum such as the backs of bathroom doors and café tables.
- Evaluate as much as you can, especially if you are testing something new, so you can understand the value in it.
- Create content that genuinely interests your audiences, that audiences search for and will want to share with others. Stay on top of trends and get creative.
- Maximise PR opportunities – identify newsworthy stories, features, and photo opportunities.

- Repurpose content that you produce for one channel or audience to other places. For example, turn content from long-form blog posts on your website to a series of snappier stories on social media.
- Focus on creating evergreen content that has relevance for years or at least months to come, as opposed to content that has a short shelf life such as content relating to certain one-off events.

If you *do* have some budget to invest, consider longer-term value. Advertising can be incredibly effective, but typically when you stop paying for it, the results stop. So, consider investing in areas where you'll reap the benefits even after the budget is gone. For example, training staff and volunteers to improve the website's SEO; a suite of strong professional photos to roll out across all channels over time; technology or software to professionalise operations and save time (for example a ring light, tripod, microphone, subscription to graphic design software); consultancy support that will ease your future workload or improve its effectiveness, such as to undertake a review of data and make strategic recommendations.

A simple yet effective example of a low-budget marketing activity was Manchester Museum's competition to find its "first official visitor" to open its doors and cut a red ribbon after being closed for 18 months for a £15 million transformation. To enter, people were asked to explain why the museum holds a special place in their heart, with the winner invited to cut the red ribbon on 18 February 2023 and receive a gift bag full of products from the new museum shop. The competition gained local media coverage, for example, in the *Manchester Evening News* (Callow, 2022) and social media interest.

Budget tips

Below are some tips on making the most of your marketing budget:

- Distribute your budget across the year according to need; it's likely that there will be seasonal peaks and troughs to your spending.
- Consider what balance of investment you want between short-term performance and longer-term brand building.
- Take account of inflation and likely annual supplier price increases, especially if your marketing strategy covers more than 12 months.
- Aim to allocate some budget (such as 5%) as a contingency to provide flexibility.
- Track spending monthly or quarterly against your projections to ensure you are not left with a substantial overspend or underspend at the end of the year.
- Ensure you evaluate your work and marketing spend to provide insights into value and input into future spending plans.
- Aim to include marketing costs in funding applications, where permissible – it is a valid and valuable investment.

- Evaluate your work (see the next chapter), and share your achievements internally.
- Consider allocating a small allowance (such as 1–5%) to innovation or experimentation, for example to create a new type of content; advertise on a new website; or undertake A/B testing of different social media ads (see next chapter). Providing you have a clear objective and evaluate the results, this can test different ideas without committing bigger budgets and taking big risks.

Questions to consider

- What is your current annual marketing budget as a percentage of your museum's overall revenue?
- How does your museum make the most of no or low marketing budgets?
- If your museum's marketing budget were halved or doubled for the next year, what would you change?

References

Callow, F. (2022) *You could be Manchester Museum's first visitor following a £15 million transformation* Available at: https://www.manchestereveningnews.co.uk/special-features/you-could-manchester-museums-first-25641215 (Accessed: 7 April 2023).

HubSpot (2022) *Marketing Budget: How Much Should Your Team Spend in 2023?* Available at: https://blog.hubspot.com/marketing/marketing-budget-percentage (Accessed: 19 April 2023).

ICOM (2022) *Museums, museum professionals and COVID-19*. Available at: https://icom.museum/wp-content/uploads/2020/05/Report-Museums-and-COVID-19.pdf (Accessed: 13 December 2022).

Moorman, C. (2023) *The CMO Survey. Managing Brand, Growth, and Metrics. Highlights and Insights Report March 2023*. Available at: https://cmosurvey.org/results/ (Accessed: 3 May 2023).

One Further (2022) *The Cultural Content Report 2022*. Available at: https://onefurther.com/resources/cultural-content-report-2022 (Accessed: 7 April 2023).

5g   Monitoring and evaluation
How will we know if we've got there?

Introduction

When there is limited time, it can be easy to skip monitoring and evaluation, and choose to spend all available time on delivering the marketing activity itself or leave it until the end of the year. With so much data available (in particular digitally), it can be tempting to solely focus on automatically generated data, rather than taking a step back and considering what is meaningful evaluation and how to achieve this. However, marketing and evaluation is a crucial and ongoing part of the framework. This chapter starts with definitions of monitoring, evaluation, quantitative and qualitative evaluation, outputs, and outcomes. It talks about how to decide what to monitor and evaluate, and meaningful evaluation rather than vanity metrics. It shares a range of different evaluation methods to consider and finishes with looking at common challenges and tips.

Monitoring

Monitoring is ongoing activity to help you keep track of what you're doing, *while* you're doing it. As well as spotting whether you're on track to meet your objectives, it's worth reflecting on the reasons why, then consider what (if any) action to take before it's too late. You may already have set SMART objectives that break down by month or quarter. If not, you can take an average from your annual target, but be mindful of seasonal variations and factors that can create natural fluctuations and may not require corrective action. It's also worth looking at your marketing spend across the year to see if this is in line with your allocations. Are there aspects that turned out to be more expensive than forecast? If so, where can you make up the difference? Or if there is something you haven't ended up spending as much on – where can you redirect that money?

Monitoring as you go along also gives you the opportunity to undertake some A/B, or split, testing, where you create two versions of a variable, each of which you show to a randomly assigned half of your audience (Group A and B), with a view to comparing the results. Providing you have a large

DOI: 10.4324/9781003309147-15

enough sample (and ideally you do this several times to gather more data and identify patterns), this should provide you with feedback about what is resonating with audiences, which you can then use to finetune what you're doing. For example:

- Send the same e-newsletter *content* to your subscriber list, but with a different *subject heading* for each half of the recipients, and compare open rates.
- Create two social media ads with the same layout and call to action, but each with a different image, and compare the conversion rates of each.

Evaluation

Evaluation takes place at a specific point in time. *Front-end* evaluation occurs at a project or campaign's *planning* stages before it begins and may include a lot of the research set out in the situational analysis in Chapter 5a, such as consulting potential audiences about their needs or a survey about your existing audiences' awareness of your products. *Formative* evaluation occurs *during* a project or campaign's development or implementation stages. For example, consulting on a new website wireframe or prototype; and gaining audience feedback on campaign straplines, exhibition copy, and photography before they are used. *Summative* marketing evaluation will help you determine whether you have achieved what you planned at the end of your chosen time period. It can be used to advocate for the role of marketing within the museum and help you set budgets for the next year. Most of this chapter focuses on summative evaluation.

Quantitative and qualitative marketing evaluation

Both quantitative and qualitative evaluation serve a purpose. *Quantitative* evaluation deals with numbers, quantities, and statistics – information that can be counted, compared, measured on a scale, and easily shown visually or graphically. It generally involves large data sets and bigger sample sizes and will often form the bulk of marketing evaluation. A lot of this data will be automatically generated from website, social media, and email platforms and analytics; and from ticketing, booking, and CRM (customer relationship management) systems. For example, the number of tickets booked, the increase in e-news subscribers, or memberships sold. The data can show trends and allow comparisons over time and with benchmarks, but it doesn't offer much depth.

Qualitative evaluation involves non-numerical insights such as opinions. Information is presented in narrative form, usually text-rich in description. It can provide more in-depth insights and help to answer questions such as "why" and "how". Examples include analysis of media coverage, exhibition, and visitor reviews; focus groups to understand how marketing messages are being received; and feedback interviews with sponsors. However, it is likely to take more time to set up, undertake, and analyse, and it can be subjective and susceptible to bias.

Deciding what to monitor and evaluate

Broadly speaking, evaluate what you and your museum value. Focus on what is relevant, and use your marketing goals and SMART objectives as a guide. At the outset, plan what information you need to collect, how and when, who will be responsible, and whether you need to allocate any budget to this.

Outputs and outcomes

It's important to distinguish between *outputs* and *outcomes*. *Outputs* are activities that you undertake and what you deliver. They are usually quantitative and often easier and free to track. *Outcomes* are the actual difference made, the results or impact achieved by your outputs, such as a change in behaviour, a transaction, or a change in attitude or belief. They may be harder to track and certainly require effort to link to your marketing activity. Table 5g.1 shows examples of both.

Outputs are generally a means to an end. Whilst they may be a success on their own, there is often limited (albeit not negligible) value in achieving your outputs if they never result in any outcomes – consider the value of the outputs in Table 5g.1 if the outcomes column were blank. However, tracking outputs can still be useful and certainly may be easier than measuring outcomes. If you really can't measure outcomes, outputs still tell part of the story and can be used to indicate progress toward your outcome. For example, the reach (total number of people who see your content) and impressions (the number of times your content is displayed) of your social media are easy numbers to pull off your social media platforms. But they do not tell the whole story; they don't tell you what anyone thought of your content or whether they engaged with it, clicked on it, or did anything as a result of seeing it.

Table 5g.1 Example outputs and outcomes

Outputs	Outcomes
One business magazine article generated from a news release	10 venue hire enquiries 2 venue hire bookings as a result
3,000 links clicked through to your web page from an online ad you placed	1,500 tickets sold as a result
10,000 impressions on a social media post about your membership scheme	100 new memberships as a result of the post
500 free family tickets given out at a community fayre	75 of the tickets redeemed at the museum

Vanity metrics

Don't be tempted to succumb to the trap of just measuring vanity metrics – metrics that look good but don't directly translate into meaningful results. They are typically free and the easiest metrics to obtain. They may show progress in the short term but only tell part of the story. For example, if you have 100,000 social media followers, that is easy to determine and sounds impressive. But what does that mean on its own? Who are the followers? Why do they follow you? How many see your content? How many engage with your content? What do they think of your museum? How many become email subscribers, visitors, or donors?

A discredited vanity metric that was used heavily by the PR industry in the past (and still used by some) is Advertising Value Equivalency (AVE). It aims to calculate the monetary value of media coverage based on the size of print coverage achieved, and the rate the publication charges for advertising, then multiplying this by a factor (often three to eight), since earned media coverage is seen as more valuable than paid-for advertising. The factor is arbitrary and unreliable; AVE is no indication of how positive the piece was about your museum, and it confuses cost with value. The figure you end up with doesn't relate to how many people read the article, absorbed any of the messages in it, or did anything as a result.

Establishing the impact of your marketing

Establishing the *impact* of your marketing can unfortunately be harder. Marketing is not carried out in isolation, and a complex web of many interrelating factors can make it difficult to establish the link between cause and effect. If the number of visitors to your museum rises, is that necessarily down to your marketing efforts and, if so, *just* your marketing efforts or *partly* due to your marketing efforts and, furthermore, *which* marketing efforts? It is rare that one data point will tell you everything you need to know. For example, a high website bounce rate (single-page sessions divided by all sessions on a website) can be down to a number of reasons or a combination of them, such as a slow-to-load page; the title tag (the headline that appears by the URL on the search engine results page) and/or meta description (a summary of what the webpage is about for search engines and searchers) are misleading so they drive visitors to the web page with expectations that are not met; a technical error; or that the user found what they wanted and left. Evaluating marketing is a bit like a jigsaw puzzle you need to piece together to see the whole story.

Marketing evaluation methods

No measure is all-encompassing on its own, and there are pros and cons with each. Aim to achieve a balance between robustness and pragmatism. Below are several marketing evaluation methods – not an exhaustive or compulsory list – to showcase a range of options and principles. I have focused on methods that are feasible for most museums to undertake in-house. Others, such as Marketing Attribution, Marketing Mix Modelling, and Customer Lifetime Value are more complex to undertake and are most likely to be carried out with a specialist external agency or by the biggest museums only.

Data at your fingertips

Chances are that your museum amasses a lot of data you can use. For example, from pre-booking data and ePOS data (electronic point of sale from your front-of-house tills, shops, and cafés). Websites, social media channels, email platforms, and digital advertising should all also provide a host of free analytics, such as the number of website visitors, new visitors, popular pages, time on your website, and the average transaction value for your online or physical shop. Qualitative comments from online review sites or written or verbal communication directly to the museum can also be very useful to go through, ideally coding responses as well as looking at numeric ratings.

Audience growth

In-person audience growth is often a mainstay of museum goals and can be measured through ticket sales, manual clickers, or automated people counters. Digital audience growth can also be valuable to measure through analytics available.

Visitor surveys and questions

Marketing and promotion encountered

Many museums ask visitors which of the museum's communication platforms or content they have come across prior to visiting. However, visitors can't always recall what they have encountered, and a visitor survey doesn't allow for any discussion or comparison of the importance of each channel and what it was about the message or timings that motivated the visitor to come along. Some visitors may answer along the lines of "I just knew about it", since they don't remember what marketing they originally saw years ago. Or if a particular social media channel is a popular answer, it might be useful to also know what content resonated or what drove the visit – was it the museum's organic or paid content, a review someone read, or a share by an influencer? It is also worth bearing in mind that some communication channels are more suited to – and mainly used for – engagement with audiences, as opposed to focusing on driving in-person visits. Therefore, even if those channels are barely represented as visit drivers in your surveys, this doesn't automatically mean they are ineffective.

Identifying audience segments

If you have identified particular audience segments to target, you need to have a method for evaluating which segment the audiences are a part of.

This might involve asking visitors for their postcode or which country they live in; demographic information such as how old they are; or why they visited. A key goal of many museums is to reach out to and engage new audiences. Understanding how many and the proportion of your audiences are first-timers is therefore a key measure. A question can be included in online booking forms and visitor surveys, asked by front-of-house teams as they welcome visitors, or using a range of creative methods, such as token drops.

Base drivers vs incremental drivers

Base *outcomes* are the actions (visits, donations, participation, shop sales, and so on) that a museum achieves without any specific shorter-term marketing interventions. Base *drivers* are elements such as the museum's reputation, location, opening hours, and price that tend to be fixed in the short or medium term. If you track base outcomes – what your outcomes are *without* a specific marketing intervention or campaign – then you can compare your results with those *after* a specific marketing intervention or campaign. These are known as *incremental* drivers, controllable factors implemented by the marketing team such as advertising, temporary price discounts, or a direct email campaign. For example, say you haven't undertaken any promotion for memberships in the past three Decembers. If you then implement a campaign to drive membership sales as a festive gift this year, comparing membership sales figures to your previous figures or averages will help you see if that campaign made a difference (although there may of course still be other factors at play too).

Loyalty measures

We can also look at audience loyalty and the relationships we build with them, for example:

Repeat visits

Look at what proportion of museum visitors are repeat visitors and how frequently they return. A high rate of repeat visits is in many cases attractive, indicating that you have satisfied audiences who feel a return visit is of value to them. It is also often cheaper to encourage previous audiences to return than convince new ones to come in the first place. However, the proportion of our visitors that are repeats is not a measure of success on its own if your priority is to increase new audiences or diversify your audiences, for example. And some museums are naturally likely to have lower repeat rates for other reasons – typically big national museums or special interest museums that attract many international tourists or enthusiasts from further afield are more likely to have lower repeat visitor proportions.

Renewal and retention rates

Renewal rates look at the percentage of audiences who renew their membership at the end of each membership period. A high figure is usually an indicator of value, satisfied customers, and an easy renewal system. If you have an online shop, retention rates (the percentage of customers that come back and shop again) is also useful to track.

Negative measures

It is also worth noting measures such as email unsubscribe rates, membership churn rates, and social media unfollow rates. Take membership churn rates (the rate at which your audiences *stop* being members with you over a given time period: divide the number of lost members by the total number of members at the start of the time period in question and multiply this by 100 to get a percentage figure). For example, if you had 2,000 members at the start of the year and you lost 400 whose memberships expired and didn't renew, this gives you a churn rate of 20%, and this is higher than in previous years, which averaged 10%. Consider why this might be, and undertake some research with lapsed members to help you understand the reasons behind the higher churn rate.

- You sent only one renewal reminder one month before renewals, whereas in previous years you also sent a second reminder one week before renewals?
- Your museum raised its membership prices?
- The membership offer has been changed, and perceived value for money is less than it was?
- External factors, such as an economic downturn, affected people's disposable income?
- Do members view memberships mainly in terms of transactional benefits, so they are waiting for the next paid exhibition they want to see before they renew?

Return on investment

Marketing Return on Investment (ROI) involves attributing revenue growth to the impact of marketing activities. The simplest ROI is calculated by taking revenue, subtracting the marketing costs involved, dividing that figure by the marketing cost, and multiplying this by 100 to get a percentage:

$$ROI = \frac{(Revenue - marketing\ costs)}{Marketing\ cost} \times 100$$

For example, you spend £500 on online ads to promote your membership as a festive gift. All your digital ads click through to a specific URL you have set up on your website, only used for the campaign, which generates £5,000 in membership gift sales. This gives you a ROI of 900%, meaning that for every

120 *Marketing strategy in practice*

£1 spent on marketing, £9 of revenue is achieved, a ratio of 1:9. You can then compare this with other campaigns you run.

You can also look at leads generated compared to conversions, in other words, tracking how many unique website users that page had, and what percentage of them then went on to buy the membership, comparing the conversion rate with past data if you have it and reflect on ways to further improve future campaigns. Did the ads drive a huge number of visitors to the web page but only 0.1% ended up converting to buy the membership (worked out by the number of transactions divided by the total number of webpage visitors)? If so, how can you make the landing page content more compelling, the transaction easier, and so on?

However not everything at museums is charged for and therefore doesn't generate profit or revenue growth. Some products and services may be charged for but simply to cover costs and certainly not with a prime aim of maximising profit. Instead of focusing on revenue generated, you can also look at audience or visitor numbers linked to marketing investment.

Measuring awareness and perceptions

If your objective is around raising awareness, changing perceptions, or tweaking attitudes around something, you need to identify the baseline starting point, and then use the same method to measure awareness, perceptions, or understanding at a chosen end point. Depending on who your audience is, this could be an online survey to your members, e-newsletter subscribers, or a random sample of people within a particular geographic area, or it could be carried out through in-person surveys or interviews with visitors. If this is not possible, consider a range of proxy measures, such as online audience engagement around the topic in question (social media shares, comments, tags, use of your hashtag); key message inclusion in media coverage; website traffic to a particular web page; form submissions; PDF downloads; user "read more" clicks; or video view analytics such as average view duration/average percentage viewed. Just remember not to stretch the results to fit the narrative you want; just because someone can recall seeing your advert doesn't mean it resonated with them or changed their understanding of something.

Measuring engagement

Not every goal is about a financial return, so it is also worth considering measures around audience engagement. "Engagement" is a vague concept, so you need to define the engagement you want to measure, for example:

- Social media engagement rate (audience interactions with your content such as comments, shares, tags, saves): [Total engagements divided by the reach or impressions] × 100.

- Email click-through rates (CTR), the percentage of users that click on a link: [Number of clicks divided by the number of subscribers] × 100.
- The conversion rate (CR) for actions you'd like your audiences to undertake, such as book, fill out a form, sign up to an e-newsletter. For example, for a digital ad: [Number of conversions divided by the number of ad clicks] × 100.

Customer acquisition cost

Customer acquisition cost (CAC) calculates the money spent to acquire a new customer or visitor and can be useful whether or not you charge for the product or service in question. The calculation involves dividing the costs spent on acquiring more audiences by the number of audiences acquired in the time that the money relates to. Comparing CAC per marketing channel can be useful, and using this data can make your marketing budget go further: if your marketing budget is fixed, allocating more budget into channels with a lower CAC will bring in more audiences. However, just looking at CAC doesn't consider the *value* of each audience. For example, you advertise your venue hire services on two websites and your CAC for both works out about the same, so you might assume that advertising on both websites is equally worthwhile. However, on further investigation, you find that the average revenue from bookings that come from one of the websites is 75% higher than bookings via the other website.

Lessons learned

Spend some time reflecting on your experiences of marketing planning, delivery, and the results, and what you can learn from them and apply in the future. For example:

- Were the goals and objectives met? Why or why not?
- What is the data telling you? What is the overall narrative?
- How can you learn from this for the future?
- Were the resources well used?
- What would you do again?
- What would you change?

Aim to foster a culture that enables honest and constructive reflections. If you didn't meet all or any of the objectives, what were the main reasons? For example:

- Did you use the wrong assumptions or base decisions on a lack of, or inaccurate, data?
- Did you misinterpret the data?
- Were the objectives unrealistic?
- Did you choose a strategy that didn't work?

- Did you run out of time?
- Was it due to a lack of team experience?
- Was the brief to the supplier inadequate, or did suppliers let you down?
- Were the communication channels you chose appropriate for the target audiences?
- Was there something beyond your control that affected the results?

Common challenges

In an ideal world, all our data would be perfectly robust and representative. But budgets, time, and other factors may not allow this. As covered in Chapter 5b, some goals and objectives will be easier to evaluate than others. For example, whether you have met a target of a 10% increase in traffic year-on-year to your website will take seconds to establish (assuming you have basic website analytics). In comparison, a breakdown of who visits your museum requires more effort to establish accurately, especially those that are not ticketed.

Broadly speaking, it tends to be easier to accurately track and evaluate digital channels compared with non-digital channels such as posters and leaflets. You may therefore need to be more proactive in considering evaluation for non-digital channels. For example, can you include a QR code on a poster that takes people who scan it straight to a particular page on your website, accessible from that QR code? Can you include a special offer code in a leaflet or magazine advert so you can count how many are redeemed?

Some of the earlier steps in the audience journey are not directly linked to final desired audience actions such as visiting the museum, taking part in an event, buying something from the shop, or donating online. This makes it very difficult to place a monetary value on approaches such as content marketing, which is a longer-term strategy useful for brand awareness and connecting with audiences, as opposed to directly selling something to them. But you can consider evaluating micro engagement moments (such as an e-news sign-up) as well as macro engagement moments (a visit or membership purchase).

Another challenge is that setting up evaluation systems doesn't always equate to getting the information. For example, not all visitors will want to, feel comfortable with, have time for, or be able to complete a visitor survey. And not all staff or volunteers feel comfortable asking visitors to complete surveys or take part in interviews. Data available to you online may also change; for example, legislation may change what information you can track and store about audiences. And finally, remember that correlation does not automatically imply causation – just because there is a link or relationship between two elements does not mean that one has caused the other.

Tips for your monitoring and evaluation

Evaluation can be onerous, so here are some steps you can take to make it more feasible yet robust:

Consider evaluation at the outset

Consider monitoring and evaluation from the outset of your strategy development as opposed to the end of its implementation so you can set systems up accordingly. If you are measuring change, ensure you have baselines before you start. Collect data and evidence as you go along – retrospectively trying to do it may be inaccurate or impossible.

Evaluate against goals and objectives

Be focused on what data you collect and analyse, letting your goals and objectives guide you. This will help ensure you are not too overwhelmed with data and get tempted by those vanity metrics.

Be pragmatic

Focus on what information is of value to you and the museum – you can't measure and interpret everything. Prioritise – can you create a set of Big Three or Big Five outcomes and supporting KPIs?

Be consistent and compare

Compare your data to previous years and/or sector benchmark data where available. Use sector standardised definitions and criteria, and demographic profile breakdowns that match national census data to allow for like-for-like comparisons. For example, don't structure your age categories in visitor surveys as 21–25 and 26–30 and so on if the sector benchmarks and national data uses 20–24 and 25–29. Keep as much consistency in your methods and questions year-on-year as possible (providing they are valid and useful) to allow for comparison between years.

Involve the right people and tools

Ensure the right people are involved, onboarded, and trained if necessary. In many instances, marketing evaluation is not just reliant on people working directly in the marketing team. Use free tools available to you, such as social media and website analytics. Automate as much as possible, such as with standardised templates and snapshot reports that can easily or automatically be updated and colour coded to show whether targets are being met.

Ensure integrity and transparency

Ensure that your evaluation methodology is clear, valid, and transparent. Ensure visitor surveys are as robust as possible; for example, through adequate sample sizes and random sampling so that the responses are more likely to be representative of your visitors as a whole. Recognise the potential for bias, including sample bias, human bias, and algorithm bias. Adhere to data privacy legislation and best practice, as well as evaluation and market research codes of conducts (such as the Market Research Society's Code of Conduct, 2023). When drawing conclusions, writing, or presenting your evaluation, make sure to acknowledge any limitations with your methodology or results, and be transparent with your sample sizes. Recognise and learn from failure.

Use your insights

Share your results with the team, such as in a team meeting to motivate volunteers and the visitor services team or at a board meeting to enable trustees to understand the value of marketing. And crucially, act on your results – use them to improve what you plan and deliver next year or next time.

Questions to consider

- If you had to choose a Big Three or Big Five key outcomes to evaluate, what would they be?
- How can you ensure that your evaluation is relevant and robust?
- Are there any methods from the list above that you want to start using, or would add to the list?

Reference

Market Research Society (2023) *Code of Conduct*. Available at: https://www.mrs.org.uk/standards/code-of-conduct (Accessed: 21 May 2023).

6 Planning and delivering a marketing campaign

Introduction

This chapter focuses on how to develop a marketing plan for a specific campaign. There are similarities in the process with the steps for developing your museum's overarching marketing strategy, so the previous chapters can be a useful reference point too. However, marketing campaigns are for a more limited duration, with a more focused remit, and may only be for some target audiences. You may run several across the year, but they should all support your museum's marketing strategy and goals in some way. There are many different types; for example, one might relate to a purpose, such as a product marketing campaign or brand awareness campaign; another might relate to a channel, such as an email marketing campaign, social media campaign, or direct mail campaign. This chapter shares typical steps for developing marketing campaigns that can be scaled up or down and finishes by showcasing examples of museum marketing campaigns, which highlight a breadth of purposes, budgets, and approaches.

Campaign framework

The framework discussed next is one you can adapt to work for your museum. The steps include:

- Situational analysis or context.
- Goals and objectives: Why?
- Target audiences: Who?
- Strategy: How?
- Action plan: What, when, and by whom?
- Resources: How much?
- Monitoring and evaluation: So what?

Situational analysis or context

Gather information about the campaign's context and purpose. Consider questions such as:

DOI: 10.4324/9781003309147-16

- Why is a marketing campaign needed? What is the purpose?
- What is the value, benefit, or experience for audiences that you will offer?
- Who are the key partners and sponsors involved (if any)? What are their requirements and expectations?
- Are there other marketing and PR teams you will need to work with (for example, representing loans, touring exhibitions, or artists)? Will they provide any marketing collateral or requests such as photography, media spokespeople, key messages? And what (if anything) will they need to approve and sign off (for example, news releases)?
- Is there already an allocated budget to work with, or do you need to set it?
- What are the timescales and key deadlines?
- What is the likely competition?
- Has the museum done anything similar in the past? Were there any lessons learned from that experience?

SWOT analysis

You can use a SWOT analysis to summarise your situational analysis. What are the main strengths and weaknesses with regard to the campaign (for example, are timescales tight)? And what opportunities and threats can you identify to be aware of?

Goals and objectives: Why?

Goals may already be determined, or they need to be set in conjunction with other departments. Are there already income, audience, and attendance targets for a temporary exhibition or event? Is it about developing new audiences, extending your reach, increasing loyalty, or increasing engagement with certain audiences? Or undertaking a membership drive? Recruiting volunteers? Are you launching something new? Raising brand awareness and familiarity more broadly? Boosting digital engagement? Do you want to increase awareness among certain stakeholders or build relationships with new partners? Drive leads for commercial services? And from that, can you break those down to create SMART marketing objectives and KPIs?

Target audiences: Who?

Target audiences may already have been identified; for example, as part of a funding application or in the early stages of planning the project. If not, work with relevant departments and team members (such as curators, engagement teams, and events teams) to identify the campaign's target audiences, key partners, and stakeholders. Your target audiences for campaigns may be the same as in your marketing strategy, a smaller subset, or on occasion, a different set altogether. Consider who is most relevant or likely to be interested in what your campaign is all about. Summarise who the target audiences are: Are they new, existing, or lapsed audiences, or a combination? Where are they based? What are their likely motivations and barriers for engaging? A table summarising key information for each audience segment can provide a useful snapshot.

Think about who the likely early adopters or attendees will be, as they should be engaged first. They may be your members, subject enthusiasts, or audiences who love new things and being the first to experience them. For example, Morris Hargreaves McIntyre's Essence ("Discerning, Confident, Independent, Arts-essential") and Stimulation segments ("Active, Experimental, Ideas, Social") (Morris Hargreaves McIntyre, no date). They may or may not already be on your radar and core audiences – a temporary exhibition may well appeal to people who have never been to your museum before.

Strategy: How?

As well as making strategic decisions about which audiences to reach and engage with the campaign, consider your marketing campaign concept. Do you need to create a "big splash", or sustain consistent interest over several months? Do you need to undertake some front-end or formative research or consultation? For example, The National Gallery in London runs Your Canvas, an online research panel where audiences and potential audiences can share their views on a range of topics, including draft exhibition titles and promotional copy (The National Gallery, 2023).

The big idea

A big idea is not always needed for a campaign, but it can be valuable as a basis on which to build it. This might take some time to evolve, through workshops, looking at previous audience and campaign research, and even sometimes popping up as a lightbulb moment when you least expect it. Think about what the key hooks or points of interest are. Is it the first time something has happened? What is new; is anything innovative? Is there anything of regional, national, or international interest? What is the "so what" factor? Is there mainstream or more niche appeal? Can you get inspiration from audience motivations or barriers?

When I worked with the Museum of Cambridge several years ago, the idea that evolved was "A small museum with a big story to tell". This was about both managing and exceeding audience expectations – the museum is small and is not a full day out. But there's more than meets the eye, and its collections and stories it tells are rich, diverse, and relevant. However, the campaign concept or idea doesn't have to become a strapline or anything that the public sees; it can also just be used behind the scenes.

Positioning

Consider how you will position the product or service in the campaign if appropriate. This will feed into your key messages and tone of voice. For example, a hands-on science exhibition will be positioned differently than an exhibition exploring racial injustice or an exhibition on Renaissance art.

Key messages

What are the main key messages you want to convey with your campaign? Can you ensure they are clear, are memorable, and resonate with target audiences? (See Chapter 10 for more.)

Action plan: What, when, and by whom?

Bring your key actions together in a plan, setting out the activities that need delivering, along with dates, deadlines, and whose responsibilities they are. Use a format that works for everyone involved, whether that is an online spreadsheet or project management software. Start with the known deadlines and work backwards, factoring in time for sign-off, and timescales involved with different distribution methods. You can also include budget allocations.

Thinking about your target audiences, which communication channels will you use to reach them? If you need to reach new audiences, don't just default to your existing channels such as your e-newsletter, social media accounts, and website. Consider your budget – where will this be best spent? Your marketing campaign assets are the tools, materials, and resources you will use, such as posters, leaflets, flyers, blog posts, press releases, images, video, emails, website landing pages, digital banner ads, and digital posters. Think about what content formats will help you reach your target audiences and are feasible for your museum to develop and pay for. You might want to develop a content plan, setting out the format of content you will develop (short- or long-form videos, images, Stories, live videos, blogs, user-generated content, and so on); the content topics; who will create these; how and where you will publish and distribute these; and the timescales – consider the regularity needed for activities such as social media posts and when optimum times are for driving actions like booking.

The funnel

If your campaign's purpose links to a clear action that you'd like audiences to take, consider planning your campaign using the idea of a funnel (typically a sales funnel, but the action doesn't have to finish with a sale). I find the funnel is a helpful visual tool as it highlights that you start off reaching more people at the wide top of the funnel, and the number of people who progress to each subsequent stage naturally drops. You can tailor the desired steps to suit your campaign. The example shown in Table 6.1 suggests a potential funnel for a pre-bookable event that I have kept simple with just three steps (you may have one or two more). The audience stages in this example are awareness, interest, and purchase, and the corresponding phases for the museum's marketing aims are reach, engage, and convert. You need to be conscious of how to encourage more people to each stage and consider the appropriate channels, messages,

Table 6.1 The stages, channels, and KPIs of an example sales funnel

Desired audience action	Marketing aim	Example channels/tools	Example KPIs
Awareness	Reach	Organic social media content	Social media impressions / reach
		Paid social media	Impressions/reach
			Cost per 1,000 impressions
			Click-through rate
		E-news	Open rates
Interest	Engage	Organic social media content	Engagement (comments, shares, reactions)
			Video completion rate
		Website landing page	Web page hits / unique users
		E-news	E-news click-through rates
Purchase	Convert	Website	Basket abandonment rate
			Conversion rate
			Tickets sold (ultimate goal)

and associated KPIs. By tracking key KPIs at each stage and comparing these for different campaigns, you can also build up an idea of which stages of which campaigns see the most success and aim to identify the reasons.

Resources: How much?

Decide how to break down the allocated budget or put forward a suggested budget. What does your evaluation tell you about the success of previous campaigns, tactics, and channels? Think about which of the objectives can be achieved, or which of the target audiences can be reached, only through channels and activities that require a budget.

Monitoring and evaluation: So what?

Agree on how you will monitor and evaluate the success of the campaign by referring back to your SMART objectives. How regularly will you monitor the results, and what are you looking for? Are there key milestones you should check progress around? What KPIs can you track, such as campaign landing page views, email open rate, click-through rate, and social media engagement? Who will undertake the evaluation, and who needs to see it? What are their expectations for what this will look like (a presentation, a report)?

Outsourcing campaigns

It may be that you outsource whole campaigns or parts of them, such as photography, media buying, or media relations. Factor in sufficient time to commission and brief suppliers, freelancers, consultants, or agencies. Write a clear brief with key information: background information and context, campaign purpose and goals, target audiences, timescales, budgets, and deliverables.

Campaign examples

Below is a range of snapshots of marketing campaigns that showcase a breadth of purposes, budgets, and approaches, representing the strategic and creative talent of marketing teams and their colleagues in museums. See also the IWM case study in Chapter 12 for poignant and sensitive campaign examples.

Beamish Museum

Open air museum Beamish Museum tells the story of life in North East England in the 19th and 20th centuries. The museum runs competitions highlighting their online and in-person shop gifts, many of which they make themselves or are made with local suppliers to create bespoke items. For a 2022 competition, they hid five golden tickets in their sweet shop tins for sale, with the winners winning an exclusive, money-can't-buy VIP experience that included entry to the museum before normal opening, a sweet shop demonstration where they could invent their own sweet, a private tour around the site in a vintage car, an afternoon tea, and a behind-the-scenes tour of the museum's stores (Beamish, 2022).

The Museum of Old and New Art (Mona)

In Australia, Tasmania's private Museum of Old and New Art (Mona) took a different approach, developing a campaign called "Best of Our Worst Reviews", featuring some of the most critical online reviews they have received, including: "I got yodelled at for no valid reason" and "I left with a feeling of disdain for all galleries and museums" (Mona, 2022). The museum's campaign site shares over 100 one-star ratings mirroring a cinema poster in look, and you can click on each to see the review, such as "You'll either love it or hate it (I wish I could just forget it)" (Mona, no date). It's a bold approach that may not sit well with all museums but is in keeping with Mona's personality and tone of voice.

Barnsley Museums

Barnsley Museums in England adopted two unloved traditional red telephone boxes in the town centre in 2021. They transformed them into mini museum spaces and works of art in themselves, but the boxes also served as promotions for the main museum venue and exhibitions. In 2022 the museum installed a life-size replica of the innermost coffin of Tutankhamun into one of the telephone boxes as part of a new Egyptian exhibition at Experience Barnsley Museum (Barnsley Metropolitan Borough Council, 2022).

York Museums Trust

A collaborative campaign example is Curator Battle, run by York Museums Trust on Twitter from March to July 2020, as a way for the organisation to engage audiences during the first Covid-19 pandemic. They challenged other museums and museum visitors to share images of objects under a different theme each week such as #CreepiestObject, #BestMuseumBum and #BestBling, resulting in huge engagement from across the world, over 17,000 new Twitter followers, and international media coverage. A survey of more than 200 participants found that 83% agreed or strongly agreed that Curator Battle helped them to feel connected to other people during lockdown. Nearly 50% of those engaging had not engaged with York Museums Trust before, and for nearly one-fifth of the audience, it was the first time they had engaged with cultural works digitally (Carroll, 2021).

Museum of Art & Photography (MAP)

The Museum of Art & Photography, Bengaluru, India, opened its physical doors for the first time in early 2023, after initially launching digitally during the Covid-19 pandemic. MAP's Head of Communications & PR Shaina Jagtiani says that one of the museum's aims is to create a museum-going culture in India, changing perceptions of museums as dusty and elitist, encouraging people to "come and hang out", explore their thoughts and reactions to objects, and not feel intimidated. Wanting to reach young people, the museum uses social media extensively, creating fast-paced and vibrant content and taking a conversational approach: "We are serious yet want to keep it approachable, light and relatable" (Jagtiani, 2023). The museum worked with influencers and celebrities in the city to create a sense of buzz around the museum opening. MAP provided them with merchandise and invited them to visit the museum, join a curated walk-through, and pick their favourite artwork to create fun videos about for social media, in particular Instagram. The museum has seen excellent organic growth and engagement with its social channels and exceeded its opening visitor targets (ibid.).

The Natural History Museum

With a brief of reigniting curiosity and increasing visitor numbers, agency SomeOne was commissioned to create a new campaign for London's Natural History Museum to break the mould of traditional exhibition-by-exhibition campaigns and refresh the positioning of the museum in 2018. The overarching campaign idea was "Come to life", both as an invitation for people to visit the museum and as a concept of bringing objects from the museum to life in the campaign. The campaign included billboards, posters, bus ads, and social media posts across owned, earned, and paid channels, all with vibrant colours, a distinctive bold graphic approach, and amusing copy giving personality to the objects (see Figure 6.1 and Figure 6.2 for examples from the campaign). Results included a 24% increase of visitors year-on-year and the highest number of visitors in one day since the museum opened (Someone, 2019).

132 *Marketing strategy in practice*

Figure 6.1 A billboard from the Natural History Museum's "Come to life" campaign. © The Trustees of the Natural History Museum. Creative by Beth Baines, Tim Green, Cosmo Jameson, Simon Manchipp, and Rich Rhodes at SomeOne.

Figure 6.2 Posters from the Natural History Museum's "Come to life" campaign. © The Trustees of the Natural History Museum. Creative by Beth Baines, Tim Green, Cosmo Jameson, Simon Manchipp, and Rich Rhodes at SomeOne.

The Rijksmuseum

For the bigger budgets, I love the flashmob recreation of Rembrandt's painting *The Night Watch*, which the Rijksmuseum in Amsterdam and its sponsor ING staged in a shopping centre in Breda to promote the painting's return to the museum and the reopening after a 10-year renovation. The campaign slogan "Our heroes are back" announced that all the major objects in the museum's collections were back together. The resulting video has been viewed millions of times (see reference list for a link to view, ING, 2013). It has everything – drama, intrigue, suspense, surprise – and worked both as a live stunt and as a 90-second viral video. Ten years later, it still feels fresh and impressive.

Questions to consider

- What makes a good marketing campaign?
- Are there any standout museum marketing campaigns that you remember?
- Which audiences are likely to be innovators and early adopters for your next marketing campaign?

References

Barnsley Metropolitan Borough Council (2022) *Smallest Museum in South Yorkshire is Home to Tutankhamun*. Available at: https://www.barnsley.gov.uk/news/smallest-museum-in-south-yorkshire-is-home-to-tutankhamun/ (Accessed 12 December 2022).

Beamish (2022) *Beamish Golden Ticket Competition*. Available at: https://www.beamish.org.uk/news/beamish-golden-ticket-com (Accessed: 14 December 2022).

Carroll, M. (2021) *The impact of Curator Battle*. Available at: https://www.yorkmuseumstrust.org.uk/blog/the-impact-of-curator-battle/ (Accessed: 21 April 2023).

ING (2013) *Onze Helden Zijn Terug!* [online video] Available at: https://youtu.be/a6W2ZMpsxhg (Accessed: 21 April 2023).

Jagtiani, S. (2023). Zoom with Christina Lister, 31 March.

Mona, Museum of New and Old Art (no date) *The Best of Our Worst Reviews*. Available at: https://mona.net.au/the-best-of-our-worst-reviews (Accessed 25 April 2023).

Mona, Museum of New and Old Art (2022) *The Museum of Old and New Art*. [online video] Available at: https://www.youtube.com/watch?v=J3lWuNOBGqc (Accessed: 10 May 2023).

Morris Hargreaves McIntyre (no date) *Culture Segments*. Available at: https://www.mhminsight.com/culture-segments/ (Accessed: 15 December 2022).

The National Gallery (2023) *Welcome to Your Canvas*. Available at: https://your-canvas.co.uk/ (Accessed: 7 March 2023).

SomeOne (2019) *Attracting the Most Visitors to the Natural History Museum in 145 years …* Available at: https://someoneinlondon.com/projects/rewriting-history (Accessed: 24 April 2023).

Part III
Deeper dives

7 Branding

Introduction

Brand and *branding* are arguably even more ubiquitous and nebulous terms than *marketing* and *museum*. In the museums sector, thoughts on brands and branding vary enormously, from ardent fans to sceptical critics. Enthusiasts recognise their financial, creative, and cultural power. Detractors see them as a waste of resources, are uncomfortable with the perceived commodification and commercialisation associated with them, and find their construct at odds with the authenticity of museum objects. Since a lot of branding involves intangible and abstract concepts (and some jargon), there can be confusion about what it is. Just as marketing is often conflated with promotion, branding is often conflated with logos.

Branding and how to develop a brand could be a whole other book. The focus of this chapter is a light-touch introduction to *brands* and *branding*, their importance and relationship to museum marketing. The chapter finishes with a longer case study about the rebranding of the Museum of East Anglian Life to the Food Museum in England, which sets branding and positioning within a big strategic journey that the museum took.

Context

Branding is sometimes seen as a contemporary phenomenon, and arguably more has been spent on creating and building brands in recent decades than earlier in history. However, the use of logos or trademarks dates back thousands of years, for example, to identify cattle as personal property (how branding gets its name) and in masonry to identify the source of the stone and the labourer who undertook the work. Trade guilds in the medieval period used marks as signs of quality, to help build trust and loyalty with customers and differentiate their products, and hallmarks have long been used to certify the origin and purity of products, typically of metals such as gold and silver. The introduction and expansion of trademark law has supported the development of brands and branding over the years; as companies could protect their names, products, and logos, they were incentivised to invest more in them. Branding has been used extensively to decommodify products and entice consumers,

DOI: 10.4324/9781003309147-18

creating a billion-dollar industry and prompting countermovements, including anti-consumerist activism and culture jamming (criticising advertising and consumerism by parodying adverts and logos). Today, the principles and tools of branding are used beyond for-profit products to apply to services, not-for-profit organisations, experiences, political parties, cities, regions, countries, celebrities, and freelancers and jobseekers looking to stand out in a busy marketplace. Whether you like them or not, brands are omnipresent in our lives.

Definitions of museum brands and branding

A *brand* is much more than a name, logo, or strapline, even though these are part of the brand identity and its visual manifestation and are elements that a museum can develop and control. But more than that, a brand is the associations that people have with the museum, the stories, attributes, and values they connect with it. The associations can be rational, functional, or emotional; and positive or negative. For example, cool, inclusive, innovative, educational, aspirational, welcoming; or intimidating, boring, patronising, pretentious, expensive, irrelevant.

Branding is a long-term strategy and process used to create positive perceptions of and associations with the museum and its offer. It is how the museum expresses its brand and includes the proactive process of creating the museum's brand identity. It provides prompts and shortcuts around the museum's attributes and values as a whole and those of its products, services, and experiences; helping people to know what the museum stands for and what they can expect from it. Elements of branding can include the museum's:

- Mission and vision, providing the "why" and giving the brand a clear direction.
- Lived values.
- Value proposition (what the museum offers its audiences).
- Personality and tone of voice it conveys to audiences.
- Brand or visual identity – the logo, colours, fonts, image concepts.

But also, the museum's:

- Quality of products, services, and experiences.
- Choice of communication channels.
- Pricing policies.
- Choice of partners, sponsors, and collaborators.
- Contact with its audiences, from front-of-house staff and volunteers to point-of-sales materials.
- Staff, volunteers, trustees, leadership.

There are many elements that marketers can control, but there are also many elements beyond their direct sphere of influence, which can have a huge impact on perceptions of the museum, such as visitor reviews or front-of-house teams' interactions with visitors. And even for the elements that you can influence, you can't fully control whether audiences encounter those cues and how audiences interpret them if they do.

The importance of museum branding

Marketing and branding are interdependent on one another and support the same end goals, but they are not interchangeable. In simple terms, if branding is about the identity of the museum, marketing is about identifying and connecting that identity with relevant audiences. The responsibility for branding varies between museums, and it may be part of the marketing team's remit or sit separately. Branding may be viewed strategically – with corresponding budget and time invested in it accordingly – or viewed tactically and mainly be about plastering the museum logo on marketing collateral.

A strong museum brand is one that plays an integral and effective role in supporting the museum to achieve its goals, and a solid foundation for marketing. I'd suggest that common factors that make a strong brand include a compelling purpose; authenticity; consistency; distinctiveness; relevance and resonance; credibility and trustworthiness; words and actions aligning; clarity; and legal protection.

A brand is a cue that can cut through the noise and overwhelm of information that audiences are bombarded with each day, helping your museum to stand out from the competition. Name recognition, brand recall, and familiarity can speed up decision-making around days out or donations. Branding can help to build awareness and trust with audiences. For example, if the museum has a new exhibition about a niche subject or an artist that is not so familiar, a strong brand can provide a trustworthy recommendation – if the exhibition is on at that museum, it must be good and worth a visit.

Consistency means delivering the same type of experience and the same quality each time, which can be reassuring and reduce risk for audiences. And the benefits compound over time, meaning that each marketing campaign is not starting from scratch in generating awareness of the museum. Having a strong brand also supports a museum's reputation, building up goodwill that can be useful to draw on in the event of a scandal.

Furthermore, a strong brand has concrete financial benefits – brand equity is the commercial value of a brand determined by audience perceptions, elements such as name awareness, customer loyalty and satisfaction (rather than the product or service itself). Strong museum brands can typically more easily develop successful branded product lines, attract sponsorship and celebrity endorsements, and build brand extensions, setting up new offshoots in other regions and countries. For example, the Louvre signed a deal for 440 million euros ($525 million) for the Louvre Abu Dhabi in the United Arab Emirates to use the Louvre name for 30 years (Noueihed, 2007).

Case study: The Food Museum

The case study I'm featuring in this chapter is a fascinating story of the rebranding and repositioning of a museum. But more than that, it also perfectly encapsulates so much of what museum marketing and this book is championing. It charts one museum's journey to stay relevant. To consult, listen, and learn. To develop a bold, long-term vision that remains authentic and loyal to its collections and values, but also tells new stories for new generations. To commit to it in the face of limited – but vocal and nasty – backlash. And doing all of this without a large capital development.

Background

The Museum of East Anglian Life[1] in Stowmarket, a market town in Suffolk in the east of England, began as a rural life museum in 1967, one of a swathe of such museums that were created across the country during the 1960s to 1970s in particular, as a way of collecting and preserving objects and stories relating to a fading way of life. Advancements in agricultural technology were transforming farming and the countryside, making many of the old farm tools and machinery obsolete, and with them some of the related traditions and communities. The original aim of the group that founded the museum was "to collect and preserve material for research and study" and not primarily display for the education of the public (Cousins, 2022). It was a rural estate comprising farmland, a big house, and ancillary buildings, and over the years, other historic buildings and objects were added, and horses and steam power became part of the museum experience.

Proposition

Over time, the museum developed from a volunteer group to a professional and accredited museum. But by 2015, it was facing challenges, with reduced local authority funding and declining visitor numbers. The Board identified the need for a new direction with a big idea, and that was the challenge given to Jenny Cousins, who was appointed director in 2016.

Research with visitors and non-visitors, coupled with the wider context of rural life museums closing or struggling (as documented by the Mapping Museums project) suggested there was an issue around the museum concept. Out of this came "a recognition that the impulse that set up the museum was unlikely to be the one that would also sustain it [...] We needed to interpret our collection for a 21st-century audience and collect and programme accordingly to reflect their lives and interests. We wanted to pursue a proposition which had wider public appeal whilst also remaining true to the museum's core purpose" (Cousins, 2023a).

"A key question for living history museums is about how they remain relevant. If you don't have memories of what is on display, and it doesn't have a visual or historical wow factor, can you relate to it?" (Cousins, 2022). Food was the theme that suggested itself because of the collection the museum had. And Cousins describes this as a lightbulb moment for the team: "When we looked at our collection through this lens, most things made sense" (2023a). The museum homed in on what it could do that others couldn't. It is in a good location to tell a food story since East Anglia is considered "Britain's breadbasket" as its climate, landscape, and soil are suited for growing wheat (National Farmers' Union, 2016) and the museum has a significant amount of land.

Consultation

The team put together a series of proposals and consulted on them and the ideas behind them. One of the questions asked was, "What should a Museum of Food be saying?" with answers ranging from the preparation of food from the ground through to eating; different farming methods for producing food; cooking workshops; and different cultures and their food. The team undertook a consultation process over three years that included:

- Consultation with existing audiences and stakeholders, including volunteers, members and funders, staff, and trustees, through meetings, emails, and workshops.
- Surveys to the public on local streets, in libraries, and at other organisations' events in the town and vicinity.
- Regularly updated display boards at the museum with opportunities to comment.
- An online survey that received around 350 responses.
- An open evening for local people, publicised in the local media.
- Around 20 workshops with groups including local schoolchildren, farmers, environmental campaigners, refugee groups, disability groups, and food writers.
- Giving talks and receiving feedback, for example, to local history societies and council meetings.

New plans

Cousins produced a 10-year masterplan that the Board adopted, and they set up a development board to bring in more external help and new ideas. Without a large-scale redevelopment project, the initial plans focused on using the museum's existing objects but interpreting them differently to tell different stories. The museum has divided the visitor experience into Grow, Make and Eat. It has restored exhibits, planted an orchard, put in a crop rotation, and largely reinterpreted what it has. Telling the bread story, the museum has created a trail that starts with a seed and ends with a loaf, going via a watermill, threshing equipment, and bread oven. Future plans include conserving and redisplaying objects with potential that are not currently on display, such as several period kitchens.

Programming includes the Skills Kitchen refugee cooking group; the Thrills and Grills programme for children in receipt of free school meals, preparing and eating food together; community allotments; and a walled garden where the museum runs volunteering and National Health Service green therapy to improve participants' health and well-being by spending time or doing activities in green spaces. The museum has also adopted a strong environmental focus; for example, it has a co-curated exhibit produced with a local Eco Future group called *Every Garden Matters: How to Save the World One Garden at a Time*. It printed the *Hedgerow* exhibition interpretation on seed paper that can be planted at the end of its life, and this project was a joint winner of the Sustainable Project of the Year at the Museums + Heritage Awards 2023.

New mission, values, and name

The decision to rename the museum was a logical outcome of the process of retheming and reinterpreting the site, rather than something that was decided at the outset. In April 2022, the museum changed its name from the Museum of East Anglian Life to the Food Museum, the new name and visual identity being the culmination of years of behind-the-scenes work. The logo therefore changed too (see Figure 7.1 and Figure 7.2). The museum's new vision is "that people are inspired by the past to make positive change in their own lives" and its mission is "to connect people with where food comes from and the impact of our choices: past, present and future". Its values are:

Figure 7.1 The logo of the Museum of East Anglian Life. © The Food Museum.

Figure 7.2 The logo of the Food Museum. © The Food Museum.

- **Relevant**, for example: "'We make our collections relatable to a 21st-century audience".
- **Challenging**: "We encourage people to debate and give them the tools and information to make up their own minds".
- **Sustainable**: "We explore human impact on the natural world" (Food Museum, 2022).

Criticisms faced

Just ahead of the launch of the new name, the museum faced some criticisms from a small group of people alleging that the museum wanted to get rid of the collection and undermine East Anglian identity. One started an online petition. Almost none of these people were previously known to the museum as members or regular users. Weeks later, some national media picked up on this story, with headlines such as "East Anglian museum gets 'inclusive' name change – and locals are furious" (Rowan, 2022) and leaning into the so-called culture wars. Comments to one of the online articles included: "Boycott it and boycott it hard" and "Dumbing down as usual"; but there were also personal attacks on staff such as, "Another woke idiot", "What a silly woman, she needs sacking", "Not harsh enough, needs eradicating" (all online comments to a piece by Warren, 2022).

However, the online pile-on outweighed criticisms directly to the museum – only three people turned up to a Town Council meeting to object to the name change, and several months on, the museum has received fewer than 30 letters about it (Cousins, 2023a). Countering the accusations, Cousins says that whilst the museum was undertaking some rationalisation, this was in line with good museum practice and a necessity after decades of more indiscriminate collecting resulted in duplication, which they would have undertaken regardless of any change of direction. "Removing it [East Anglia] from our name is not removing it from our approach. In many ways, we are trying to get people more interested in the local by starting with something universal" (2022).

Looking ahead

The coverage did at least raise awareness of the Food Museum on a national level, albeit not the angle that the museum would have liked. One year on, the museum team members are happy with how the revitalised museum is evolving. Visitor numbers have risen by 30% from the 2017–18 baseline. Promotion is a key focus for the year ahead. A recent appointment of a Digital Assistant will help the museum to extend its reach and promote the daily museum experience, not just its events (Cousins, 2023b). Cousins notes that while adopting a new business model is not easy, it is exciting and has given the team a renewed purpose and energy as an organisation, with positive visitor feedback and reviews (2023a). As Cousins said, "We cannot live in the past. We have to remake our museums for today's audiences. Just because we've inherited a thing, it does not mean that it should remain the same forever. We have to work out what we want to hold onto, and what we can let go of and what we can see differently. We have to make space for new ideas and new baselines and allow our sector to evolve" (Cousins, 2022).

Questions to consider

- What do you feel makes a strong brand?
- What is a museum brand you admire? Why?
- What lessons can you draw from The Food Museum case study that you can apply to your museum?

Note

1 East Anglia is a region that takes in the eastern counties of Suffolk and Norfolk and by some definitions Essex and Cambridgeshire as well.

Further reading

Klein, N. (2010) *No Logo*. London: Fourth Estate.

Miltenburg, A. (2017) *Brand the Change. The Branding Guide for Social Entrepreneurs, Disruptors, Not-For-Profits and Corporate Troublemakers*. Amsterdam: BIS Publishers.
Sinek, S. (2019) *Start with why*. London: Penguin Business.

References

Cousins, J. (2022) *Independent Museums in an Interdependent World*. Presentation at the AIM Conference, 17 June.
Cousins, J. (2023a) Email to Christina Lister, 12 April.
Cousins, J. (2023b) Email to Christina Lister, 2 May.
Food Museum (2022) *Vision, Mission and Values*. Available at: https://foodmuseum.org.uk/about/vision-mission-and-values/ (Accessed: 14 April 2023).
Mapping Museums project website (no date) *Mapping Museums*. Available at: www.mappingmuseums.org. (Accessed: 14 April 2023).
National Farmers' Union (2016) *Farming in East Anglia*. Available at: https://www.nfuonline.com/updates-and-information/farming-in-east-anglia/ (Accessed: 14 April 2023).
Noueihed, L. (2007) *France Signs Deal to Open Louvre in Abu Dhabi*. Available at: https://www.reuters.com/article/us-abudhabi-louvre-idUSL0657417920070306 (Accessed: 12 May 2023).
Rowan, C. (2022) *East Anglian Museum Gets 'Inclusive' Name Change – And Locals Are Furious*. Available at: https://www.telegraph.co.uk/news/2022/05/30/east-anglian-museum-gets-inclusive-name-change-locals-furious/ (Accessed: 23 April 2023).
Warren, J. (2022) *Fury as Historic Rural Museum About 'Britain's Breadbasket' of East Anglia is Stripped of its 'Cherished' Regional Heritage and Given Eco-friendly Focus on 'Sustainability' and Food Production*. Available at: https://www.dailymail.co.uk/news/article-10766563/Fury-historic-East-Anglian-farming-museum-stripped-cherished-rural-heritage.html#comments (Accessed: 15 April 2023).

8 Pricing

Introduction

Discussions around museum admission charging highlight the balancing act between maintaining the principle of broad access and the pragmatic need to generate income. Historically many museums have been free to enter, there is a moral imperative, and sometimes there is an audience expectation of this. However, with the traditional sources of museum funding increasingly being eroded in many countries, many museums rely on income from admissions. This chapter discusses factors that affect pricing including price elasticity of demand; research on the impact of charging and free admission; the importance of communicating pricing well; inclusive pricing; and different types of pricing strategies. The charges cited in the examples were accurate during December 2022 to May 2023.

What to charge for and who should pay

There are many decisions to be made: first, in terms of *what* products, programmes, events, and services should be charged for; second, in terms of *how* they should be priced; and third, *who* should pay. Even museums with free admission are likely to charge for ancillary products and services, typically refreshments and merchandise, and often special temporary exhibitions and some activities. There are also questions in terms of what is included in free or paid-for admission – is an audio guide, a guided tour, a children's activity pack, or an exhibition programme included or extra? In addition, many museums have commercial income streams such as venue hire, consultancy work, research, reproduction, and copyright fees.

Who should pay is another big question. Pricing policies are often based on the principle that audiences with a propensity to pay – ability and willingness – should pay, whilst audiences who are not able to pay and may not otherwise attend or engage should not pay at all, or not pay in full. Museum pricing policies often seek to appeal to and attract new (often under-served) audiences, but there is also a need to ensure that core audiences don't feel penalised, or that their loyalty is disincentivised. Memberships and annual passes are a common way to reward loyalty, increase repeat visits, and build closer

DOI: 10.4324/9781003309147-19

relationships with audiences. Annual passes provide unlimited free return to the museum within 12 months, often for the price of one admission. Memberships can offer a range of benefits to audiences, such as free or discounted entry or access to special exhibitions; priority booking or entry; news and members' magazines; exclusive events; discounts in the museum shop, café, and restaurant; and access to members' rooms.

Factors affecting pricing

There is a big interplay of factors that may affect your pricing, including:

- **Your museum's mission and values:** For example, are more expensive admission tickets for early and exclusive access in-keeping with a policy of inclusivity and accessibility? Who are the discounts and concessions for?
- **Your goals:** If you want to reach *new* audiences through a discount, how can you make sure that the discount isn't also snapped up by existing visitors? Or is your priority to incentivise loyalty from *existing* audiences or bring back *lapsed* audiences?
- **Your target audiences:** What are they able and prepared to pay? To what extent is price a barrier to engagement? Which audiences do you want and need to support? What constitutes value for money for them?
- **Your costs and income targets:** What income do you need to make from different aspects of the museum? What costs do you need to cover?
- **Funding and subsidies:** The availability of local and national government funding, political ideology, and policies.
- **The economic climate:** In an economic downturn, many audiences are likely to have less disposable income and are less able to take holidays and costlier excursions.
- **Your competition:** How are key competitors priced and how does your offer compare? If you are a smaller site with a smaller average dwell time to local competitors, is it appropriate to charge more?
- **Past experience:** What does your evaluation from previous exhibitions, events and projects say? Have different pricing points impacted audience numbers and types?
- **Tradition:** Linked to both competition and past experience are the accepted norms in museum pricing, for example around concessions. Audiences may expect them, but tradition on its own is not a reason to continue.
- **Price elasticity of demand:** To what extent will a price increase result in a noticeable fall in demand? Will a discount result in an increase in audiences and/or breadth of audiences or just eat into your income? (See below).
- **Your capacity:** If you are already at visitor capacity, a discount is likely to lose you income rather than attract more audiences. If you have quiet and off-peak spells, discounts for those times may help attract new visitors and/ or spread audiences away from busy times.

- **Funders' requirements:** Some funders may require free access for all or some audiences for programmes they fund.
- **External factors such as socio-demographic trends:** For example, factors such as schools' policies and budgets may impact the price you can charge for school visits.

Price elasticity of demand

Price elasticity of demand is an economic theory (originally developed by Alfred Marshall over a century ago) used to understand how demand for a product or service changes, or is likely to change, when its price is changed, if all other variables are constant. With *inelastic* products or services, a change in price leads to a *smaller* percentage change in demand. Examples of inelastic products are petrol, utilities, tobacco products, and peak commuter rail tickets. The goods or services are needed despite price hikes, there aren't directly compatible substitutes, or there are barriers or perceived barriers to alternatives. In contrast, *elastic* products are less likely to be necessities or considered essentials by most customers, and there are also often a range of cheaper substitutes available. A *small* price increase will lead to a *bigger* percentage fall in demand and vice versa. Examples are branded food items such as cereals, which can be replaced by supermarket own brand versions, many electronics, flights, and holidays.

Turning to museums and thinking back to discussions about segmentation, there will be some people for whom art, history, museums, supporting them and visiting the venues is an intrinsic part of who they are. For them, there is no substitute for seeing a Van Gogh painting in real life and so their behaviour is less likely to change as a result of price increases (especially for audiences who have more disposable income). Exclusivity, novelty and buzz around museum exhibitions, programmes and events also make demand for them more inelastic. However, for others, for example audiences who see museums as more of a social outing, there will be plenty of alternative trips and activities they could turn to if they feel that a museum visit has become too expensive. Price elasticity of demand may be different for different audiences depending on the event, programme, or exhibition in question as they will value some more than others. And it may also change over time as audiences' preferences, life circumstances and disposable income change.

Audiences' value for money

Value for money is subjective, individual, and complex, and may not correlate directly to price – just because something is more expensive, does not mean that audiences or customers feel it provides inferior value for money. For some people, a higher price signals higher quality, and vice versa. Some people are prepared to pay £50 for a ticket to a theme park or football match but not £5 for a museum visit. Value is about weighing up benefits and costs to the audience or potential audience. Costs may include functional costs such as the price of admission and travel to the museum, as well as psychic costs such as frustration from queuing or travel stress. Paying is a form of commitment, so whilst audience expectations may increase when they pay so, too, may their buy-in – free, pre-bookable events tend to have higher rates of no-shows than events that are charged for.

To charge or not to charge

It might feel counterintuitive, but lowering prices or making something free doesn't necessarily increase the demand for it from everyone. Price is only one barrier to engagement and one factor affecting demand for museums, albeit perhaps simpler to adjust than more institutional or structural barriers. There are people who never visit museums that are free to enter and access. There are many debates and research around whether and how charging for entry to museums affects visitor numbers and diversity, and it can be hard to draw universal conclusions as there are so many other factors at play for each individual museum and its audiences. Below, I touch on some research to highlight some key points.

Data from the UK's Department for Culture, Media, and Sport and MORI showed that there was a 62% increase in visitor numbers in the seven months after entry charges were scrapped at most national museums in the UK in 2001, an increase of 2.7 million people year-on-year (Martin, 2003, p. 1). However, whilst there was an increase in the number of visitors who were socially excluded, the most significant impact was on the increase in visits from existing audiences (ibid., p. 10), and overall, the general visitor base of the museums remained fairly stable (ibid., p. 4). Similarly, research conducted by DC Research into museums across the UK on behalf of the Association of Independent Museums found that "charging does not affect the social mix of visitors to museums. [...] there is very little difference between the proportions of different social grades of visitors to free admission sites and to paid admission sites" (2016, p. 15). A more recent report looking at the impact of free entry to museums in Sweden also found that whilst visitor numbers increased by around 50%, free entry did not lead to a big change in the social-demographic make-up of visitors or a substantial number of new visitors (Kulturanalys, Swedish Agency for Cultural Policy Analysis, 2023, pp. 56–7).

However, there *can* be differences in audiences at museums that charge compared with those that have free entry. For example, analysis from the Audience Agency found that free entrance museums in England attract a higher proportion of visitors who are less culturally engaged, who are local audiences, and who are under 35 years old (2018, p. 11). Whilst the number and diversity of visitors is a primary focus of discussions around charging, there are also other motivations around charging policies, and other impacts as a result. For example, DC Research's report found that visitors to charging museums are slightly more likely to have purchased from the shop or used on-site catering than visitors to free-entry museums; museums that charge tend to have longer visitor dwell times than those that don't, and lower rates of repeat visits (31%) than museums that don't charge for admission (39%) (2016, p. 17). Aside from revenue, other benefits of charging are that it provides the museum with data on visitors through the types of tickets bought and when they visit, and charging provides a focal point for visitors when they first enter the museum. For museums that don't charge entry, alternatives for these benefits need to be considered.

Inclusive pricing

Museum pricing policies need to be linked to their audience development programmes, with decisions made on which audiences require different charges and where they will make a difference. Many charging museums provide a concessionary rate to disabled visitors (and free entry to their carers), in recognition both that a disabled visitor's experience is not always fully comparable with the experience of someone who is not disabled, and of the "disability price tag" – disability equality charity Scope found that on average, disabled households (with at least one disabled adult or child) need an additional £975 a month to have the same standard of living as non-disabled households (Scope, 2023).

There has been progress on what constitutes a family ticket, since research by Kids in Museums found that 96% of single parents felt that family tickets didn't work for them (2010, p. 3). The two-adults-plus-two-children ticket has in many museums been replaced with more flexible ticketing options that cater for a variety of sizes and composition of families such as single-parent families, families with more or less than two children, and different generations such as grandparents.

The language used in marketing materials and by museum staff and volunteers is also important to consider. For example, consultant Margaret Middleton sets out examples of family-inclusive language such as saying "grownup, adult, or caregiver" rather than "parents, mom, dad" since not everyone accompanying a child is a parent; and "family members" instead of "members of a household" since not all families live together, for example, families with divorced or incarcerated parents (2022, p. 32).

The Accessibility and Diversity Checklist for Museums by Culture for All Service and ICOM Finland offers a range of recommendations on inclusive pricing for museums, including considerations such as:

- There are regular times, events, and programme contents with free admission for all.
- There are targeted free services for people on low income to gain free admission.
- There is an option of free cloakroom facilities.

- There is an area where visitors can bring their own food and refreshments.
- There is no fee for using assistive devices; for example, visitors who are blind or partially sighted are not charged for audio guides (Salonlahti and Salovaara, 2022, pp. 50–5).

Communicating prices

Your pricing sends out signals on how you position your museum (affordable, accessible, exclusive, quality, inclusive). Within museums that charge for entry, there isn't always consistency around pricing policy – for example, there are different cut-off points for child tickets (often between 14 and 17 years old) and different starting ages for senior tickets (usually between 60 and 65 years old). Ideally, pricing should be clear and straightforward – you don't want audiences having to undertake advanced mathematical calculations to determine which type of ticket they would benefit most from buying and what is included. I counted 14 different adult rates for a special exhibition at one gallery, which also makes promoting the cost of admission convoluted.

I often hear from smaller and independent museums in the UK that some visitors and potential visitors criticise their entry charges, when the much larger national museums (with a bigger offer) are free to enter. Similarly, some local authority museums that charge for admission are criticised by people who feel they have already paid for the museum through their local council tax. There is an understandable confusion from the public around how museums are funded differently within and between countries. If your museum is free to visit, this should be a core part of your communications – don't assume that audiences will know. A survey of a representative cross-section of the British public seven months after most of the UK's national museums were made free to enter in 2001 found that 40% of respondents were not aware of the charges being scrapped (Martin, 2003, p. 6).

Another issue is ensuring that any free or discounted tickets and opportunities for certain audiences are actually made available and communicated to those audiences. IMPACTS Experience's data from 48 cultural organisations in the United States that offer regular, scheduled free days to reach affordable-access audiences shows that on average, people who visit on free days have a *higher* household income and educational attainment than people who visit on non-free days and are more likely to be repeat visitors (Dilenschneider, 2015). IMPACTS Experience's analysis also shows that households reporting annual incomes above $250,000 are significantly more likely to be aware of an organisation's affordable access programming than households with annual incomes of less than $25,000, even though the latter are the target audience for them (ibid., 2016). As well as a lack of communication with the intended audiences, reasons for low uptake of such access programmes may include other costs for participants, such as transport to the venue, stigma, and audiences not feeling welcomed.

Changing prices

Making changes to pricing is sometimes necessary and/or beneficial as a result of fundamental changes to government funding or policy; wanting to attract new audiences or spread out visitors; needing to account for inflation and cost increases; or an improvement in the offer, such as new facilities and gallery spaces. Understanding what competitors charge, undertaking consultation with audiences, and testing to see what impact price changes make is advisable. Communicate the changes and the reasons behind them clearly to audiences, especially existing audiences if you are increasing prices. Ensure that visitor-facing teams understand the changes and can explain the reasons behind this confidently. Make sure you consider ways of evaluating any price changes you make, although isolating the impact of price alone can be difficult.

Different types of pricing

Museums typically have a range of price points for their admissions and memberships, aiming both to be accessible and attract a range of visitors, and to generate income. Below are a series of different pricing strategies and examples to consider, which can be combined.

Economy pricing

Economy pricing is a low price for a low-frills option, similar to a supermarket basic house brand. I wouldn't say it is that common in museums, but the idea of a more basic offering at a cheaper price is sometimes used. For example, The Museum of Norwich in England offers a "Twilight ticket" for £2.50 one hour before closing (compared with the standard adult entry of £7) (2023).

Premium pricing

Premium pricing involves charging a higher price for something with higher quality or perceived quality. For example, a corporate membership scheme's more expensive tiers with exclusive benefits such as invitations to private views.

Competition-based pricing

With competition-based pricing, you are influenced by the prices charged by your key competitors. I wouldn't suggest using this model on its own, but as part of a range of factors. It is worth knowing what competitors charge and how your offer compares to theirs in terms of site size, average visit duration, the number of changing exhibitions and events, and so on, and how audiences *perceive* your offer in comparison. Interestingly, when I researched things to do for a weekend with friends in Antwerp, Belgium, in 2022, nine out of the 10 museums or heritage sites I shortlisted charged €10–12 for a standard adult ticket, with only one outlier at €20.

Cost-based or mark-up pricing

Cost-based or mark-up pricing involves working out what the cost of producing and distributing a product is and adding a mark-up (typically a certain percentage). It is important to understand what the costs of producing something are and to consider whether to absorb cost increases, such as from suppliers or inflation. However, this method does not account for what different audiences value and are prepared to pay, and what competitors charge. Sometimes break-even pricing – a version of cost-based pricing – is relevant in museums, when the aim is not to make any profit, but rather to only recover costs from the product or service, for example, for a children's workshop.

Time or task-based pricing

Time or task-based pricing has a similar principle behind it to cost-based pricing but is more relevant to service-based offerings. For example, charging by the hour or day for consultancy services, curatorial work, or research support.

Psychology pricing

Psychology pricing involves setting a price that your audiences respond to emotionally; for example, selling items in your shop for 99p, or a main course and drink offer for €9.95.

Concessions and discounts

Concession tickets provide a discount to those who qualify, typically children, students, retired people or people over a certain age, disabled people, the unwaged or unemployed, families, and members of larger groups. Some museums also provide discounts for young people; military staff and veterans; and emergency service, health, and social care workers. It is a complicated area to decide who qualifies for a concessionary rate, at what rate it should be set, and how – if at all – visitors need to prove they qualify in a way that is not exclusionary or embarrassing for them.

Concessionary rates for older people are standard in many countries, but there is discussion around whether it is appropriate to offer a blanket discount to *all* older people, since as many countries' older populations are growing, many older people have time and disposable income available and are often very culturally engaged. The Carolee Schneemann *Body Politics* exhibition at the Barbican in London charged over-65s £13 during the week but the full price of £18 at weekends, whilst the other concession discounts (unwaged, students, National Health Service staff, and Art Fund members) were available at any time (Barbican, 2022).

There are also opportunities to provide one-off or temporary discounts as part of special offers for particular audiences or time-limited offers as part of tourism campaigns, often with other attractions. A report for Kids in Museums suggests that the number of new visitors resulting from an attractive discount offer can provide an uplift in sales volume of 20–25%, providing it is marketed effectively (Culture Label, 2018, p. 6). Dedicated codes will help the evaluation of these. Avoid setting a precedence of running such discounts so regularly that audiences wait for them before they buy. Some museums provide discounts for their local community. The Tower of London provides local residents within the borough of Tower Hamlets (the borough it is situated in, with high levels of deprivation) who have a local library card entry for only £1 through an agreement with Tower Hamlets Council, compared with a standard adult rate of £29.90–£32.90 and child rate of £14.90–£16.40 (Historic Royal Palaces, 2023).

Variable pricing

Variable pricing changes the price depending on the supply and demand, for example off-peak pricing aims to encourage visitors who can visit during quieter times to do so – quieter times of the day, days of the week and of the year. For example, an Off-Peak Annual Pass for entry to the London Transport Museum on weekdays after 2 pm during term time and in the summer school holidays is £22, compared with a standard unlimited annual pass at £24 (2023). Some museums also provide price incentives for audiences who pre-book online early and/or who pre-book online rather than pay at the door on the day.

Dynamic pricing

Whilst variable pricing is set in advance and remains constant – for example, £10 weekend rates and £8 weekday rates – dynamic pricing adjusts prices up or down on an ongoing, real-time basis. It can help spread out audiences and maximise income from those who are able to pay whilst still offering cheaper options to more price-sensitive audiences. However, you need to consider to what extent it serves your audiences, who might benefit, and who is disadvantaged through it. It also makes it harder to promote admission prices accurately and simply in advance and requires more advanced software to achieve.

Dynamic pricing is common with airline and train tickets, hotels, and supermarket delivery slots. Some theatres have started using this pricing method, and though it is less common with museums, it is receiving increased interest. Research into dynamic pricing carried out in 2022 with 550 UK-based adults who plan to visit a visitor attraction in the next 12 months highlighted clear opportunities and challenges for museums that may wish to implement dynamic pricing (Convious and Baker Richards, 2022, pp. 4–7) including:

- Only 23% of consumers had heard of dynamic or demand-based pricing before.

- 60.5% think it is OK for visitor attractions to *lower* admission prices when they expect to be less busy than usual, but only 22.5% think it's OK to *increase* admission prices when they expect to be busier than usual.
- If a visitor attraction offered them a 20% discount for booking in advance, 91% said they would be likely to book earlier.
- Price incentives could redistribute many visitors' intentions of visiting from popular morning arrival slots to quieter midday and afternoon slots.

The Children's Museum of Indianapolis, USA has what it calls Plan-Ahead Pricing, with discounts of up to 20% for buying general admission tickets at least two weeks in advance. The website says that prices will never fall below what is listed today but may increase until the visit date, with an adult ticket varying from $25.75 to $37.75 for the month ahead on 6 May 2023 (The Children's Museum of Indianapolis, 2023).

Value-based pricing

Value-based pricing is a pricing strategy focused on what the product or service is worth to the customer. However, this can be hard to accurately ascertain, is likely to be different for different audiences, and changes over time and in different circumstances for each individual. That's where what I call audience choice pricing comes in to play for museums, perhaps the ultimate form of value-based pricing. There are different iterations of this model, set out below, but the principle is that the choice of how much (and in some cases, whether or not) to pay rests with audiences. Some museums operate such a model across the board, whilst others are experimenting with it, using it in conjunction with other pricing options or in a limited way. There is a danger that frequent and core audiences who would otherwise pay the full price end up paying less than they would otherwise have done.

Donations or voluntary suggested charges

Some museums are free to visit but ask for donations, sometimes with voluntary suggested donation amounts. The location and types of requests can vary, including for example, a traditional donation box for cash, a contactless card donation box, and QR codes to help visitors donate on the way out.

Pay What You Can (PWYC) and Pay What You Decide (PWYD)

These have seen increased interest and experimentation over the past few years both within the museums sector and performing arts. Pay What You Can (PWYC) asks for payment upfront at time of booking or entry, whilst Pay What You Decide (PWYD) asks for payment after the experience. Schemes can also be called Pay What you Think, Feel, or Wish. Whatever their name, the question for audiences is, what is this worth to you?

London's National Gallery announced the first blockbuster exhibition to be available on a Pay What You Wish (PWYW) basis for *Lucian Freud: New Perspectives*, in response to the cost-of-living crisis (National Gallery, 2022). The exhibition was available for a minimum of £1 on Fridays after 5.30 pm, compared to its peak pricing of £26 and off-peak of £24. This was clearly popular – when I looked in mid-December at pre-bookable availability for the last month of the exhibition (January 2023), the only slots that were full were Fridays at 5.30–7 pm.

Price bundling

Price bundling involves grouping together more than one product or service and offering them jointly at a lower price than if they were sold individually. It cuts your profit margin but supports upselling and cross-selling, encourages more spend and increases audiences' value. Examples: having a group tour package that includes refreshments or selling an exhibition admission ticket with an exhibition catalogue.

Bespoke pricing

Bespoke pricing involves museums working up a quote specific to the particular product, service, circumstances and client, such as with regard to different client requests for venue hire.

Penetration pricing

Penetration pricing involves setting a very low early price to get a foot in the door, then increasing prices over time. This isn't a commonly used strategy in museums, but inadvertently ended up being used for much of the sector's digital engagement offerings, which were provided for free – or at very little cost or suggested donations – at the start of the Covid-19 pandemic. A key issue with penetration pricing is whether audiences will subsequently be prepared to pay more or whether a precedent has been set. A report analysing Indigo's audience sentiment data on willingness to pay for digital content from around 90,000 regular cultural attenders in the UK found that people who have previously paid for digital content are more willing to do so again, whereas people who have consumed for free are less likely to be willing to pay (Baker Richards, 2020, p. 5).

Pricing for digital products

Many museums are grappling with how to price their digital products. The Covid-19 pandemic saw an explosion of digital experimentation and output as most museums across the world were forced to close their doors, including increased social media content, virtual museum tours, video live streams, talks, presentations, and craft workshops. Initially much of this was made available for free, to support and engage audiences during a very difficult time. But as the pandemic rumbled on, many museums found they needed to generate more income to cover the costs of creating the digital output and/or to plug gaps in visitor revenue, so they started charging. Not all pandemic digital initiatives are still running. However, many museums are offering various digital products, some for free and some for a fee. For example, Denver Museum of Nature & Science runs a Virtual Science Academy, which charges $140 for a class of up to 30 children for a 45-minute live and interactive science session (2023); and London's Design Museum provides free access to some digital events as part of the museum's membership offer (2023).

Questions to consider

- What message does your pricing policy communicate about your museum?
- What does inclusive pricing mean to you?
- To what extent is pricing a barrier to visiting or engagement with your museum, and with which audiences? What can you do about this?

Further reading

Baker Richards resources around pricing: https://www.baker-richards.com/blog/.
Connolly, S., Durnin, J., and Berriman, C. (2016) *Success Guide: Successfully Setting Admissions Policy and Pricing*. Available at: https://aim-museums.co.uk/wp-content/uploads/2017/03/Successfully-Setting-Admissions-Policy-and-Pricing-.pdf.
Merritt, E. (2020). *Museum Pricing for Affordability and Profit*. Available at: https://www.aam-us.org/2020/01/20/variable-pricing/.

References

Audience Agency (2018) *Museums Audience Report*. Available at: https://www.theaudienceagency.org/resources/museums-audience-report (Accessed: 4 May 2023).
Baker Richards (2020) *After the Interval: Act 2. An Analysis of Willingness to Pay for Digital*. Available at: https://www.baker-richards.com/wp-content/uploads/2020/10/After-the-Interval-Act-II-Analysis.pdf (Accessed: 18 December 2022).
Barbican (2022) *Carolee Schneemann. Body Politics*. Available at: https://www.barbican.org.uk/whats-on/2022/event/carolee-schneemann-body-politics (Accessed: 15 December 2022).
The Children's Museum of Indianapolis (2023) *Buy or Reserve Tickets*. Available at: https://www.childrensmuseum.org/visit/buy-tickets (Accessed: 8 March 2023).
Convious and Baker Richards (2022) *Consumer Attitudes to Dynamic Pricing for Visitor Attractions in the UK*. Available at: https://blog.convious.com/eblog/consumer-attitudes-to-dynamic-pricing-for-visitor-attractions-in-the-uk (Accessed: 8 March 2023).
Culture Label (2018) *Flexible Family Tickets. Commercial Considerations*. Available at: https://kidsinmuseums.org.uk/wp-content/uploads/2018/12/Family-Ticket-Commercial-Report.pdf (Accessed: 19 December 2022).

DC Research (2016) *Taking Charge – Evaluating the Evidence: The Impact of Charging or Not for Admissions on Museums.* Available at: https://aim-museums.co.uk/wp-content/uploads/2017/04/Final-Report-Taking-Charge-%E2%80%93-Evaluating-the-Evidence-The-Impact-of-Charging-or-Not-for-Admissions-on-Museums.pdf (Accessed: 16 December 2022).

Denver Museum of Nature & Science (2023) *Virtual Science Academy.* Available at: https://www.dmns.org/learn/virtual-experiences/virtual-science-academy/ (Accessed: 8 March 2023).

Design Museum (2023) *Membership for You: Membership Plus.* Available at: https://designmuseum.org/become-a-member/membership-for-you-membership-plus (Accessed: 9 March 2023).

Dilenschneider, C. (2015) *Free Admission Days Do Not Actually Attract Underserved Visitors to Cultural Organizations (DATA).* Available at: https://www.colleendilen.com/2015/11/04/free-admission-days-do-not-actually-attract-underserved-visitors-to-cultural-organizations-data/ (Accessed: 16 December 2022).

Dilenschneider, C. (2016) *Why Cultural Organizations Are Not Reaching Low-Income Visitors (DATA).* Available at: https://www.colleendilen.com/2016/05/18/why-cultural-organizations-are-not-reaching-low-income-visitors-data/ (Accessed: 16 December 2022).

Historic Royal Palaces (2023) *Tower of London Ticket Prices.* Available at: https://www.hrp.org.uk/tower-of-london/visit/tickets-and-prices/ (Accessed: 25 February 2023).

Kids in Museums (2010) *Family Ticket Watch.* Available at: https://kidsinmuseums.org.uk/wp-content/uploads/2018/12/Family-Ticket-Watch-Report.pdf (Accessed: 16 December 2022).

Kulturanalys, Swedish Agency for Cultural Policy Analysis (2023). *Fri Entré till Museer.* [Report in Swedish]. Available at: https://kulturanalys.se/wp-content/uploads/2023/04/Fri-entre-till-museer-webb.pdf (Accessed: 4 May 2023).

London Transport Museum (2023) *Annual Passes.* Available at: https://www.ltmuseum.co.uk/visit/tickets (Accessed: 5 May 2023).

Martin, A. (2003) *The Impact of Free Entry to Museums.* Available at: https://www.ipsos.com/sites/default/files/publication/1970-01/sri-the-impact-of-free-entry-to-museums-2003.pdf (Accessed: 19 December 2022).

Middleton, M. (2022) 'Early Childhood Education: Laying the Foundation' in *Welcoming Young Children into Museums. A Practical Guide.* Oxon: Routledge, pp. 16–39.

The Museum of Norwich (2023) *Admission Prices.* Available at: https://www.museums.norfolk.gov.uk/museum-of-norwich/plan-your-visit/admission-prices (Accessed: 3 April 2023).

The National Gallery (2022) *Friday Night Visitors to Pay What They Wish for the National Gallery's Lucian Freud Exhibition.* Available at: https://www.nationalgallery.org.uk/about-us/press-and-media/press-releases/the-credit-suisse-exhibition-lucian-freud-new-perspectives-1 (Accessed: 18 December 2022).

Salonlahti, O. and Salovaara, S. (eds.) (2022) *Accessibility and Diversity Checklist for Museums.* Translated by Heiskanen, S. Culture for All Service / For Culture on Equal Terms and The Finnish National Committee of ICOM. Available at: https://www.kulttuuriakaikille.fi/accessibility_checklists (Accessed: 14 March 2023).

Scope (2023) *Disability Price Tag 2023: The Extra Cost of Disability.* Available at: https://www.scope.org.uk/campaigns/extra-costs/disability-price-tag-2023/ (Accessed: 9 March 2023).

9 Communication channels

Introduction

These days we are spoilt for choice when it comes to the amount and variety of communication channels we can use to reach our audiences. But that is a double-edged sword. Audiences are more fragmented, no single channel will reach everyone; decision-making can be overwhelming; and planning and delivery can be intricate. Media, channels, and platforms are also constantly evolving.

Average magazine and newspaper circulations are dwindling, and in some cases, print editions have been replaced by digital-only offerings (such as the UK's *The Independent* newspaper). A digital graveyard is littered with former social media platforms and digital media outfits seen as the latest hot thing that either failed to make it in the long run (Friends Reunited social networking site; short-form video hosting Vine; social network Google+) or failed to fully break through despite the hype (audio-based social media platform Clubhouse). Whilst traditional media has long been subject to legislation, the past decade has also increasingly seen governments and legislation try to keep up with the evolution of digital media and how to tackle issues such as fake news; the usage of consumer data (in particular following the Cambridge Analytica scandal over the company's harvesting and use of millions of Facebook profiles without consent); and security concerns (some countries have introduced an outright ban or banned government devices from social media app TikTok amid security concerns that the Chinese government could access stored user data from the China-based app).

But more than that, our *thinking* around audiences and how we communicate with them has evolved over the last decades – from selling *to* them and talking *at* them, to having conversations *with* them and building a community *with* and *around* them. Just as exhibitions are now sometimes co-curated with partners and community groups, museum marketing and communication is also more participatory, with a proliferation of User-Generated Content, memes, selfies, comments, questions, and reviews from audiences.

This chapter delves into more detail about communication channels and how to choose them, featuring a range of examples. Rather than provide an

DOI: 10.4324/9781003309147-20

exhaustive list of channels and how to use them, which may quickly become redundant, I focus on how to categorise and think about them, including the PESO Model™ and push/pull approaches. Since channels, their algorithms, and their audiences are constantly evolving, and their ownership and legislation of them change, this chapter focuses on strategic considerations and reflections to guide your planning. The chapter also covers audience journey mapping as a useful process for thinking about channels and audiences.

Deciding on which channels and platforms to use

The most important factor affecting which channels and platforms you use should be who your target audiences are and which channels and platforms they use and encounter. Your marketing goals and objectives should also steer your decisions: Do you want to reach a broad audience, in which case so-called Above the Line channels like billboards; posters; and TV, radio, and newspaper advertising can be an effective way to reach big numbers of people. Or is your identified audience smaller and more niche, in which case you will want to develop a more targeted approach (Below the Line), for example, by using social media advertising, emails to a strand of your email list, or partnering with a community organisation. Attracting first-time visits from international tourists will require different channels to building longer term relationships with local families. And even *within* the broader international tourism segment, there may be differences. For example, cultural aficionados who book a trip around the dates of a particular exhibition may look at different channels – and much earlier – than tourists who want to fill a wet morning when they have already arrived in your city.

Evaluation of previous campaigns and data can also guide you on what is cost- and time-effective, linking back to your goals and objectives and looking at data such as conversion rates and Return on Investment (see Chapter 5g). Your museum's values and ethical considerations are also likely to play an increasingly important role in the channels and approaches you choose (see Chapter 12), as do pragmatic factors like budgets, team skills, and time available. And realistically, what staff and volunteers feel comfortable and confident doing is also a factor; it is hard for museums (especially smaller ones and those that are volunteer-run) to keep up with new platforms and skills needed. Whilst we often talk of "social media" as a catch-all phrase, the reality is that each platform has its own rules, personality, best practices, and often formatting requirements. Online how-to guides can tell you the technical requirements, such as optimal image sizes for each platform and how to add alt text for images, but picking up on the personalities and quirks of each platform is likely to take longer and require time spent on the platform observing and testing things.

It is a balance of not spreading yourself too thinly with a presence on so many platforms that you risk your output quality, and not putting all your eggs in one or two baskets. If there's one key takeaway from the last few years of social media turbulence, it's that whilst having a presence on such platforms can be an effective way to reach and engage your audiences, you don't want to be too dependent on them, leaving you exposed and vulnerable if things change. Key channels that I therefore usually advocate ongoing investment in (whether that is money or time) are the museum website and e-newsletter, both of which are channels you control, and SEO to help draw audiences to them. I often ask training workshop participants: If you had to drop one channel over the next year, which one would you drop? And if you could only use one channel, which one would you keep? This can lead to interesting reflections about the value of different channels for different organisations, how we invest our time, and when it is time to come off a channel.

Identifying where your audiences are

Asking your audiences which media they consume and which social media platforms they use is a good starting point, whether that's as part of your visitor survey, a survey to your e-newsletter subscribers, or something more anecdotal from questions at the front desk. If you want to reach new audiences, be specific on who they are and remember they are unlikely to already be engaging with you via your own channels. Many governments publish data on their populations' media habits and usage and trends over time, and there are guides online that summarise the audience demographics and trends of key social media platforms globally and by country. Media channels also tend to publish – or share on request – media packs summarising the demographics of their audiences. If your budget enables you to work with marketing or advertising agencies, they will have expertise and experience to guide you too.

Setting out your channels visually can help to show if there are audience segments that are underserved in terms of channels, whether you need to trim or expand your list of channels and platforms, and how much time or budget you commit to each. This could be a simple audience/channel table as outlined in Chapter 5a or a more detailed audience journey map (see below). If you want to reach new audiences, you might want to try something new and/or an element of experimentation; for example, the Royal Ontario Museum in Canada created a dating profile for its T. rex mascot Teddy on the dating app Tinder (Dodge, 2017); and the Getty Museum's Animal Crossing Art Generator allows users of the video game series Animal Crossing to add any image in the museum's open-access collection to the game (Zawacki and Waldorf, 2020).

Digital and non-digital channels

Digital communication channels provide cost-effective global reach that can be targeted, changed immediately, and evaluated, providing automated and granular analytics that are hard or impossible to achieve with a lot of offline marketing channels and the "spray and pray" approach of billboards, posters, and leaflets. Huge swathes of audiences now spend much of their time and money online, and we need to go where our audiences are. Many museums – like other organisations – have switched to a digital-by-default or digital-first approach to marketing in the recent years, in particular as a result of the Covid-19 pandemic.

However, there are still many people who choose not to engage digitally or who are digitally excluded, not out of choice. The World Economic Forum says that around a third of the world's population – 2.9 billion people – don't use the internet (2022), and whilst figures vary enormously, every country has pockets of their populations who are digitally excluded, so can't necessarily be reached through online marketing channels. A lack of access to devices (mobile phones, tablets, laptops, or desktops); a lack of access to data (broadband or mobile data services); a lack of skills; and a lack of confidence are all factors at play. The digital inclusion charity Good Things Foundation reports that being unemployed, retired, disabled, living on a low income, and/or having no or few qualifications are the biggest predictors of being digitally excluded (2020, p. 3). This means that some of the typically most underrepresented audiences in museums are also digitally excluded, so we need to bear this in mind when undertaking marketing campaigns and audience development initiatives.

Case study: Wonderbound

Although this case study is not from a museum, its lessons are interesting and transferable in terms of taking a considered approach and doing what is right for your organisation, staff, and audiences. Wonderbound – a contemporary ballet company in Denver, USA – chose to come off social media channels in 2022 (Moore, 2022). Garrett Ammon, Wonderbound's Artistic Director, says that the decision was motivated by a combination of ethical, artistic, and business reasons. Ammon is concerned by the way social media companies downgrade artists' and arts organisations' work to "content" that the companies can exploit for their own profit; the constant pressure to game the algorithms, pay for visibility, and feed the beast; as well as the broader negative impacts: "The toll that social media is taking on the mental and physical health of individuals and the harm it is doing to relationships and societal cohesion is dramatic. I'm willing to take the long road to build brand awareness and refrain from participating in something that is doing legitimate harm".

The decision to leave social media was taken after a monitored trial period that gave them the confidence to delete their social media presence. Having decreased the organisation's social media activity to around two posts a month per platform for a year and diverted the time saved to other marketing and sales activity (such as personalised emails, phone calls, and taking part in events), the team actually found that financial outcomes had *improved,* including a substantial rise in season subscriptions compared with pre-pandemic numbers (Ammon, 2023).

Budgets

It's safe to say that one size does not fit all, and most museums will always welcome more marketing budget. Spending on printed channels such as the design, print, and distribution of leaflets and flyers has historically been the biggest outlay. This was reflected in the UK Arts Marketing Association's member benchmarking survey, which also found that the next biggest categories of budget spend for museums tended to be advertising in print publications; posters or other outdoor advertising; and online advertising (excluding social media) (2019, pp. 18–22). Budgets spent on print have been decreasing over time due to such factors as decreasing marketing budgets; the environmental impact of printing and distributing materials; the lack of flexibility in terms of not being able to change content once printed; changing audience behaviour and increased preference for digital communication; the improved ability for targeting, tracking, and evaluation using digital communications; and broken habits from Covid-19 pandemic lockdowns.

Detailed breakdowns of sector marketing spending are hard to come by, but the 2023 CMO survey with responses from marketing leaders at US for-profit companies showed that on average, chief marketing officers spent 53.8% of their marketing budgets on digital marketing activities (Moorman, 2023, p. 17) and 17% on social media, with respondents expecting this to increase to 26.4% in the next five years (ibid., p. 55). There may also be some one-off investments that are necessary, in particular the development or redevelopment of a museum website, which often requires a big initial investment but then more minimal ongoing spend on hosting and support.

There is no such thing as a free communication tool if you also consider the time needed to run it. Content marketing is a popular approach that can be very successful for brand awareness, engaging with audiences, and sharing expertise. It involves creating and sharing online content (social media posts, videos, blogs, podcasts, and so on) that does not explicitly sell a company or product. Although it doesn't have to cost anything, it can require a huge amount of research and often planning, design, and editing time.

Deciding on **how** *to use different platforms*

Consider the purpose of your channels and platforms. To generate awareness? To engage audiences more long term? To drive visits? To reach certain audience segments? Are you keen to do something new or experiment? And consider the interplay of different channels. For example, what support can your organic social media channels provide to a paid advertising campaign? An understanding of how each platform works and what it can best be used for is needed. For example, Instagram is more likely to be effective at brand awareness and engagement, whilst Facebook is typically better than Instagram at promoting events and generating website traffic, although all social media platforms aim to keep users on their platforms for as long as possible.

As well as choosing your channels, you need to think about *how* to use them. For example, Wellcome Collection's 2017 strategy "recognised that our website and social channels *were* Wellcome Collection rather than *promoted* Wellcome Collection", explained Jen Staves, former Digital Manager at the museum and gallery in London. The team changed their digital editorial strategy from blogging to magazine-style storytelling as a result. This involved using a journalistic approach to storytelling, "creating high-quality, regular content with all the parts stories have – narrators, protagonists and antagonists, arguments, opinions, climaxes, resolutions – in formats readers know and recognise". The team chose six familiar and well-loved formats for their content – serials, essays, interviews, photo galleries, book extracts, and comics – and set up a regular publishing schedule so that readers know what to expect and when (Staves, 2019).

Audience journey

A useful exercise I often run with clients is audience journey mapping. It helps you to take an audience perspective and a more holistic approach to marketing, using your resources more effectively where and when they are most needed. It helps you consider different communication channels at different stages of the journey. There are often "Aha" moments as a result about what needs to change. Visitor-services teams may also use visitor journey mapping to focus more on the actual visiting experience. But in this marketing audience journey framework, the visiting or engagement experience is only one part of the evolution of the relationship between the museum and its audiences. It is more interested in audiences' *metaphorical,* not necessarily *physical,* journey.

Table 9.1 shows an example audience journey you can use or adapt, charting typical audience phases, from not being aware of your museum; to becoming more interested; committing to an action (typically visiting, but can also be

Table 9.1 A template example audience journey grid

Journey phase	*Awareness*	*Consideration*	*Decision/ Booking*	*Visiting/ Attending/ Participating*	*Retention*	*Advocacy*
Touchpoints or communication channels						
Activities						
Audience considerations/ thoughts/feelings						
Pain points						
Insights and opportunities						

donating, purchasing a membership, and so on); to returning; and then advocating on your behalf, such as by sharing positive experiences with others. You can base your input on data and insights such as website analytics, team knowledge, visitor surveys, visitor interviews, and observations of visitors. If your data from audiences is very limited, consider asking colleagues, friends, or family to act as mystery shoppers and take on the role of a potential audience member, reflecting on, testing, and jotting down their considerations and channels used at each step. Or if time and budget allow, undertake fresh research and consultation. Bring together a range of people to share ideas and thoughts in a workshop, using sticky notes or cards for ideas.

Touchpoints are any interactions or points of contact that audiences have with the organisation or brand. What part(s) of the museum do they come across and interact with at each stage? What information sources do they look at? In the awareness phase, this might be a poster by the escalators at an underground station, whilst in the retention phase, your e-newsletter.

Activities are what audiences do at each stage. At the consideration phase, this might include looking at prices, opening hours, and how to get to the museum. At the advocacy phase, this could be writing an online review or sharing a museum selfie on their social media.

Audience considerations, thoughts, or feelings set out more detail: What affects whether they undertake your desired action? For example, they might be frustrated at the number of steps in the online booking process, excited for a day out, or worried about whether the facilities will cater to them.

Pain points are friction or obstacles that audiences might come across at each stage, such as a web link that doesn't work or online tickets going straight to their email spam folder. They can range from minor inconveniences that irritate, to major issues that result in audiences not progressing further along the journey and having a very negative experience.

And finally, aim to draw conclusions and identify areas to fix or build on in the **insights and opportunities** row.

In reality, audience journeys are individual and, in many cases, not linear. Some audiences may never return, stay in touch, or recommend your museum, and others may bounce around the steps. But you can aim for an average or ideal representation. If you want more detail, develop different audience journey maps for different audience groups or segments, or for different products and programmes.

The PESO Model™

The PESO Model™ is one way of categorising channels and approaches into groups – Paid, Earned, Shared, and Owned – developed by Gini Dietrich in 2014 (Dietrich, 2020). It can be a useful way of considering which channels to use, their purpose, and their limitations. Whilst some activities fit in the intersection between categories (influencer marketing can straddle paid and earned), here I focus on the four main categories: Paid, Earned, Shared, and Owned.

Paid media

Paid channels involve placing content that you generate and pay for – essentially all forms of advertising such as newspaper, magazine, radio, and TV adverts; social media advertising; billboards and posters; flyers; paid influencer marketing; and sponsored content. They tend to have a large and broad reach beyond your existing audiences; you have control of the message and placement; they are scalable; and if done well, results can be immediate. However, they can be expensive; there is often less credibility as audiences know you are behind the message; some audiences can avoid them (whether deliberately through ad blocker browser extensions or more subconsciously by tuning them out); and once the paying stops, the results tend to stop.

Earned media

Earned media is generated by an authoritative third party, such as articles and reviews by journalists and influencers' social shares (that aren't paid for). They tend to be credible and provide endorsements that are valued by many audiences; they don't tend to cost a lot (or anything). However, you have less control over them, and there are no guarantees that you will receive *any* coverage, let alone *positive* coverage; they can require a lot of time to nurture and see results; and they are unlikely to be easily scalable.

Shared media

Shared media involves content created, amplified, and shared by others, including your audiences themselves. Examples include user-generated photos from your museum; visitor reviews; and comments, shares, and other engagement on your social media. Advantages and disadvantages are very similar to earned media, but the reach of each is likely to be smaller.

Owned media

Owned media is generated by you or your suppliers in channels that you control; for example, your website, e-news, podcast, and a launch event that you organise. Your organic social media content falls into this category to *some* extent – you create the content and control when and where it is placed, although ultimate control rests with the social media companies and their algorithms. Advantages of owned media are that you have control and the channels are at your fingertips, so using them is easy, free or low-cost, and lower risk. However, they are less likely to reach new audiences or huge volumes of people.

Push and outbound marketing vs pull and inbound marketing

Another way of differentiating between channels and approaches is to consider the distinction between push or outbound marketing and pull or inbound marketing. Both can be effective and can be used separately to achieve different goals, or together to support each other. For example, you use a Facebook advert (push) to boost an organic video post you created on an object from your collection (pull).

Push marketing

Push marketing – as the name indicates – involves "pushing" products, services, or messages out to audiences, even when and where they don't ask for it. It therefore interrupts the audience or user in what they are doing, so is also sometimes called interruption marketing. Whilst explicit permission hasn't been sought from audiences for the communication, I'm talking about legal ways to grab attention, not shady practices such as selling email lists without permission. It typically involves a broader and bigger audience, and the communication is usually one way from the museum. It is often transaction-focused, aiming to drive a purchase, lead, or sign-up from audiences.

Examples of channels and approaches are direct mail, display adverts, billboards, and posters, Pay Per Click ads, and radio adverts, primarily linking to the Paid category in the PESO Model™ above. If done well, results are often more immediate. Push marketing can be useful to reach new audiences, promote short-term campaigns, one-off offers, and boost new exhibition launches and events. However, the cost tends to be higher, and there are ways for audiences to filter or block them out.

Pull marketing

In contrast, pull marketing is about *drawing* audiences *to* you, to discover your museum, products and services; to spread awareness; and ultimately, to build relationships with your audiences. It is a longer-term approach to build your museum's overall brand and reputation as benefits are not necessarily immediate but compound over time with consistent effort. You are *earning* the right to communicate with audiences and gain their interest and loyalty. Whilst pull marketing can be used to spread awareness of your museum in the first place, it can also be very useful in building and maintaining relationships with audiences, helping you to stay relevant and keep them interested, and providing them with engaging content (and potentially, less explicitly, to encourage repeat interactions and visits).

Examples include Search Engine Optimisation (SEO – optimising your website so that it is found more easily on search engines such as Google) and content marketing. Pull marketing covers earned, shared, and owned categories from the PESO Model™ above. The idea is that you meet your target audiences' needs at a time and location that suits them. Therefore, permission marketing is a type of pull marketing – audiences are given a choice to opt in to communication with you, for example, for email communication and loyalty programmes, so that marketing is consensual, relevant, and tailored to them.

Questions to consider

- Which channels and platforms are of most value for communicating with your audiences?
- If you had to drop one channel, which one would you drop? If you could only use one channel, which one would you keep?
- If you have digitally excluded audiences you want to reach, how do you reach them?

Further recommended reading

Digital Culture Network (2023) *Knowledge Hub*. Available at: https://digitalculturenetwork.org.uk/knowledge/.

Good Things Foundation (2023) *The Digital Divide*. Available at: https://www.goodthingsfoundation.org/the-digital-divide/.

Gregory, A. (2021) *Planning and Managing Public Relations Campaigns. A Strategic Approach*. 5th ed. London: Kogan Page.

References

Ammon, G. (2023). Email to Christina Lister, 12 May.

Arts Marketing Association (2019) *AMA Benchmarking Survey 2019 – member report*. Available at: https://www.a-m-a.co.uk/wp-content/uploads/2021/12/AMA-Benchmarking-Survey-2019-_Member-Report.pdf (member-only resource). (Accessed: 5 January 2023).

Dietrich, G. (2020) *What is the PESO Model™?* Available at: https://spinsucks.com/communication/peso-model-breakdown/ (Accessed: 5 January 2023).

Dodge, R. (2017) *Museum Puts T. rex on Tinder to Make New Audiences Fall in Love with Them*. Available at: https://www.museumnext.com/article/this-museum-put-a-t-rex-on-tinder/ (Accessed: 21 April 2023).

Good Things Foundation (2020) *Blueprint for a 100% Digitally Included UK*. Available at: https://www.goodthingsfoundation.org/wp-content/uploads/2021/01/blueprint-for-a-100-digitally-included-uk-0.pdf (Accessed: 5 January 2023).

Moore, J. (2022) *Denver Dance Company Takes a Giant Leap off Social Media*. Available at: https://denvergazette.com/arts-entertainment/denver-dance-company-takes-a-giant-leap-off-social-media-john-moore/article_ddd0bf32-411b-11ed-bdf7-a7a602845490.html (Accessed: 16 March 2023).

Moorman, C. (2023) *The CMO Survey. Managing Brand, Growth, and Metrics. Highlights and Insights Report March 2023*. Available at: https://cmosurvey.org/results/ (Accessed: 3 May 2023).

Staves, J. (2019) *The Story Behind Stories and Our Journalistic Approach to Digital Content*. Available at: https://stacks.wellcomecollection.org/the-story-behind-stories-and-our-journalistic-approach-to-digital-content-ad196b8665ab (Accessed: 12 March 2023).

World Economic Forum (2022) *The First Alliance to Accelerate Digital Inclusion*. Available at: https://www.weforum.org/impact/digital-inclusion/ (Accessed: 5 January 2023).

Zawacki, S. C., and Waldorf, S. (2020) *How to Build an Art Museum in Animal Crossing*. Available at: https://www.getty.edu/news/how-to-build-an-art-museum-in-animal-crossing/ (Accessed: 5 May 2023).

10 Messaging

Introduction

This chapter digs deeper into your marketing messaging – what you are saying to your audiences, what you want to convey, and what you communicate. Communication is not simply about your museum's intentions behind the message, but about how the recipient receives and interprets the message. Today, we are bombarded with ads and messages from brands and have access to almost unlimited information through the internet. Attention spans online are short, with high expectations – Google's research shows that 53% of website visits are abandoned if a mobile site takes longer than three seconds to load (An, 2017).

Your messaging and communication should reflect your museum's values, and it goes without saying that it should be honest and truthful. Deceptive advertising is not only generally illegal, but also unethical and is not going to win you any support in the longer term. You need to be able to deliver on your marketing promises and build trust with your audiences. Museums tend to be brilliant storytellers and aren't short of stories to tell. But however powerful and targeted your messaging is, it can't achieve all your goals in isolation. It's not just a lack of awareness that is stopping potential audiences from visiting, so just telling them about something that's coming up is not going to be enough for everyone. Messaging clearly can't overcome physical barriers to engagement, and even if your messaging resonates and leads audiences to your website to book, if the booking process is too complicated or the pricing is too high, many won't follow through with the desired actions. So messaging needs to be seen as part of a broader strategy and process.

This chapter looks at the purpose of your communication and relates messaging to your audiences, segmentation, and personalisation. It covers key messages, powerful messaging, and calls to action, and it discusses message timing and frequency. It finishes with visual messaging and tone of voice, which can also be used to great effect to get your message across.

The purpose of your communication

Consider what you want to achieve with your marketing campaign or communication. Is it to raise awareness or inform audiences of something;

prompt or remind them; persuade or convince them; entertain or inspire them; prompt other emotions such as to move or shock audiences; or encourage an action such as a visit, a donation, a ticket purchase, or an e-news sign-up?

And crucially, consider *who* the audiences are that you want to reach. For example, if you are running a temporary exhibition with lesser-known artists or themes, can you use social proof, such as testimonials from early visitors and reviews from journalists, to reassure people it's worth a visit and create a sense of FOMO (fear of missing out)? Or for schools' bookings, you might focus on how you can make the teachers' lives and workload easier, emphasising how your workshops support the school curriculum and that you can provide example risk assessments.

People do not primarily use social media to be sold to. The top five reasons according to We Are Social's Digital Report 2023 are: Keeping in touch with friends and family (47%); filling spare time (36%); reading news stories (34%); finding content such as articles and videos (30%); and seeing what's being talked about (29%). However, 27% do use social media to find inspiration for things to do and buy, 26% to find products to purchase, and 23% to see content from their favourite brands (Kemp, 2023, p. 179). The Audience Agency's Cultural Participation Monitor research found that people who follow arts and culture organisations on social media are more likely to be female, under 45, and have children under the age of 10. Motivations for following arts and culture organisation accounts on social media varied by audience segment. A higher proportion of the more culturally engaged segments said that they follow social media for information about events/activities to attend in person compared with the segments with lower cultural engagement, which showed a higher proportion who follow for entertainment. The research showed the top three main reasons for following were a general interest in the topic; for entertainment; and for information about events/activities to attend in person (2023).

Segmentation and messaging

Since audiences aren't a homogenous bloc, your messaging shouldn't be either. You might need to tailor messages to emphasise different elements of your museum's offer for different audiences. New audiences are likely to need more signposting to find key information about facilities than existing audiences. It may be that you need to create marketing copy in several languages.

Some positioning and messaging designed to appeal to one audience segment may in fact put off another. A colleague undertook on-street research asking passers-by in a local town for their opinions on five local museums and attractions' tourism leaflets some years ago. One of the findings was that older people found the emphasis on family audiences (with images of children enjoying the new outdoor play area) in one museum leaflet off-putting. So, a balance is needed to minimise these clashes; for example, by using different channels for different audiences or emphasising different times of the day or week for different activities.

Features and benefits

There is a debate around whether communication should describe and promote the features or benefits of products and services. *Features* are aspects of your product or service that describe what it is or has, whereas *benefits* describe the importance of those features, their impact, or their implication. As a simple example, key *features* of an umbrella are that it is made of waterproof nylon, is lightweight, and is collapsible. Its *benefits* are that it will keep you dry and is easily portable in a small bag. Or even one stage further – you'll arrive at your meeting feeling confident, not looking dishevelled.

Turning to museums, it's not as easy to say one or the other – it will largely depend on your audiences. For some – often core audiences and those who are very culturally engaged – features of an exhibition will resonate and sell it to them: the name of an artist, the theme of the exhibition, the fact that the works are shown together for the first time or that a well-respected curator is giving a talk. For other audiences, a more benefit-led messaging approach will be more appropriate: highlighting aspects such as a social day out or opportunity for some escapism.

As cultural organisations looked to reopen after the initial 2020 Covid-19 pandemic lockdowns, Morris Hargreaves McIntyre's audience research identified seven big motivations for audiences looking to engage with cultural organisations (2020). These were all benefit-led, beyond a focus on objects and collections, and made for excellent messaging:

- Spending quality time with loved ones in a different space that's not local.
- Escaping and releasing the pressure valve of the home.
- Reuniting with favourites, whether that's a favourite animal or painting.
- Healthier bodies and minds.
- Getting closer to nature and wildlife.
- Seeing beautiful things in ways you can't appreciate on a screen.
- Stimulating children's imagination.

Personalisation

Linked to segmentation is personalisation, using data to communicate directly with audiences based on their needs, interests, and behaviours, such as their visiting history, communication preferences, and purchase history. For example, providing relevant product, exhibition, and event recommendations; a discount offer to celebrate a birthday; personally addressing communications to each audience member. When personalisation is done well, both the museum and audience benefit, delivering more relevant content and support to busy audiences, which in turn builds trust, loyalty, and repeat audiences for the museum.

Of course, this is not always easy to do. It is harder to obtain and use data from drop-in visitors, compared with audiences who book online and subscribe to an e-newsletter. And even then, you might not have enough data to enable successful personalisation. For example, say someone books tickets online and signs up to receive future events news. You don't know *why* they booked those tickets to a Claude Monet exhibition and what else might they be interested in (unless you ask them). Was it because they are interested in Monet? In art by French painters? In Impressionism? Or perhaps they were buying tickets as a gift for someone else and aren't interested at all. Personalisation also extends to allowing audiences to opt out of specific content when they want to, the way many supermarkets enable e-newsletter subscribers to opt out of receiving Mother's and Father's Day promotional messages.

A simple way of getting more data on what your audiences want is having a few tick box options at the point of sign-up to your e-newsletter so they can opt in to receiving information on what they are most interested in and then segment your e-news lists accordingly. Some communication may go out to the whole list, whilst others are sent to only part of it; local audiences are likely to be more interested in the latest events and activities in the museum than international subscribers, for example.

Key messages

Key messages are the main points you want to get across and that you want your audiences to hear, see, understand, and ultimately remember or even act on. It can be tempting to come up with a long list, but you have very little time and space, and audiences are busy and often preoccupied, so too many messages will get lost. Ideally you want your key messages to be:

- Limited in number, so as not to overcomplicate or dilute them.
- Concise and simple, so they can be understood.
- Relevant – to the museum *and* its audiences.
- Memorable – so your audiences can easily recall them.
- Tailored to different audiences.

You might have a suite of key messages around your museum as a whole that fit strategically and are used on a longer-term, ongoing basis. You might also have specific key messages for particular projects, programmes, and exhibitions. They aren't straplines but guides as to what you want to communicate. Key messages will help you to define your content (not just using words, but also visually). Take your museum's mission, overall goals, and marketing goals and objectives as a starting point. Consider your audiences' needs, barriers, and motivations. It can be helpful to include a range of staff or volunteers, if you are running an ideas session around key messages, to get a broad range of initial ideas that can be narrowed down.

Powerful messaging

Messages can be powerful for a range of reasons, and they can appeal to emotions or logic. Stories about the museum's collections may be absorbing and moving; a fundraising campaign may by compelling; and a behind-the-scenes anecdote might be amusing. Elements of scarcity, time sensitivity, or exclusivity are also usually effective in encouraging immediate action, for example: "Only 10 tickets left", "Only 20 days left to see ... ", and "Join now for instant access".

Calls to action

A call to action (CTA) is a message or piece of content that prompts a viewer, reader, listener, user, or follower to undertake a particular action, such as sign up to receive e-news, book a ticket, or donate. It's essentially a clear instruction. Not all pieces of content need a call to action – content marketing is more concerned with brand awareness than explicitly trying to sell anything – but many benefit from one. On digital media, a CTA will often appear in a button that users are drawn to click on. You need to balance expected and common calls to action that audiences are used to digesting (such as "Click here") with ones that provide a bit more interest and are tailored to your museum's personality. If you want audiences to sign up to your e-newsletter, you could simply say "Sign up to our e-news" – it does what it says on the tin. Or you could make it a bit more enticing, for example:

- "Be the first to find out about our upcoming events and exhibitions".
- "Enjoy exclusive stories from behind the scenes".
- "Never miss our latest news".
- "Subscribe now and receive 10% off our annual memberships".
- "Join our community of 2,000 supporters".

The timing of your messages

The timing of your messages is critical to consider. You want to reach your audiences and convey the message at a time when they are likely to be receptive and able to respond in the way you want. This is why if you scroll social media in the early hours of the morning you might come across insomnia cures being advertised. For example, consider:

- Can you use your data to understand how far in advance of key event days your audiences like to book?
- Short time windows can create a sense of urgency and lead to action, for example, a final opportunity to see an exhibition before it closes.

- When is the most appropriate time to have a website pop-up with a plea for donations or a survey completion?

Mapping audience journeys (covered in the previous chapter) provides a useful basis for thinking about messages that you want to convey to audiences at different times along the journey, and in response to any pain points or opportunities you identified.

Message frequency and reiteration

There is an old "Rule of 7" that is often bandied about in marketing, that a potential customer needs to hear or see the marketing message at least seven times before they'll take action to buy that product or service. But this apparently originated with research by 1930s Hollywood movie studios showing that moviegoers on average needed to see a movie poster seven times before buying a ticket (Corfman, 2022). Although this number was specific to a particular sector almost 100 years ago, the rule still circulates. And certainly, the principle is still important – it is likely to take more effort than just one ad to convince someone to visit, buy, or donate, even if the number seven is not universally applicable. Reiterating our messages can be more persuasive, as long it doesn't become repetitive – make the same point but in different ways, keeping the content fresh.

With digital marketing and e-commerce, this "rule" is no longer as relevant. On the one hand, a consumer might be exposed to several marketing messages from a brand weekly or even daily over a long period of time before purchasing; it can take more than seven interactions, or they may never take that leap. Brand awareness that has built up over time does play a role – if a consumer has heard of a museum, is familiar with it, and trusts it, they are more likely to need fewer prompts to convince them for a particular exhibition. But on the other hand, it's easier for consumers to act after only one "touch" from a brand – a well-placed and constructed social media ad can be clicked on and takes the consumer straight to an e-commerce product page.

There is also research that shows that *overexposure* to marketing campaigns can have a negative impact on consumers – for example, research by UK advertising's thinktank Credos shows that bombardment is the most important driver of the public's distrust in advertising (2021). Social media platforms have also cottoned on to this, giving users the option to hide ads with "I see it too often" as one of the reasons you can give as feedback.

Visual messaging

Messaging isn't just or always about words. Images and videos also send clear messages to, and are interpreted by, audiences. Contrast a photo of children laughing and using interactives at a museum with a photo of children standing behind a rope barrier with "Do not touch" signs nearby. Similarly, different fonts can have different messages and personalities – serif fonts are often considered to be more traditional and formal; sans serif fonts clean and contemporary; script typefaces traditional and elegant; slab typefaces (with thick stroke weights) bold.

Visual cues such as photos and simple graphics are also used in Easy Read guides to museums to make messages, information, and instructions easier to understand. And the use of colour can – deliberately or inadvertently – send out messages to audiences, influencing our behaviour and decision-making. In the UK, you often see red and yellow used to draw attention to and emphasise urgency with price promotions and discounts, whilst green is often used to denote nature, natural, eco-friendly. However, there is added complexity for organisations operating globally, since there can be different associations with colours in different cultures.

Tone of voice

As well as *what* you say, messaging is also about *how* you say it and the impression that it makes on everyone who encounters it. Brand *voice* is about how the character or personality of your museum comes through in your communication, whether it is written, spoken or visual. It is consistent and unchanging, a skeleton or framework. From that, your *tone* refines that voice; it is how you express that personality, the emotional inflection adding interest. It can be adjusted to different channels, topics, and audiences. An appropriate voice and tone help humanise your brand and museum, connecting more with audiences, helping your museum to be approachable, supporting your storytelling, and making your marketing more memorable. It needs to be authentic, distinctive, and relevant – a memorial museum is clearly going to have a very different tone of voice than a children's museum.

Questions to consider

- Can you recall any effective messaging you have come across, from museums or other sectors? What made it effective?
- What are two or three key messages about your museum that you want to convey in your communications?
- How would you differentiate messaging for different audience segments for an event or exhibition?

Further reading

Albrighton, T. (2018). *Copywriting made simple. How to write powerful and persuasive copy that sells.* Kibworth Beauchamp: Matador.
Halpern, D. (2019) *Inside the Nudge Unit. How small changes can make a big difference.* London: WH Allen.
Münster, M. (2021) *I'm afraid Debbie from marketing has left for the day.* London: Laurence King Publishing.

References

An, D. (2017) *Find Out How You Stack up to New Industry Benchmarks for Mobile Page Speed*. Available at: https://www.thinkwithgoogle.com/intl/en-gb/marketing-strategies/app-and-mobile/mobile-page-speed-new-industry-benchmarks/ (Accessed: 20 December 2022).

The Audience Agency (2023) *Spring 2023 Cultural Participation Monitor*. Available at: https://www.theaudienceagency.org/evidence/covid-19-cultural-participation-monitor/recent-key-insights/spring-2023#Social_Media_Behaviour (Accessed: 5 May 2023).

Corfman, T. (2022) *How to Make Journalists Your Partner in Pitching*. Available at: https://www.prdaily.com/how-to-make-journalists-your-partner-in-pitching/ (Accessed: 11 May 2023).

Credos (2021) *New Credos Research Shows Signs Of Improvement In Public Trust In Advertising*. Available at: https://adassoc.org.uk/our-work/new-credos-research-trust/ (Accessed: 10 May 2023).

Kemp, S. (2023) *Digital 2023 Global Overview Report*. Available at: https://wearesocial.com/uk/blog/2023/01/digital-2023/ (Accessed: 13 March 2023).

Morris Hargreaves McIntyre (2020) *What Audiences Want on Reopening*. Available at: https://www.mhminsight.com/what-audiences-want-on-reopening/ (Accessed: 31 March 2023).

11 Accessible and inclusive marketing

Introduction

The accessible and inclusive design of museums' physical spaces, interpretation, and programmes have been increasingly developed over the past years, and there are some venues that do a phenomenal job. However, there is still a way to go in terms of consistency – not all museums go beyond basic compliance with the law; disabled and neurodivergent visitors cannot access everything; and the representation of their experiences and perspectives is also limited. The same often applies to museum marketing. Just taking websites as an example, a report on the accessibility of UK museums and heritage sites showed that whilst online information about access provision at museums and heritage sites had increased significantly in the four years since 2018, there had been no major improvements in information for blind and visually impaired, D/deaf, hard of hearing, and neurodivergent visitors (who the report points out are historically underrecognised as requiring accessibility measures). It also found that 19% of museums and heritage sites surveyed had no online access information in either 2018 or 2022. The report, by VocalEyes in partnership with Stagetext, Autism in Museums, and the Centre for Accessible Environments, presented research from digital volunteer researchers who included people with personal experience of access barriers (Vocal Eyes, 2022).

Accessibility and inclusivity should be an integrated part of all marketing, and this chapter explores this in more depth. The chapter starts with definitions, looks at principles, and includes practical tips and examples of what museums are doing and can implement at no cost. It includes examples of accessible formats and content, as well as inclusive content and language. Guidance that reflects the latest technology and country-specific guidelines can be found online.

Definitions

The terms *accessible marketing* and *inclusive marketing* are sometimes used interchangeably, and certainly there is a degree of overlap. The purpose behind them is the same: they aim to ensure our marketing is for a broad range of different people. They complement each other, but there is a distinction

DOI: 10.4324/9781003309147-22

between the two. *Accessible* marketing ensures your audiences *can* access your marketing content, whilst *inclusive* marketing ensures that they *want* to access it and that it resonates with them.

Accessible marketing involves ensuring that all of your audiences can access your marketing and can experience and engage with your content. This means understanding and removing the barriers that prevent them from doing so, ensuring that the functionality can be operated by them (for example, can the email be opened and content viewed on any type of digital device? Can screen readers make sense of the content?), with measurable improvements based on aspects such as font sizes and colour contrast ratios. Accessibility measures are becoming more standardised and can be applied across museum departments.

Inclusive marketing involves creating content that is mindful of and resonates with different audiences. It is typically more concerned with strategy and content, rather than platform and mechanics, and can be more subjective. For example, does your language alienate some audiences? Do your promotional images represent diversity in your audiences? The *principles* behind inclusive marketing may be universal, but what this looks like for marketing *delivery* may be more nuanced and vary across cultures, needing to be tailored to each museum, its audiences, communities, collections, and history.

Accessible marketing

Marketing accessibility is about making sure our marketing activity can be seen, heard, used, enjoyed, digested, and understood by as many people as possible, removing the barriers preventing people from doing so. As well as often being a legal requirement, it is best practice, a social responsibility, and good business sense. Accessible marketing can be beneficial for a broad range of people. For example, captions on videos might be used by commuters scrolling on their phones on a busy train; and alt text, which describes digital images (read aloud by screen readers used by visually impaired users), is also displayed if the image fails to load correctly on your website and is indexed by search engines to better understand and rank your webpage's content. Making sure that your marketing is accessible is not a niche issue for a handful of potential audience members. For example, the World Health Organization (WHO) states that, globally, 2.2 billion people have a near or distance visual impairment (2022), over 1.5 billion people live with hearing loss (WHO, 2021), and both numbers will rise in the coming years.

Principles

Consider what principles to base your accessible marketing on and how these can translate into practical actions. For example:

Identify your starting point

You can commission an accessibility audit or undertake this internally; for example, the Accessibility and Diversity Checklist for Museums by Culture for All Service and ICOM Finland has a section on communication. You can tick whether you are meeting each suggested statement, and if not, set out what to change and by when (Salonlahti and Salovaara, 2022, pp. 56–79). For example: "We provide information in our communications on the typical hours when it is quiet or crowded at the museum" (ibid., p. 63).

Consider accessibility from the outset

Consider accessibility from the outset when you are planning a campaign, rather than trying to retrofit accessibility in at a later stage when you have already committed to marketing channels and approaches and spent your budget.

Don't make any assumptions

The Accessible Marketing Guide by Unlimited (arts commissioning body that supports, funds, and promotes new work by disabled artists) advises not to make any assumptions. Disabilities and their implications are wide-ranging: not all disabilities are visible, not all disabled people see themselves as disabled, and a broad range of people may find accessibility information valuable, including visitors coming with pushchairs or older people who have a range of impairments and may not necessarily look at a website page labelled with "disability" or "accessibility" (2020). Individuals may have different preferences for how they communicate with you, so aim to provide a range of options.

Consult and research

Building on that is the importance of consultation and research with audiences and potential audiences with different backgrounds and experiences. If you have no budget, start by using free online guides and looking at best practice in the sector and beyond (such as the guides listed as further reading). Free and paid-for tools can also support work you do in-house; for example, some graphic design software can simulate colour blindness so you can test artwork with this in mind. If you are commissioning consultants and agencies for graphic design and website development, make sure that accessibility expertise is a key requirement in your brief. Include budgets for consultation, research, and provision of accessible marketing materials in your funding applications. If budgets allow, undertake consultation directly with users with lived experience of disability and neurodivergence, and/or take advice from charities representing them.

Commit to an ongoing process

Make a commitment to improving the accessibility of your marketing, and recognise that not everything can be done overnight. Expectations and requirements are likely to vary according to your museum's size and budgets. Start with making the free changes you can. For example:

- Capitalise the first letter of each word in hashtags so they can more easily be read by people and screen readers.
- Avoid flashing and flickering video content that can trigger seizures in people with photosensitive epilepsy.
- Use a matte or uncoated paper for printed materials, rather than glossy paper that glares.

Make the most of free tools available

Many digital and communication platforms have inbuilt functionality that improves accessibility; for example, YouTube can provide automatically generated captions that you can edit to finetune. The World Wide Web Consortium's Web Accessibility Initiative (WAI) provides guidelines that are seen as the international standard for web accessibility, as well as free resources, such as checks you can carry out on your website and considerations for useability testing with disabled people (2023).

Accessible formats

We often provide *different* content in *different* formats – perhaps a printed leaflet aimed at tourists, a blog post to share more information about an object for core museum fans and researchers. But we also need to consider how to provide the *same* content in *different* formats to enable more people to access them, in particular, key information that audiences need when considering or planning a visit, as well as evergreen content (that has a long shelf life) that you can invest in. Avoid a reliance on PDF files on websites since they are typically less likely to be accessible; they make navigation harder; it is harder to track their use; and they are less likely to be kept up to date.

Large print

Provide versions of your content in large print, which the Royal National Institute of Blind People states is generally 16–18 point size (no date).

Video captions

Provide captions on your videos. Autogenerated captions can give you a head start, but whilst automatic speech-recognition technology is improving, it is not yet entirely accurate, so you need to manually edit captions. Providing a transcript of the video content is also valuable as people can read it at their own pace, especially if it is a longer and/or fast-paced video. This also feeds into your search engine optimisation (SEO), since search engines index text but can't index audio in a video (yet anyway).

Audio recordings

Consider creating audio recordings of key marketing information, and include a transcript of the recording as a text file and/or web page. Again, software can auto-generate transcripts, which can then be manually improved.

Sign language

Consider making marketing information available in sign language. There are an estimated 25,000 people who use British Sign Language (BSL) as their main language across the UK and a total of around 151,000 users (Royal National Institute for Deaf People, no date). Sign languages differ from spoken languages – for example, with their own grammar – and subtitles are not necessarily an adequate substitute, especially for people who use BSL as their main or only language. In England, a judicial review following the #WhereIsTheInterpreter campaign around the lack of BSL interpreters for two of the UK Government's Covid-19 data briefings in 2020 found that the Government had breached the Equality Act 2010. The judge rejected the notion that subtitles were sufficient: "Without BSL interpretation there was a clear barrier, for a vulnerable and marginalised group, undermining accessibility of information […] The lack of provision – the provision of subtitles only – was a failure of inclusion" (Mr Justice Fordham, 2021).

Braille

Providing marketing material in braille (patterns of raised dots representing letters and words felt by fingertips on paper or braille display devices) can be considered through consultation with your audiences of blind and visually impaired people. Of people who are registered blind or partially sighted in the UK, 7% use braille (Royal National Institute of Blind People, 2022), but Unlimited notes that many blind and visually impaired people are now using sound-based formats in preference to braille (2020). Specialist agencies can produce content in braille, or you can buy the kit required to produce it in-house.

Easy Read Guides

Provide your key marketing information as an Easy Read Guide, which presents information in a way to help many people – including people with learning disabilities – to access it more clearly. These typically feature simple and short words and sentences; straightforward photos, symbols, and drawings to support the meaning of the text; a clear layout; and a bigger font size.

Visual stories

Many museums now have a visual or social story as an additional information source to allow potential audiences to familiarise themselves with the museum ahead of a visit, typically with simple text and photographs of what visitors can expect at the museum. The Science Museum in London also has a Sensory Map of the museum, which highlights the areas that are usually more or less crowded, have brighter or dimmer lights, are noisier or quieter, and where there are strong smells and interactives (2022).

Accessible language

Accessible language involves ensuring all audiences can understand what you are saying, including audiences who have other languages as their first or native language. It involves writing simply and clearly, without being patronising. For example, using easy and short words; writing conversationally, in the first person, using the active voice; and avoiding jargon and acronyms. Free guidelines and support for English text include:

- Content Design London's Readability Guidelines (2020).
- Microsoft Word's Editor function provides a Flesch Reading Ease score and a Flesch-Kincaid Grade Level, equivalent to the US grade level of education required to understand a text, to help you gauge whether your text can be easily read and understood (based on the number of sentences, words, and syllables).
- The Hemingway Editor provides instant feedback and tips on how to make the text you paste into the website more easily understood (no date).
- The Plain English Campaign has free guides on how to write clear and concise information (no date).

Inclusive marketing

Inclusive marketing (also called *inclusion marketing* or *diversity marketing*) considers and reflects diversity in all forms, such as age, ethnicity, gender identity, sexual orientation, body size and appearance, disability, socioeconomic status, religion, and language. It is a part of an inclusive approach to audience development and engagement and – if done authentically and sensitively – will help to build trust and foster deeper relationships with audiences from all backgrounds and walks of life. It is about being welcoming and relevant to a broad range of people, but typically focuses on audiences who are marginalised or underserved and considers protected characteristics (such as disability, religion, sexual orientation). Inclusive marketing is an ongoing journey – embed your aspirations throughout the marketing team and organisation and involve a broad range of people.

The marketing team and processes

Developing museum leadership teams, boards of trustees, and a marketing team with people from a broad range of backgrounds and lived experiences is important. I have not seen a specific breakdown for museum marketing staff, but a report comparing representation gaps in the creative industries with other industry sectors in the UK found that the underrepresentation of disabled workers in advertising and marketing is second only to mining (Carey, Giles, and O'Brien, 2023, p. 24). Inclusive marketing needs to be intentional and proactive, and the external layer of the organisational culture. A spotlight was shone on many museums following a range of anti-racist statements and commitments in the aftermath of George Floyd's murder in 2020 and subsequent protests. Some media and campaigns have been holding museums to account, tracking their progress and actions since, and calling out hypocrisy and inaction (for example, Attiah, 2021).

Seek to understand others' perspectives, whether through social listening, online research into best practice, undertaking inclusivity training, or running focus groups and insight panels with audiences and non-users. Internal advocacy and discussions may also be necessary as there can be different perspectives and priorities between marketing staff, trustees, and the senior management team. Extend your considerations of diversity to external suppliers who support your marketing team, in terms of who you commission, their approach, and commitment to inclusivity.

Ensure that processes are set up to support your inclusive marketing, such as clear guidelines about inclusive language, appropriate sign-off procedures, and time and space to discuss content and tone to use. Whilst automation and scheduling social media content can be time-efficient, there are pitfalls to watch out for. For example, fast food giant KFC Germany blamed a bot using automated push notifications "linked to calendars that include national observances" for its wholly inappropriate Tweet: "It's memorial day for Kristallnacht! Treat yourself with more tender cheese on your crispy chicken" (as quoted by Binley, 2022) (Kristallnacht being Nazi-led attacks across Germany in 1938 that killed Jewish people and destroyed Jewish-owned businesses and synagogues).

Inclusive content

Ensuring your inclusive content is authentic and meaningful is paramount, and this is about more than simply posting a rainbow flag during LGBT+ History Month. Museums are well placed to provide educational and informative content around anniversaries, events, and significant dates such as the International Holocaust Remembrance Day. Different museums with their varying collections, remits, ownership, and leadership may vary in what they cover and how. How museums cover a range of topics may also evolve over time; for example, the increased recognition and celebration of Indigenous Peoples' Day as an alternative to Columbus Day in the United States (President

Biden Jr., 2021). As well as considering what content you *include,* consider what you *don't* include. Sometimes museums choose to stay silent on issues (for a range of reasons), but silence can be interpreted in different ways.

There is a polarisation of views around some topics inflamed by social media, leading to many museums receiving negative comments and, in some cases, hateful, abusive, and trolling responses. Marketing and engagement teams need to make choices about what content they put out, and the stance they take, knowing that not all audiences may agree. They also need processes and policies in place with clear guidelines on how to handle vitriol online, and to protect social media teams' mental health and well-being, such as clear social media policies, online group rules, expectations around hours that social media is monitored, and thresholds for blocking users, such as for offensive language or behaviour.

A positive example of inclusive content is from Historic Royal Palaces, which challenged the assumption that people from the past were "teeny, teeny tiny" in an Instagram Reel showing court stays (a type of boned corset) in a UK size 20–22 from around 1750. In the video, curator Polly Putnam says, "It's rare to see clothes this big because most museums only collected clothes that would fit on a standard-sized mannequin. Just like today, where everyone is different shapes and sizes, this was exactly the same in the Georgian era" (2023). The Reel received excellent engagement and positive comments, and was shared by several body-diversity and body-positivity influencers. Sharing a range of user-generated content from different audiences and their perspectives and experiences is another way of valuing inclusive content, providing you seek permission and give credit to content creators.

Audience portrayal in marketing

Using photography and video that reflects a diverse range of visitors in marketing materials is often the first idea that springs to mind as a visible statement saying, "everyone is welcome". Consider the *presence* of difference audiences as well as their *portrayal* in content and advertising. But make sure this is authentic and not performative and that you don't resort to an over-reliance of photos of some visitors or models.

Content warnings

Some museums use content warnings or trigger warnings to help visitors understand what to expect from particular galleries or exhibits, briefly describing content to help audiences choose whether or not to engage at that particular time. Warnings are also used in marketing to flag upcoming content to audiences that they might find distressing, traumatic, or offensive and that might affect them negatively. This gives audiences a chance to scroll past or turn it off if they don't want to encounter it at that time (or at all). A content warning can be an introductory sentence at the top of a social media post or website page, a verbal and captioned introduction at the start of a video, or a description in the first image of an image carousel post.

In social media, "trigger warning" or "content warning" is often abbreviated to "TW" or "CW" and followed by a colon and keywords that introduce the content – for example, eating disorders, self-harm, hate speech, suicide, and pregnancy loss – or to warn about content with flashing images. Whilst the two are often used interchangeably online, a trigger warning is a specific type of content warning that aims to highlight content that may cause intense distress for audiences with Post Traumatic Stress Disorder and other anxiety disorders, for example, from hearing a gunshot.

There can be a huge range of reasons why someone might not want or be able to engage with particular content, from personal experiences and trauma, to being with children, to being in a public space. A content warning in marketing acknowledges and shows respect for this and gives audiences agency. Independent exhibit designer Margaret Middleton's tips about content warnings in museums also apply to marketing (2022, pp. 172–73):

- Give a detailed description of what to expect in the gallery (or marketing) content so that audiences can make up their own minds.
- Avoid making assumptions about *whom* the content is or is not for – if there is an appropriate warning, audiences can make decisions for themselves.
- Offer alternative routes should audiences wish to avoid this particular content. In terms of marketing, make sure that key information such as ticketing information isn't buried under or after content that some audiences may wish to avoid.

For example, "Content warning: the upcoming post contains content that some younger people may find offensive" is unnecessarily specific on who might be affected, but too general on the reason for the warning. In contrast, the People's History Museum in Manchester, UK, shared the following content warning on its website about its Nothing About Us Without Us exhibition, exploring the history of disabled people's activism and ongoing fight for rights and inclusion: "This exhibition is a celebration of the determination of disabled people in the face of hardship and abuse. Some of the items in this exhibition show disabled people in distressing or even life-threatening situations. Stories covered include disabled people's responses to lived experiences of abuse, assaults, suicide, and incarceration in hospital and other settings" (2023). This content warning has more detail on the content but does not make any assumptions about whom the content is for or not for. It can be useful to agree on themes and types of content that your museum defines as needing a content warning and include these in your marketing or social media content guide.

Content warnings are not about censoring ideas or content; hiding uncomfortable content or differences of opinions; patronising or mollycoddling audiences. And they should absolutely not be used to perpetuate stigma, prejudice, hate, or discrimination. For example, the purpose of a content warning about racism should not be to shy away from discussions around the harmful impact of racism, but rather to help protect people with lived experience of racism from further harm; and a content warning might be used to flag a reference to homophobic language or a slur, but should not be used to flag that the content is about LGBTQ+ people or their lives.

Inclusive language

It may be necessary and beneficial to create marketing content in more than one language – for example, from legal requirements such as the Welsh Language Standards in Wales; to cater to different languages spoken within the museum's country; or for international tourists. But inclusive language also refers to the *choice* of words you use. Words carry meaning and can cause harm and offence, even if unintentional. There is a range of language to stay clear of:

- Acronyms and jargon without explanations, which could keep some audiences from understanding your message.
- Exclusionary assumptions about audiences' knowledge, for example, namedropping art movements without context.
- Relying on references from a single culture, which may have different connotations for other cultures or not be universally known or understood (for example, saying that something is a "Marmite issue", meaning it's a love or hate issue, referencing the British yeast extract spread).
- Cultural appropriation (the inappropriate or unacknowledged adoption of a part of one culture or identity by members of another culture or identity, in particular when people from a dominant culture appropriate from a minority culture). For example, don't use terms such as *Pow wow* (use *meeting* or *gathering*) unless using the term in the correct context and honouring the culture it originates with.
- Terms that originate from harmful historical events and beliefs. For example, *pioneer* is rooted in colonialism (replace with *innovator, inventor, trendsetter*).
- Ableist language such as *crippling, crazy,* and *depressing* used out of context.
- Unnecessarily gendered language such as *mankind* (use *humankind, people, humanity*) and default to genderless pronouns (*they/them/theirs*) if you are unable to confirm the pronouns of someone.
- Sweeping, collective terms or acronyms such as "BAME" (Black, Asian, Minority Ethnic): the #BAMEOver campaign shares guidance on why 'BAME' is a problematic term and different alternatives, for example, "African Diaspora people", "People of South Asian heritage", based on survey results and discussions with over 250 people who came together to reset the terms of reference for people with lived experience of racism in the UK (What Next?, 2021).

Just like many museums and organisations have tone-of-voice guidelines, create an inclusive language guide that can easily be referred to and updated as needed. This should not be confined to the marketing department – ensure it is developed in consultation with audiences and other departments for consistency, for example, with language used in exhibition interpretation.

Case study: The Postal Museum

London's Postal Museum won the Kids in Museum Best Accessible Museum award in 2021, and the judges mentioned online information as one element that impressed them (The Postal Museum, 2021). The Head of Marketing and Communication, Annie Duffield, makes the point that accessibility is "a journey we are right in the middle of, and I expect we always will be as best practice evolves" (2023). Below are just a few examples showcasing their approach and highlighting some of the points I have made above:

- The museum worked with the charity Ambitious about Autism and a group of their Youth Patrons to develop a visual story as a PDF and pre-visit films about what to expect from a visit.
- The marketing team is working toward making sure that the museum's website is WCAG Level AA compliant.
- The team follows best practice for online content, such as alt text and captions on videos.
- Plain English is part of the tone-of-voice guidelines for marketing and online content and is now also a standard approach to exhibitions and onsite content too.
- The whole museum team is also offered disability awareness training, which is carried out cross-departmentally for a more holistic understanding of what is and is not working across the museum experience.
- The Postal Museum's marketing team works with its access team to co-produce content. For example, for a BSL tour, the Access and Community Engagement Manager, with guidance from the BSL guide running the tour, suggested the promotional video should not just have captions but should be in BSL. The marketing team supported the access team with writing a brief and scripting the video, which was then produced by a Deaf filmmaker. Edits of the video were shared across the museum's channels. The tour was a sell-out, and Duffield notes that the results "far exceeded what we could have achieved trying to advertise this event without a collaborative and co-produced approach" (2023).

Questions to consider

- What values and principles will guide your museum's accessible and inclusive marketing?

- What are your priorities for developing the accessibility of your marketing?
- What does inclusive content and language mean for your museum?

Further reading

Middleton, M. (no date) *Museums and content warnings*. Available at: https://www.margaretmiddleton.com/post/museums-and-content-warnings.

Salonlahti, O. and Salovaara, S. (eds.) (2022) *Accessibility and diversity checklist for museums*. Translated by Heiskanen, S. Culture for All Service / For Culture on Equal Terms and The Finnish National Committee of ICOM. Available at: https://www.kulttuuriakaikille.fi/accessibility_checklists.

Unlimited (2020) *Accessible Marketing Guide*. Available at: https://weareunlimited.org.uk/resource/accessible-marketing-guide/.

References

Attiah, K. (2021) *If U.S. Museums Say Black Lives Matter, Then They Should Return Africa's Stolen Art*. Available at: https://www.washingtonpost.com/opinions/2021/05/12/if-us-museums-say-black-lives-matter-then-they-should-return-africas-stolen-art/ (Accessed: 14 March 2023).

Biden Jr., President J. R. (2021) *A Proclamation on Indigenous Peoples' Day, 2021*. Available at: https://www.whitehouse.gov/briefing-room/presidential-actions/2021/10/08/a-proclamation-indigenous-peoples-day-2021/ (Accessed: 17 March 2023).

Binley, A. (2022) *KFC Apologises after German Kristallnacht Promotion*. Available at: https://www.bbc.co.uk/news/world-europe-63499057 (Accessed: 12 January 2023).

Carey, H., Giles, L., and O'Brien, D. (2023) *Job Quality in the Creative Industries*. Available from: https://cdn2.assets-servd.host/creative-pec/production/assets/publications/PEC-GWR-Job-quality-in-the-Creative-Industries-v7.pdf (Accessed: 17 April 2023).

Content Design London (2020) *Readability Guidelines*. Available at: https://readabilityguidelines.co.uk/ (Accessed: 12 January 2023).

Duffield, A. (2023) Email to Christina Lister, 17 March.

Hemingway Editor (no date) *Hemingway App Makes Your Writing Bold and Clear*. Available at: https://hemingwayapp.com/ (Accessed: 14 March 2023).

Mr Justice Fordham (2021) *Rowley v Minister for the Cabinet Office Approved Judgment*. Available at: https://www.judiciary.uk/wp-content/uploads/2022/07/R-on-the-application-of-Katherine-Rowley-v-Minister-for-the-Cabinet-Office.pdf (Accessed: 12 January 2023).

Middleton, M. (2022) 'Queer Museum Narratives and the Family Audience', in A. Langar (ed.) *Storytelling in Museums*, pp. 163–175. London: Rowman & Littlefield.

People's History Museum (2023) *Exhibition | Nothing About Us Without Us*. Available at: https://phm.org.uk/exhibitions/nothing-about-us-without-us/ (Accessed: 8 April 2023).

The Plain English Campaign (no date) *Free Guides*. Available at: https://www.plainenglish.co.uk/free-guides.html (Accessed: 16 April 2023).

The Postal Museum (2021) *The Postal Museum wins Best Accessible Museum*. Available at: https://www.postalmuseum.org/news/family-friendly-museum-award-2021/# (Accessed: 4 May 2023).

Putnam, P. (2023) *Were People in the Past All Small?* [Instagram Reel from Historic Royal Palaces]. 20 March. Available at: https://www.instagram.com/reel/CqAYsB4jwDe/?hl=en (Accessed: 8 April 2023).

Royal National Institute for Deaf People (no date) *Facts and Figures*. Available at: https://rnid.org.uk/about-us/research-and-policy/facts-and-figures/ (Accessed: 12 January 2023).

Royal National Institute of Blind People (no date) *Large and Giant Print*. Available at: https://www.rnib.org.uk/living-with-sight-loss/independent-living/reading-and-books/large-and-giant-print/ (Accessed: 11 January 2023).

Royal National Institute of Blind People (2022) *Reading and Braille Research*. Available at: https://www.rnib.org.uk/professionals/health-social-care-education-professionals/knowledge-and-research-hub/reports-and-insight/reading-and-braille-research (Accessed: 13 March 2023).

Salonlahti, O. and Salovaara, S. (eds.) (2022) *Accessibility and Diversity Checklist for Museums*. Translated by Heiskanen, S. Culture for All Service / For Culture on Equal Terms and The Finnish National Committee of ICOM. Available at: https://www.kulttuuriakaikille.fi/accessibility_checklists (Accessed: 14 March 2023).

Science Museum (2022) *Sensory Map*. Available at: https://www.sciencemuseum.org.uk/sites/default/files/2022-07/Sensory-Map-Science-Museum-July-2022.pdf (Accessed: 8 April 2023).

Unlimited (2020) *Accessible Marketing Guide*. Available at: https://weareunlimited.org.uk/resource/accessible-marketing-guide/ (Accessed: 10 January 2023).

VocalEyes (2022) *Heritage Access 2022*. Available at: https://vocaleyes.co.uk/research/heritage-access-2022/ (Accessed: 11 January 2023).

What Next? (2021) *#BAMEOver – A Statement for the UK*. Available at: https://www.whatnextculture.co.uk/bameover-a-statement-for-the-uk/ (Accessed: 24 April 2023).

World Wide Web Consortium (2023) *Making the Web Accessible*. Available at: https://www.w3.org/WAI/ (Accessed: 10 February 2023).

WHO, World Health Organization (2021) *Deafness and Hearing Loss*. Available at: https://www.who.int/news-room/fact-sheets/detail/deafness-and-hearing-loss (Accessed: 11 January 2023).

WHO, World Health Organization (2022) *Blindness and Vision Impairment*. Available at: https://www.who.int/news-room/fact-sheets/detail/blindness-and-visual-impairment (Accessed: 11 January 2023).

12   Ethical marketing

Introduction

I have touched on some ethical themes throughout the book, but I also wanted to give ethical museum marketing a dedicated space and finish the book with this topic, which is growing in importance and complexity. Ethical marketing constantly needs to evolve to reflect broader societal changes, legislation, public preferences, and behaviour, such as changes in attitudes and approaches toward – and the legislation of – tobacco advertising, marketing to children, data protection, and dietary claims on food. As consumer expectations change, many companies also try to align themselves with these changes. Sometimes this has been for self-serving, disingenuous reasons rather than an authentic commitment, leading to accusations of greenwashing, brownwashing, fairwashing, pinkwashing, and more (companies or governments making unsubstantiated or misleading claims to persuade consumers and stakeholders that they are committed to certain values and practices, for example, around sustainability, anti-racism, Fairtrade, or LGBTQ+ rights).

This chapter starts by defining ethics and ethical approaches and looks at the context of ethical business and consumption. It covers museum and marketing ethics, and codes of ethics for both. It charts examples of activism by and against museums. The chapter then considers marketing for good, including green museum marketing and practical frameworks to support decision-making. It ends with a case study from the Imperial War Museums Group. I don't claim to have all the answers, but I hope this chapter will be thought-provoking and encourage reflection and discussion.

Defining ethics and ethical approaches

Ethics involve moral principles that govern a person's or organisation's behaviour – norms and values that determine right from wrong. The following is a range of approaches museum marketers can take to ethical decision-making:

- A pragmatic approach to ethical museum marketing is common, considering issues practically and through deliberation, often when they come up, rather than based on specific principles or absolutes. This approach

recognises that different marketing actions may be appropriate to meet different objectives, reach different audiences, with different budgets, at different times.
- Some museums take a values-based approach, using the organisational values as a basis on which to make decisions.
- Others focus on the *effects and outcomes* of the actions; in other words, the end justifies the means. This could be the greatest good for the greatest number of people (for example, paying for advertising with a social media giant – despite concerns around its values – is acceptable if it reaches a large volume of people who enjoy learning about your museum's collections); or the benefit to the museum undertaking the action is considered worthwhile (for example, printing and distributing reams of leaflets is acceptable if it generates a huge rise in visitors and/or income to your museum).
- And finally, some museums and marketers focus on whether the *action, behaviour,* or *intention* is morally acceptable, rather than the consequences. For example, deciding not to use tracking pixels – despite them being useful to your museum in tracking behaviour and conversions – due to data privacy concerns.

If you want to explore theoretical ethical frameworks in more depth, see Eagle and Dahl's *Marketing Ethics & Society* as a useful starting point.

Ethical business and consumption

Ethical business isn't a new concept – Corporate Social Responsibility (CSR, a business model in which companies balance the creation of social and environmental benefits with more traditional business goals such as revenue and profit growth) built on earlier movements such as concerns for worker welfare during industrialisation and the growth of unions. Many initiatives now exist, including the UN Global Compact, a voluntary initiative encouraging businesses to commit to implementing sustainability principles; and B Lab Global's B Corp Certification, measuring companies' social and environmental impact, which includes looking at their ethical marketing. Brand activism is increasingly commonplace, building on innovators such as The Body Shop cosmetics company and Ben & Jerry's ice cream.

Similarly, movements to restrict or change consumption have a long history, for patriotic reasons such as wartime; for religious reasons such as Ramadan and Lent; and in more recent decades, for environmental and social reasons, such as a drive to eat more plant-based foods. Historically the focus has often been on *products,* but there has also been a rise in awareness of and interest in *services,* such as ethical banking, investment, and pensions. Individuals, community groups, protest groups, and campaigning organisations have also staged boycotts, demonstrations, and disruptive actions to raise awareness of issues they care about, mobilise others, and affect change.

Ethical museums

ICOM (2018) and key national museum associations such as the American Alliance of Museums (no date), the UK's Museums Association (2020) and New Zealand's Museums Aotearoa (2021) have codes of ethics for members, covering issues such as acquisition and disposal. In addition, many individual museums have their own codes of conduct or ethics. Arguably the biggest challenge facing museums now is the climate emergency. Many museums are tackling this proactively such as working toward carbon neutrality or net zero. There are also intense and evolving discussions around museums' reckoning with their pasts, their relevance today, and how they operate. For example, legacies of colonialism and calls for repatriation, restitution, and decolonisation; questions around underrepresented stories and who tells the stories; social justice; governance and leadership, trustee appointments, lack of staff diversity, low pay, zero-contract hours, and unpaid internships. These are often not niche, introspective debates in the sector's echo chambers; many of them break out into (or even originate in) media and public discourse. Audiences and stakeholders are often affected by and highly engaged in these questions, such as the discussion around the return of the Parthenon Marbles from The British Museum to Greece.

Activism *by* museums

Museums face a constant set of choices (such as pricing policies, which objects to show and stories to tell, who tells them and how) that can speak volumes to audiences and stakeholders, whether decision-making is proactive and intentional, or not. At the more purposeful end of the spectrum is museum activism, which seeks to bring about social, political, or environmental change. Some museums are by their very nature activist and have this explicitly embedded in their DNA from the outset. For example, the Museum of Homelessness in London says: "We fight injustice. We carry out investigations and campaign for the change we need. Our independent research and campaigns influence policymakers and the homelessness field to make changes to policy and practice" (no date). And Climate Museum UK is an experimental museum that "curates and gathers responses to the Earth crisis" (no date). Other museums have developed more of an activist approach over time. For example, the People's History Museum in Manchester, UK, has decided to speak out more on issues that are important to it, such as calling for the UK government to re-think its approach to the Nationality and Borders Bill in 2021 (Mabbott, as quoted by Kelly, 2022). How the public views museums and their potential for activism is nuanced and evolving. The public's increased experiences of organisations across industries taking a stand on key societal issues also raises their expectations of organisations doing so. Whilst speaking out is authentic and effective for some museums, it can come with a host of risks (in particular for publicly funded museums) such as a backlash from some audiences.

Activism *against* and *within* museums

There have been plenty of news headlines in the past few years covering a series of high-profile protests and stunts, but activism at museums – whether directly against them or using museums as a stage – is not new. As public spaces and often publicly supported institutions seen as bastions of culture and heritage, museums can provide a potent and prominent stage for protests. For example, suffragette Bertha Ryland slashed a painting at the Birmingham Museum and Art Gallery in 1914 in protest against the government's refusal to give women the right to vote (BBC News, 2018). Over a century later, when asked why they use cultural institutions as the site of civil disobedience, Extinction Rebellion co-founder Simon Bramwell, who joined Just Stop Oil activists when they attached themselves to the frame of Giampietrino's *The Last Supper* painting at the Royal Academy of Arts in London, said: "Politics will always follow culture, so it's absolutely vital that we hold the ideals of our cultural institutions to account" (as quoted by Escalante-De Mattei, 2022).

Activists and their goals have varied; for example, artists and creative practitioners engaging in institutional critique and protest (such as the Art Workers Coalition calling for greater inclusion of African American, Latinx, and other marginalised artists in the programming of the Museum of Modern Art – MoMA – in New York in the 1960s) (MoMA, no date); museum staff and trade unions organising and striking for higher pay and enhanced benefits at several museums across America including the Philadelphia Museum of Art and the Museum of Contemporary Art in Los Angeles (Hurdle, 2022); and sector grassroots movements and organisations calling for change within museums around inclusion and diversity, such as Museum as Muck, Museum Detox, and Fair Museum Jobs in the UK. Another notable example is the US-based *Museums Are Not Neutral*, a global advocacy initiative co-produced by La Tanya S. Autry and Mike Murawski "to expose the myth of museum neutrality and demand ethics-based transformation across institutions" saying, "Museums can be agents of social change in our communities, and it's up to us to make this happen together" (Museums Are Not Neutral, no date).

Income generation

All activism against or at museums is likely to have implications and impacts on museums' reputations, and the public's awareness and perceptions of them. Marketing teams, and in particular public relations teams responsible for issues and crisis management, need to handle these situations with care. However, whilst some forms of activism target areas not directly within the sphere of marketers' influence – such as curatorial decisions – there are some issues that are more overtly under the remit of marketing departments (and their siblings – income generation and fundraising).

Who is permitted to hire museums as event venues is a big question for museums. Questions were raised about conflicts of interest, impartiality, and governance in relation to London's Victoria and Albert Museum's (V&A) decision to host a Conservative Party fundraising event in 2022 and links between two trustees and the political party (Harris, 2022). In response, V&A Director Tristram Hunt tweeted: "Private venue hire is an important income stream to ensure the V&A stays free & open for everyone & the collections cared for. Political parties are very welcome to rent out spaces on commercial terms" (2022).

In New York, the American Museum of Natural History cancelled the hosting of an event by the non-profit Brazil-American Chamber of Commerce to honour the then President of Brazil Jair Bolsonaro with a Person of the Year award after the museum came under fire for this. Criticisms centred on Bolsonaro's disregard for the environment from staff who threatened resignations, the Decolonize This Place movement, Brazilian and American scientists, and New York Mayor Bill de Blasio (Offenhartz, 2019), as well as people on social media. Initially the museum said that the booking was an "external, private event" that was "booked at the Museum before the honoree was secured" (American Museum of Natural History, 2019a) but three days later said that the event would take place at another location (ibid., 2019b).

Two very prominent examples of toxic philanthropy and ethical issues with museum sponsorship relate to the Sackler family's donations and fossil fuel companies' sponsorship. The billionaire Sackler family behind the pharmaceutical company Purdue Pharma is accused of fuelling the opioid epidemic in the USA, which has seen nearly 500,000 Americans die of opioid overdoses between 1999 and 2019, and in 2020 pleaded guilty to criminal charges over its marketing of painkiller OxyContin, which it knew was addictive and being widely abused (BBC News, 2022). Members of the Sackler family have been prolific donors to museums (such as London's National Gallery and New York's Guggenheim Museum) and other cultural organisations for decades, with galleries, wings, and rooms named after them. Artist Nan Goldin founded Prescription Addiction Intervention Now (PAIN), made up of artists, activists, and people who have experienced addition, which has been instrumental in exposing cultural organisations' links to the Sackler families, which has included undertaking direct action at museums (PAIN, no date). Museums have had different responses, with some swiftly taking down the Sackler name; others initially saying they would no longer accept *new* donations from the Sacklers but not take down their name from *existing* donations; and some emphasising that their donations received came from Sackler family members with no ties to Purdue Pharma and/or were given before the sale of OxyContin. Difficulties in removing the Sackler name also came in part from the original contracts, which sometimes contained perpetuity clauses, and museums' fear of scaring off other future donors.

Some museums have also come under criticism for accepting sponsorship money from fossil fuel companies. Campaign group Culture Unstained alleged that London's National Portrait Gallery's sponsorship deal with oil and gas giant BP breached the gallery's clause on human rights in its Ethical Fundraising Policy (Culture Unstained, 2017); and protestors including Survival International, Extinction Rebellion Scientists, London Mining Network, Culture Unstained, UK Student Climate Network, and Coal Action Network have protested against the Science Museum's sponsorship deal with the Adani Group, in solidarity with Indigenous peoples from India, Australia, and Indonesia, where Adani operates mines on Indigenous land (Survival International, 2022).

These examples have shown the complex interplay of legal, financial, reputational, and ethical concerns around fundraising and income generation. The benefits for sponsors and donors are clear: exposure, positive brand association, credibility and respectability, influence, social legitimacy, reaching audiences, and for some, reputation laundering. Museums can benefit from the income, connections, and sometimes additional resources, skills, and expertise. But museums must ask themselves whether the income from some sources is worth it when it is weighed down by unethical baggage, compromises on the museum's integrity and independence, protests, alienation of some audiences, and negative publicity.

Ethical marketing

There is an argument that marketing is in itself neutral – it can be used for good or for bad reasons and outcomes. Just as marketing has been used to create demand for and sell cigarettes, it has been employed to encourage seatbelt use. Whilst there are some laws that govern marketing – often around advertising – a lot of the best practice, standards, and guides on ethics are self-regulated by the marketing industry in each country, and compliance is voluntary. Furthermore, self-regulation and legislation can struggle to keep up with the fast pace of technological change.

Codes of ethics

Key marketing bodies and associations have codes of conduct and/or ethics that set out the ethical and professional standards that marketers should uphold. The Chartered Institute of Marketing (CIM), the Chartered Institute of Public Relations, the Market Research Society, and Data & Marketing Association are examples of UK bodies with their own codes. For example, the CIM's Code of Professional Conduct lists 13 responsibilities for members to uphold such as: "Never knowingly or recklessly disseminate any false or misleading information, either on their own behalf or on behalf of anyone else" (2020).

Whilst acceptance of the codes is typically a pre-requisite to becoming a member of the associations, non-members can also choose to adhere to them. Members can be reprimanded or have their membership withdrawn if they are found to have broken the code after a disciplinary procedure, although this is rare. Membership of one or more of the associations can be beneficial (and sometimes requested) when seeking employment or consultancy opportunities, but it is not a pre-requisite without which you can't practise or call yourself a marketer, so the codes' influence is constrained. The codes are also not a prescriptive guide on what to do – they can be subjective and open to interpretation, and do not tell a marketer whether to advertise on a particular platform, for example. So it is up to marketers themselves to also take individual responsibility.

Marketing for good?

Below are a few subsets of marketing that are arguably more focused on doing good and are relevant to museums.

Values-based marketing

Values-based marketing builds your marketing strategy and actions from a set of values, authentic and lived by the organisation, and which also resonate with audiences' values. A lot of research shows that consumers and audiences are placing increased importance on organisations' values aligning with their own and using their purchasing power to hold brands to account. For example, Ipsos' Global Trends research of over 24,000 people aged 16–75 in 25 countries reported that 70% of people surveyed agree that they tend to buy brands that reflect their personal values (Ipsos, 2021, p.33).

Social marketing

Social marketing is marketing for a social or public good, such as anti-smoking, safety in the sun, and recycling campaigns. It involves encouraging or influencing voluntary, sustained, and positive behaviour change among the public or consumers. Some museums already incorporate social marketing in their work, overlapping with museums' learning and engagement work, such as encouraging audiences' perspectives and behaviour to change around climate change.

Cause-related marketing

Cause or cause-related marketing involves a for-profit company partnering with a not-for-profit organisation on a cause (such as reducing child poverty) for mutual benefit. Typically, the non-profit gains income, exposure, and sometimes expertise, and the for-profit organisation benefits from improved corporate image, building relationships with communities and consumers, and boosting employee morale and sales. This can include the for-profit company giving a proportion of each sale of a product to the non-profit, and/ or developing a product with ties to a cause. This can be the case with products both in museum shops and for sale by other retailers through licensing agreements.

Demarketing

Demarketing is about *discouraging* consumers and consumption, a term coined by Philip Kotler and Sidney Levy in 1971 (Kotler, 2017). It can be a temporary or permanent policy and apply to all or just a subsection of audiences or customers. Examples are to minimise unwanted consumption of harmful goods such as cigarettes; to minimise demand when demand far outstrips supply, for example, water usage during a drought; and to minimise harm to natural resources, the built environment, and local communities, for example, tourism to the Great Barrier Reef, Amsterdam, and Venice. Tactics can involve increasing prices; campaigns and messaging to encourage less consumption; cutting promotion; restricting availability and the distribution of products and services; or encouraging a redistribution of demand – for example, shifting demand from peak to off-peak travel.

Ethical museum marketing

I'd suggest that most museum marketing is more considered and ethical than marketing in many other sectors, and museums tend to be for the public good and have an educational purpose, giving them a head start. As a small tangible example, a search under the rulings of the UK's Advertising Standards Authority judging whether an ad has broken its advertising rules shows that no rulings relate to museums (2023).

Whilst there is a lot of discourse around museum ethics more broadly, there is less guidance and discussion around museum marketing ethics specifically. It is interesting to note that there is no specific mention of "marketing" and "communications" in the codes of ethics from ICOM, the American Alliance of Museums (AAM), or the UK Museums Association, although some marketing or communication themes are included – all three cover income generation. For example, the AAM Code of Ethics states that "revenue-producing activities and activities that involve relationships with external entities are compatible with the museum's mission and support its public trust responsibilities" (American Alliance of Museums, no date); and the Museums Association's Code of Ethics states that museums should "provide and generate accurate information for and with the public" (2020, p. 6). Similarly, I found that marketing and communication are also generally not included in museums' own ethics' policies, aside from in reference to income generation.

Green and sustainable museum marketing

Marketing and consumption are inextricably linked. Historically, marketing has revolved around profit generation and growth, and in the museums sector, marketing is used to grow income and audiences, typically two success markers. Culture, heritage, and tourism are also huge employers and drivers of economic growth. But pursuing unrestrained growth by exploiting finite resources is not sustainable or conscionable, and arguably this is the biggest ethical challenge facing museum marketing and museums as a whole.

International tourists are often core museum audiences and contribute income through admission, retail, and catering outlets, but should museums feel comfortable encouraging them if they have to fly to visit? Another issue is the blockbuster exhibition model that, when done well, delivers on income generation, profile, prestige, reputation, education, audiences, and national image. But criticisms have long existed (around conservation, risk issues for loans, insurance costs, and more) and in more recent years also a focus on the environmental impact such as the CO_2 emissions of mounting and touring big temporary exhibitions internationally. What are the viable alternatives? City-based museums in Central Europe are likely to have more opportunities to attract many international tourists by train than rural museums in Scotland. During the lockdowns of the Covid-19 pandemic, many museums turned to digital engagement, and then on tentative reopening focused on attracting local and hyperlocal audiences. But many museums have struggled to generate sufficient income from these approaches. These challenges need to be tackled as a sector, since one museum undertaking demarketing may just divert demand to another.

The enormity of the climate crisis can feel overwhelming, but a pragmatic approach can be a useful entry point that includes a commitment to an ongoing process, starting with achievable actions. For example, ensuring that the marketing suppliers you use have green credentials; sharing and learning from others in the sector; using recycled materials and no single-use plastics; using a carbon footprint calculator for your output to work out your baseline; using a web hosting company that is powered by renewable energy; supporting marketing staff in terms of sustainability, such as permitting working from home to minimise travel. Cutting back on producing print and increasing digital marketing is often an early green step that marketers take and should absolutely be considered. However, it is a misnomer that there is no environmental impact from digital marketing. The internet represents around 3.7% of global emissions, likely to double by 2025 (Griffiths, 2020), and a typical online ad campaign emits 5.4 tons of carbon, about half of the total annual impact of an inhabitant of the UK (Good-Loop, 2022, p. 2). So digital marketing also must form a big part of the conversation, for example, taking part in Digital Cleanup Day as a kickstart to clear digital waste such as unnecessary emails, files, apps, and duplicates of photos and videos (2023).

Practical frameworks

Marketing and communications teams are affected by all the issues set out above, whether directly – for example, in terms of sponsor selection and terms, data collection and consent, culturally sensitive marketing – or through the resulting journalist requests for interviews, negative media coverage, and social media comments. There is a huge range of nuanced micro and macro issues to navigate, for example:

- What influence do marketers have over museum policies and mechanisms for contributing to them?
- How do you balance the need for income generation without compromising the museum's ethics and values?
- Which issues do museums campaign on?
- How do you quantify reputational risk?
- What does a due diligence procedure look like, and who is responsible?
- What happens when marketing staff or volunteers don't feel comfortable – or their values are in direct conflict – with a museum's actions or values?
- How do you balance respecting audiences' data privacy whilst maximising opportunities for evaluation and personalisation, such as location-based marketing (using the location of audiences' mobile phones to distribute content or offers) and behavioural targeting (using data around audiences' behaviour – such as webpages viewed, buttons clicked, items placed in their cart) to target them more effectively?

There are many invested stakeholders whose viewpoints may not always align – from internal stakeholders (staff, volunteers, trustees) to audiences and other external stakeholders such as funding bodies, partners, and sponsors. There may be clashes between short-term and long-term priorities. There may be difficult and uncomfortable discussions to be had.

Turning to practical approaches to support decision-making, consider marketing holistically, and ethical approaches to each stage: marketing research, planning, delivery, analysis, and reporting on your marketing activities. First, museum marketers should – as a minimum – adhere to relevant laws, such as around data privacy, and second, adhere to any self-regulatory systems as required, including museum and marketing associations (even if you are not a member, it is worth being familiar with them and following them as best practice). Third, I also recommend museum marketing teams create their own guide to steer and support an ethical approach to marketing that includes clear values and principles on which to base decisions, as well as a process for decision-making and determining who should be involved (see the case study at the end of the chapter for an example). Below are some suggested approaches to guide this work.

A values-based approach

A good starting point is taking your museum's values and considering how they can inform an ethical approach to strategic marketing. Below is a list of core values from different museums. Consider how they differ and how each value might inform ethical marketing:

- **The Van Gogh Museum** in The Netherlands shares: "The Van Gogh Museum is authentic, in connection and original. These core values function as an ethical compass for the museum and staff" (no date).
- **The Hong Kong Museum of History's** values are: Professionalism, Openness, Integrity, Creativity, Focus on people, Passion (no date).
- **The Western Australian Museum's** values are: Respectful, Inclusive, Accountable, Establishment (no date).

Inspiration from sector ethic guides

Consider developing your own principles for the marketing team, based on existing sector guides as inspiration, such as:

- **The International Social Marketing Association's (iSMA) principles:** Respect and sensitivity; Social justice and fairness; Openness and transparency; Avoidance of conflicts of interest; Duty of care and nonmaleficence; Serve public interest (2022).
- **The American Marketing Association's ethical values** cover Honesty, Responsibility, Fairness, Respect, Transparency, and Citizenship content (2021).
- **The UK Evaluation Society's principles** in its Guidelines for Good Practice in Evaluation cover: Clarity, Integrity, Independence, Accessibility, Trust, Equity, Transparency, Diversity (2019, p. 5).

Using the marketing mix

To help identify what the museum's values or marketing principles look like when embedded in marketing practice, they can be mapped across the marketing mix (set out in Chapter 5a), using tangible ideas or questions. For example, if one of your values is inclusivity, you might want to consider questions such as:

- **Promotion:** Is your choice of communication platforms inclusive and appropriate for your audiences? Is content and language used inclusive?
- **Process:** Is your audience research free from bias? What is your online content moderation policy and how do you apply it? How do you credit content creators and suppliers?
- **People:** How is your recruitment inclusive? How do your marketing salaries compare to other museums, broader arts marketing roles, and other sectors? How do you protect the well-being of your staff or volunteers who manage the museum's social media? (See, for example, Dornan on social media burnout, 2019.)

Looking ahead

Marketers will increasingly need to understand and wrestle with evolving technology and the more unchartered waters of NFTs (non-fungible tokens, unique digital assets) and AI (artificial intelligence). I have come across a range of responses to AI from marketers, from not understanding what AI is, to a principled refusal to entertain it, to a resignation of its inevitability, to excitement around its possibilities. This points to the need for marketing teams to ensure they keep on top of technological developments, share their experimentation and lessons; that senior managers invest in their CPD (Continuing Professional Development) and understand what skills and experience to look for when they recruit in the future. AI has the potential to undertake, automate, speed up, and improve the accuracy of many of marketers' current activities. But it also poses big questions around transparency, bias, data privacy, and which skills and people will become redundant. And will it further exacerbate the gulf between the largest and smallest museums, if harnessing the power of AI requires a sizeable investment? Marketers need to be proactive in facing these challenges and opportunities.

Case study: The Imperial War Museum

Imperial War Museums (IWM) is a family of five museums in the UK that uncover the causes, course, and consequences of war, from the First World War through to present-day conflict. The IWM team have run award-winning and innovative marketing campaigns, and I could easily have included these as case studies in other chapters. For example, putting a vending machine into the middle of Manchester Piccadilly Station to generate awareness of a new exhibition, *Yemen: Inside a Crisis,* at IWM North. The vending machine contained snacks and drinks as you might expect, but with price tags that reflected the high inflation in Yemen due to its conflict – such as £11 for a chocolate bar – resulting in almost 10 million Yemenis suffering from extreme hunger (IWM, 2019). And in 2021, they commissioned conflict photographer Hazel Thompson to take a photo to promote the opening of the Second World War and Holocaust Galleries at IWM London. They used IWM staff and models to re-create a 1941 photograph of Londoners sheltering on escalators in a tube station during the Blitz, bringing it up to date with people on their phones and laptops. Both campaigns are excellent examples of how marketing can make exhibitions resonate and be relevant to people today, generating media interest and social media engagement in the process. The marketing, not just the exhibition content, can move people and encourage reflection. But I wanted to include IWM in this chapter due to its considered approach to marketing, showing that ethical can still be powerful, creative, and effective. This case study also highlights a clear process for making difficult decisions balancing risks and opportunities, commercial goals and values, and a pragmatic approach.

The IWM has a clear mission and values that guide their marketing, and a clear process for dealing with ethical decisions. The group has an editorial board with editorial principles derived from the museum's remit and values;

it is chaired by Assistant Director of Communications & Marketing Pete Austin and reports to the brand and reputation board. It is tasked with making decisions about issues and opportunities that come to the board from across the museum, for example, around marketing campaigns, exhibition interpretation, whether the museum should take an organisation stance on certain issues, and involvement in awareness days. The board comprises director-level staff from a cross section of the museum including public engagement and learning; exhibitions and interpretation; content and narrative (curators, subject experts); digital; and commercial. After conversations that discuss potential ramifications, risks, and opportunities, a collective decision is taken against the editorial principles and documented, then communicated back to the team that raised the issue.

A tangible example of this was IWM's participation in the Stop Hate for Profit campaign, in which 1,200 companies and non-profits paused Facebook advertising during July 2020 to hold the platform to account for hate and disinformation (Shorty Awards, 2021). The Museums Association reported that IWM was the only known English cultural institution taking part (Knott, 2020). The decision to participate was made after discussion by the editorial board in which Austin explained the risks of pausing advertising on one of the world's largest social media platforms. July would usually be a big promotional month for the summer season, and especially in 2020 as the museums were gearing up to reopen in August after their pandemic closures. Austin says that stopping the spread of disinformation and misinformation is a "poignant topic close to our hearts and crucially, our organisational cause [...] so we felt it was important that we put our weight behind it as a national institution" (2023). He acknowledges that they did see a drop-off in engagement on Facebook and Instagram as a result, although the impact was short-lived.

Austin says that considering whether the values and principles of each marketing channel align with those of your museum on a daily basis would be very time-consuming, messy, and unsustainable. Whereas it is achievable to align your museum's values and principles on bigger campaigns where you want to take a stance, in line with your organisation's role and remit (2023). Looking to the next few years, Austin agrees there will be a lot of ethical challenges for marketers and suggests that museums and cultural organisations need to speak and act more proactively: "Saying what they *are* about, they can start saying where they *do* want to be, they can start aligning their organisations' values with campaigns from the outset" (2023).

Questions to consider

- What does ethical marketing mean to you?
- How can you translate ethical principles and values to practical measures?
- How does your museum's ethics policy include marketing?

Further reading

American Marketing Association (2023)AMA *Code of Conduct.* Available at: https://myama.my.site.com/s/article/AMA-Code-of-Conduct.
Eagle, L. and Dahl, S. (2015) *Marketing Ethics & Society.* London: Sage.
Marstine, J. (ed.) (2011) *The Routledge Companion to Museum Ethics. Redefining Ethics for the Twenty-First-Century Museum.* Oxon: Routledge.

References

Advertising Standards Authority (2023) *Rulings.* Available at: https://www.asa.org.uk/codes-and-rulings/rulings.html?q=museum (Accessed: 26 January 2023).
American Alliance of Museums (no date) *Ethics.* Available at: https://www.aam-us.org/programs/ethics-standards-and-professional-practices/code-of-ethics-for-museums/ (Accessed: 25 January 2023).
American Museum of Natural History (2019a) [Twitter] 12 April. Available at: https://twitter.com/AMNH/status/1116502555247489024 (Accessed: 20 April 2023).
American Museum of Natural History (2019b) [Twitter] 15 April. Available at: https://twitter.com/AMNH/status/1117889750105354240 (Accessed: 20 April 2023).
Austin, P. (2023) What's App voice note to Christina Lister, 21 April.
BBC News (2018) *Blue Plaque for Birmingham 'Painting Attack' Suffragette.* Available at: https://www.bbc.co.uk/news/uk-england-birmingham-45892002 (Accessed: 5 May 2023).
BBC News (2022) *Sackler Family to Pay $6bn for Role in US Opioid Crisis.* Available at: https://www.bbc.co.uk/news/world-us-canada-60610707 (Accessed: 24 April 2023).
CIM, Chartered Institute of Marketing (2020) *Code of Professional Conduct.* Available at: https://www.cim.co.uk/media/7393/cim-code-of-professional-conduct-february-2020.pdf (Accessed: 24 January 2023).
Climate Museum UK (no date) *About.* Available at: https://climatemuseumuk.org/ (Accessed: 8 April 2023).
Culture Unstained (2017) *Revealed: National Portrait Gallery's Ethics Rules – and How BP Breaches Them.* Available at: https://cultureunstained.org/badcompany/ (Accessed: 21 March 2023).
Digital Cleanup Day (2023) *Join Digital Cleanup Day.* Available at: https://www.digitalcleanupday.org/ (Accessed: 22 March 2023).
Dornan, R. (2019) *Social Media Burnout.* Available at: https://medium.com/@RussellDornan/social-media-burn-out-be31286a4d59 (Accessed: 11 May 2023).
Escalante-De Mattei, S. (2022) *Why Climate Activists Are Gluing Themselves to Paintings Across the U.K.* Available at: https://www.artnews.com/art-news/news/just-stop-oil-uk-museums-gluing-protests-1234633474/ (Accessed: 25 January 2023).
Good-Loop (2022). *Counting Carbon: How U.K. Marketers are Tackling Adland's Climate Crisis.* Available at: https://counting-carbon.good-loop.com/ (Accessed: 22 March 2023).
Griffiths, S. (2020) *Why Your Internet Habits Are Not As Clean As You Think.* Available at: https://www.bbc.com/future/article/20200305-why-your-internet-habits-are-not-as-clean-as-you-think (Accessed: 22 March 2023).
Harris, G. (2022) *Activist Group's Film Projection on Victoria and Albert Museum Façade Raises Concerns about Trustees' Politics.* Available at: https://www.theartnewspaper.com/2022/06/21/activist-groups-film-projection-on-victoria-and-albert-museum-facade-raises-concerns-about-trustees-politics (Accessed: 25 January 2023).

Hong Kong Museum of History (no date) *Vision, Mission & Values*. Available at: https://hk.history.museum/en_US/web/mh/about-us/vision.html (Accessed: 27 January 2023).

Hunt, T. (2022) [Twitter] 20 June. Available at: https://twitter.com/TristramHuntVA/status/1538823047087542274 (Accessed: 20 April 2023).

Hurdle, Jo. (2022) *Strike at Philadelphia Museum of Art Is Window Into Broader Unrest*. Available at: https://www.nytimes.com/2022/09/29/arts/design/strike-philadelphia-museum-of-art.html (Accessed: 20 March 2023).

ICOM, International Council of Museums (2018) *ICOM Code of Ethics for Museums*. Available at: https://icom.museum/wp-content/uploads/2018/07/ICOM-code-En-web.pdf (Accessed: 25 January 2023).

International Social Marketing Association (2022) *Draft Social Marketing Statement of Ethics*. Available at: https://isocialmarketing.org/wp-content/uploads/sites/5/2022/10/Socal-Marketing-Ethics-guidance-for-consultation-Board-aproved-September-2022.pdf (Accessed: 25 January 2023).

Ipsos (2021) *Ipsos Global Trends 2021*. Available at: https://www.ipsos.com/sites/default/files/ct/publication/documents/2022-02/gts-2021-launch-report.pdf (Accessed: 25 January 2023).

IWM, Imperial War Museums (2019) *Yemen: Inside a Crisis | Price of War*. Available at: https://www.youtube.com/watch?v=-YUL06xSBhQ (Accessed: 13 April 2023).

Kelly, P. (2022) *A New Age of Activism?* Available at: https://www.museumsassociation.org/museums-journal/analysis/2022/01/a-new-age-of-activism/ (Accessed: 21 March 2023).

Knott, J. (2020) *Imperial War Museums Joins Facebook Advertising Boycott*. Available at: https://www.museumsassociation.org/museums-journal/news/2020/07/imperial-war-museums-joins-facebook-advertising-boycott/ (Accessed: 9 January 2023).

Kotler, P. (2017) *"Welcome to the Age of Demarketing" – Philip Kotler*. Available at: https://www.marketingjournal.org/welcome-to-the-age-of-demarketing-an-excerpt-from-philip-kotlers-autobiography-philip-kotler/ (Accessed: 13 January 2023).

MoMA, Museum of Modern Art (no date) *MoMA through Time*. Available at: https://www.moma.org/interactives/moma_through_time/1970/fighting-moma/ (Accessed: 25 January 2023).

Museums Aotearoa (2021) *Code of Ethics*. Available at: https://www.museumsaotearoa.org.nz/publications-resources/code-of-ethics (Accessed: 27 January 2023).

Museums Are Not Neutral (no date) *Join the Movement*. Available at: https://www.museumsarenotneutral.com/ (Accessed: 26 January 2023).

The Museum of Homelessness (no date) *We Fight Injustice*. Available at: https://museumofhomelessness.org/we-fight-injustice (Accessed: 25 January 2023).

The Museums Association (2020) *Code of Ethics for Museums*. Available at: https://www.museumsassociation.org/app/uploads/2020/06/20012016-code-of-ethics-single-page-8.pdf (Accessed: 25 January 2023).

Offenhartz, J. (2019) *AMNH Employees Revolt Over 'Appalling' Decision To Host Bolsonaro At Museum*. Available at: https://gothamist.com/news/amnh-employees-revolt-over-appalling-decision-to-host-bolsonaro-at-museum (Accessed: 26 January 2023).

PAIN (no date) *PAIN*. Available at: https://www.sacklerpain.org/ (Accessed: 26 January 2023).

Shorty Awards (2021) *#STOPHATEFORPROFIT* Available at: https://shortyawards.com/13th/stop-hate-for-profit-social-campaign (Accessed: 13 April 2023).

Survival International (2022) *Protest at London's Science Museum as Indigenous Peoples Slam Adani Sponsorship Deal.* Available at: https://www.survivalinternational.org/news/12710 (Accessed: 8 May 2023).

UK Evaluation Society (2019) *Guidelines for Good Practice in Evaluation.* Available at: https://www.evaluation.org.uk/app/uploads/2019/04/UK-Evaluation-Society-Guidelines-for-Good-Practice-in-Evaluation.pdf (Accessed: 9 April 2023).

Van Gogh Museum (no date) *Mission and Strategy.* Available at: https://www.vangoghmuseum.nl/en/about/organisation/mission-and-strategy (Accessed: 27 January 2023).

Western Australian Museum (no date) *Background & Mission.* Available at: https://museum.wa.gov.au/about/background-mission (Accessed: 27 January 2023).

Bibliography

Ables, K. (2022) *What Is a 'museum'? A Revised Definition Looks Forward, Not Back.* Available at: https://www.washingtonpost.com/arts-entertainment/2022/08/27/international-council-of-museums-redefines-museum/ (Accessed: 24 September 2022).

Adcock, D., Halborg, A. and Ross, C. (2001) *Marketing Principles & Practice.* 4th ed. Harlow: Pearson Education Limited.

Albrighton, T. (2018) *Copywriting Made Simple. How to Write Powerful and Persuasive Copy that Sells.* Kibworth Beauchamp: Matador.

American Alliance of Museums (no date) *Ethics.* Available at: https://www.aam-us.org/programs/ethics-standards-and-professional-practices/code-of-ethics-for-museums/ (Accessed: 25 January 2023).

American Marketing Association (2017) *Definitions of Marketing.* Available at: https://www.ama.org/the-definition-of-marketing-what-is-marketing/ (Accessed: 5 May 2022).

American Marketing Association (2021) *AMA Code of Conduct.* Available at: https://myama.my.site.com/s/article/AMA-Code-of-Conduct (Accessed: 24 January 2023).

American Marketing Association (2021) *AMA Statement of Ethics.* Available at: https://myama.my.site.com/s/article/AMA-Statement-of-Ethics (Accessed: 26 January 2023).

Anderson, I. (2019) *Pulse Report: The Art of Pricing.* Available at: https://www.baker-richards.com/pulse-report-the-art-of-pricing/ (Accessed: 19 December 2022).

Arts Council England (2022) *Equality, Diversity, and Inclusion.* Available at: https://www.artscouncil.org.uk/equality-diversity-and-inclusion-data-report-2020-2021 (Accessed: 27 February 2023).

Arts Marketing Association (2019) *AMA Benchmarking Survey 2019 – Member Report.* Available at: https://www.a-m-a.co.uk/wp-content/uploads/2021/12/AMA-Benchmarking-Survey-2019-_Member-Report.pdf (member-only resource). (Accessed: 5 January 2023).

Arts Professional (2019) *Pricing in the Arts.* Available at: https://www.artsprofessional.co.uk/sites/artsprofessional.co.uk/files/data_all_190703.pdf (Accessed: 19 December 2022).

Association of Independent Museums (2019) *Economic Value of the Independent Museum Sector Toolkit.* Available at: https://aim-museums.co.uk/wp-content/uploads/2019/10/Economic-Impact-Toolkit-2019.pdf (Accessed: 6 February 2023).

The Association of Leading Visitor Attractions (2021) *ALVA Attractions Recovery Tracker Wave 9.* Available at: https://www.alva.org.uk/documents/ALVA_

Attractions_Recovery_Tracker_Wave_9_(17-22_June)_250621_ALVA_v1-2.pdf (Accessed: 3 December 2022).

The Association of Leading Visitor Attractions and Decision House (2022) *What Is the Outlook for Visitor Attractions? ALVA Public Sentiment Research*. Available at: https://www.alva.org.uk/images/assets/210148_44547_221006.pdf (Accessed: 9 February 2023).

The Audience Agency (2018) *Museums Audience Report*. Available at: https://www.theaudienceagency.org/resources/museums-audience-report (Accessed: 31 January 2023).

The Audience Agency (2023) *Spring 2023 Cultural Participation Monitor*. Available at: https://www.theaudienceagency.org/evidence/covid-19-cultural-participation-monitor/recent-key-insights/spring-2023#Social_Media_Behaviour (Accessed: 5 May 2023).

Baker Richards (2020) *After the Interval: Act 2. An Analysis of Willingness to Pay for Digital*. Available at: https://www.baker-richards.com/wp-content/uploads/2020/10/After-the-Interval-Act-II-Analysis.pdf (Accessed: 18 December 2022).

Bounia, A., Nikiforidou, A., Nikonanou, N. and Matossian, A. D. (eds.) (2012) *Voices from the Museum: Survey Research in Europe's National Museums*. Linköping: Linköping University Electronic Press. Available at: http://liu.diva-portal.org/smash/record.jsf?pid=diva2%3A563949&dswid=4748 (Accessed: 23 February 2023).

Cantrill- Fenwick, R. (2021) *What can – and Should – You Charge Digital Audiences?* Available at: https://www.baker-richards.com/what-can-and-should-you-charge-digital-audiences/ (Accessed: 17 December 2022).

Carey, H., Giles, L. and O'Brien, D. (2023) *Job Quality in the Creative Industries*. Available from: https://cdn2.assets-servd.host/creative-pec/production/assets/publications/PEC-GWR-Job-quality-in-the-Creative-Industries-v7.pdf (Accessed: 17 April 2023).

Carvill, M., Butler, G. and Evans, G. (2021) *Sustainable Marketing. How to Drive Profits with Purpose*. London: Bloomsbury Business.

Cashman, S. (2010) *Thinking Big! A Guide to Strategic Marketing Planning for Arts Organisations*. 2nd ed. Cambridge: Arts Marketing Association. Available at: https://www.culturehive.co.uk/wp-content/uploads/2012/11/Guide_-_Thinking_Big_-_Stephen_Cashman_-_2010-2.pdf (Access: 9 November 2022).

Chartered Institute of Marketing (2015) *7Ps. A Brief Summary of Marketing and How It Works*. Available at: https://www.cim.co.uk/media/4772/7ps.pdf (Accessed: 5 May 2022).

Chartered Institute of Marketing (2020) *Code of Professional Conduct*. Available at: https://www.cim.co.uk/media/7393/cim-code-of-professional-conduct-february-2020.pdf (Accessed: 24 January 2023).

Coe, N. (2019) *The 'Pay What You can' Conundrum*. Available at: https://www.baker-richards.com/the-pay-what-you-can-conundrum/ (Accessed: 18 December 2022).

Constantinides, E. (2006) 'The Marketing Mix Revisited: Towards the 21st Century Marketing', *Journal of Marketing Management*, 22(3), pp. 407–438. Available at: 10.1362/026725706776861190 (Accessed: 6 March 2023).

Convious and Baker Richards (2022) *Consumer Attitudes to Dynamic Pricing for Visitor Attractions in the UK*. Available at: https://blog.convious.com/eblog/consumer-attitudes-to-dynamic-pricing-for-visitor-attractions-in-the-uk (Accessed: 8 March 2023).

Culture Label (2018) *Flexible Family Tickets. Commercial Considerations*. Available at: https://kidsinmuseums.org.uk/wp-content/uploads/2018/12/Family-Ticket-Commercial-Report.pdf (Accessed: 19 December 2022).

DC Research (2016) *Taking charge – Evaluating the Evidence: The Impact of Charging or not for Admissions on museums*. Available at: https://aim-museums.co.uk/wp-content/uploads/2017/04/Final-Report-Taking-Charge-%E2%80%93-Evaluating-the-Evidence-The-Impact-of-Charging-or-Not-for-Admissions-on-Museums.pdf (Accessed: 16 December 2022).

Desvallées, A. and Mairesse, F. (2010) *Key Concepts of Museology*. Paris: Armand Colin. Available at: https://icofom.mini.icom.museum/publications/key-concepts-of-museology/ (Accessed: 25 September 2022).

Dietrich, G. (2020) *What Is the PESO Model™?* Available at: https://spinsucks.com/communication/peso-model-breakdown/ (Accessed: 5 January 2023).

Diggle, K. (1994) *Arts Marketing*. London: Rhinegold Publishing Limited.

Dilenschneider, C. (2015) *Free Admission Days Do Not Actually Attract Underserved Visitors to Cultural Organizations (DATA)*. Available at: https://www.colleendilen.com/2015/11/04/free-admission-days-do-not-actually-attract-underserved-visitors-to-cultural-organizations-data/ (Accessed: 16 December 2022).

Dilenschneider, C. (2016) *Why Cultural Organizations Are not Reaching Low-income Visitors*. Available at: https://www.colleendilen.com/2016/05/18/why-cultural-organizations-are-not-reaching-low-income-visitors-data/ (Accessed: 20 September 2022).

Dilenschneider, C. (2019) *They're Just Not That Into You: What Cultural Organizations Need to Know About Non-visitors*. Available at: https://www.colleendilen.com/2019/02/06/theyre-just-not-that-into-you-what-cultural-organizations-need-to-know-about-non-visitors-data/ (Accessed: 20 September 2022).

Dilenschneider, C. (2019) *Active Visitors: Who Currently Attends Cultural Organizations?* Available at: https://www.colleendilen.com/2019/01/23/active-visitors-currently-attends-cultural-organizations-data/ (Accessed: 20 September 2022).

Dilenschneider, C. (2019) *Inactive Visitors Are Interested in Attending Cultural Organizations. Why Don't They?* Available at: https://www.colleendilen.com/2019/01/30/inactive-visitors-are-interested-in-attending-cultural-organizations-why-dont-they-data/ (Accessed: 20 September 2022).

Eagle, L. and Dahl, S. (2015) *Marketing Ethics & Society*. London: Sage.

Ekström, K. M. (ed.) (2020) *Museum Marketization. Cultural Institutions in the NeoLiberal Era*. Abingdon: Routledge.

European Union (2012) *Work Plan for Culture, 2011-14: A Report on Policies and Good Practices in the Public Arts and In Cultural Institutions to Promote Better Access to and Wider Participation in Culture*. Available at: https://ec.europa.eu/assets/eac/culture/policy/strategic-framework/documents/omc-report-access-to-culture_en.pdf (Accessed: 25 September 2022).

Ewen, S. (1996) *PR! A Social History of Spin*. New York: Basic Books.

Falk, J. (2016) 'Museum Audiences: A Visitor-Centered Perspective', *Loisir et Société / Society and Leisure*, 39(3), pp. 357–370. Available at: 10.1080/07053436.2016.1243830 (Accessed: 23 February 2023).

Fordham, Mr. J. (2021) *Rowley v Minister for the Cabinet Office Approved Judgment*. Available at: https://www.judiciary.uk/wp-content/uploads/2022/07/R-on-the-application-of-Katherine-Rowley-v-Minister-for-the-Cabinet-Office.pdf (Accessed: 12 January 2023).

French, Y. and Runyard, S. (2011) *Marketing and Public Relations for Museums, Galleries, Cultural and Heritage Attractions*. Oxon: Routledge.

Garwood, C. (2018) *Museums in Britain. A History*. Oxford: Shire Publications.

Gil, C. (2022) *The End of Marketing*. 2nd edn. London: Kogan Page.

Godin, S. (2005) *All Marketers Are Liars. The Power of Telling Authentic Stories in a Low-Trust World*. London: Penguin Books Ltd.

Godin, S. (2019) *This is Marketing. You Can't be Seen Until You Learn to See*. London: Penguin Business.

Good Things Foundation (2020) *Blueprint for a 100% Digitally Included UK*. Available at: https://www.goodthingsfoundation.org/wp-content/uploads/2021/01/blueprint-for-a-100-digitally-included-uk-0.pdf (Accessed: 5 January 2023).

Gregory, A. (2005) *Planning and Managing Public Relations Campaigns*. 2nd edn. London: Kogan Page.

Hall, C. M. and Wood, K. (2021) 'Demarketing Tourism for Sustainability: Degrowing Tourism or Moving the Deckchairs on the Titanic?', *Sustainability*, 13, pp. 1585. Available at: 10.3390/su13031585 (Accessed: 13 January 2023).

Halpern, D. (2019) *Inside the Nudge Unit. How Small Changes Can Make A Big Difference*. London: WH Allen.

Hibbins, A. and Moffat, K. (2020) *Who Are Museum Digital Visitors?* Available at: https://www.theaudienceagency.org/asset/2440 (Accessed: 27 February 2023).

Hill, L., O'Sullivan, C., O'Sullivan, T. and Whitehead, B. (2018) *Creative Arts Marketing*. Oxon: Routledge.

HubSpot (2022) *Marketing Budget: How Much Should Your Team Spend in 2023?* Available at: https://blog.hubspot.com/marketing/marketing-budget-percentage (Accessed: 19 April 2023).

International Association for the Measurement and Evaluation of Communication (no date) *Barcelona Principles 3.0*. Available at: https://amecorg.com/barcelona-principles-3-0-translations/ (Accessed: 8 December 2022).

International Council of Museums (2018) *ICOM Code of Ethics for Museums*. Available at: https://icom.museum/wp-content/uploads/2018/07/ICOM-code-En-web.pdf (Accessed: 25 January 2023).

International Council of Museums (2022) *Museums, Museum Professionals and COVID-19*. Available at: https://icom.museum/wp-content/uploads/2020/05/Report-Museums-and-COVID-19.pdf (Accessed: 25 September 2022).

International Social Marketing Association (2022) *Draft Social Marketing Statement of Ethics*. Available at: https://isocialmarketing.org/wp-content/uploads/sites/5/2022/10/Socal-Marketing-Ethics-guidance-for-consultation-Board-aproved-September-2022.pdf (Accessed: 25 January 2023).

Ipsos (2021) *Ipsos Global Trends 2021*. Available at: https://www.ipsos.com/sites/default/files/ct/publication/documents/2022-02/gts-2021-launch-report.pdf (Accessed: 25 January 2023).

Iskiev, M. (2022) *The HubSpot Blog's 2023 Marketing Strategy & Trends Report: Data from 1,200+ Global Marketers*. Available at: https://blog.hubspot.com/marketing/hubspot-blog-marketing-industry-trends-report (Accessed: 3 May 2023).

Janes, R. R. and Sandell, R. (eds.) (2019) *Museum Activism*. Oxon: Routledge.

Jones, D. G. B. and Tadajewski, M. (eds.) (2019) *The Routledge Companion to Marketing History*. Abingdon: Routledge.

Kemp, S. (2023) *Digital 2023 Global Overview Report*. Available at: https://wearesocial.com/uk/blog/2023/01/digital-2023/ (Accessed: 13 March 2023).

Kids in Museums (2010) *Family Ticket Watch*. Available at: https://kidsinmuseums.org.uk/wp-content/uploads/2018/12/Family-Ticket-Watch-Report.pdf (Accessed: 16 December 2022).

Kids in Museums (2010) *Flexible Family Ticket Guidelines.* Available at: https://kidsinmuseums.org.uk/wp-content/uploads/2018/12/Flexible-Family-Ticket-Guidelines.pdf (Accessed: 19 December 2022).

Kingsnorth, S. (2019). *Digital Marketing Strategy. An Integrated Approach to Online Marketing.* 2nd ed. London: Kogan Page.

Kolb, B. M. (2021) *Marketing Strategy for the Creative and Cultural Industries.* 2nd ed. Abingdon: Routledge.

Kotler, N. G., Kotler, P. and Kotler, W. I. (2008) *Museum Marketing & Strategy: Designing Missions, Building Audiences, Generating Revenue and Resources.* San Francisco: Jossey-Bass.

Kotler, P. (2017) *"Welcome to the Age of Demarketing" – Philip Kotler.* Available at: https://www.marketingjournal.org/welcome-to-the-age-of-demarketing-an-excerpt-from-philip-kotlers-autobiography-philip-kotler/ (Accessed: 13 January 2023).

Kotler, P. (2018) *'Father of Modern Marketing' Philip Kotler on Avoiding Brand Decay and Preparing for Disruption.* Available at: https://www.marketingweek.com/philip-kotler-modern-marketing/ (Accessed: 22 February 2023).

Kulturanalys, Swedish Agency for Cultural Policy Analysis (2023). *Fri entré till museer.* [Report in Swedish]. Available at: https://kulturanalys.se/wp-content/uploads/2023/04/Fri-entre-till-museer-webb.pdf (Accessed: 4 May 2023).

Latapí Agudelo, M. A., Jóhannsdóttir, L. and Davídsdóttir, B. (2019) 'A Literature Review of the History and Evolution of Corporate Social Responsibility', *International Journal of Corporate Social Responsibility*, 4(1). Available at: 10.1186/s40991-018-0039-y (Accessed: 25 January 2023).

Lehmannová, M. (2020) *224 years of Defining the Museum.* Available at: https://icom.museum/wp-content/uploads/2020/12/2020_ICOM-Czech-Republic_224-years-of-defining-the-museum.pdf. (Accessed: 16 September 2022).

Lindstrom, M. (2008) *buy•ology. How Everything We Believe About Why We Buy is Wrong.* London: Random House Business Books.

Market Research Society (2023) *Code of Conduct.* Available at: https://www.mrs.org.uk/standards/code-of-conduct (Accessed: 21 May 2023).

Martin, A. (2003) *The Impact of Free Entry to Museums.* Available at: https://www.ipsos.com/sites/default/files/publication/1970-01/sri-the-impact-of-free-entry-to-museums-2003.pdf (Accessed: 19 December 2022).

Mason, R., Robinson, A. and Coffield, E. (2018) *Museum and Gallery Studies. The Basics.* Oxon: Routledge.

McLean, F. (2002) *Marketing the Museum.* London: Routledge.

Middleton, M. (2022) 'Early Childhood Education: Laying the Foundation', in *Welcoming Young Children into Museums*, pp. 16–39. A Practical Guide. Oxon: Routledge.

Middleton, M. (2022) 'Queer museum narratives and the family audience', in A. Langar (ed.) *Storytelling in Museums*, pp. 163–175. London: Rowman & Littlefield.

Miltenburg, A. (2017) *Brand the Change.* Amsterdam: BIS Publishers.

Molson, K. (2022) *2022 Visitor Attraction Website Report.* Available at: https://www.rubbercheese.com/insights/2022-visitor-attraction-website-report/ (Accessed: 9 December 2022).

Moorman, C. (2023) *The CMO Survey. Managing Brand, Growth, and Metrics. Highlights and Insights Report March 2023.* Available at: https://cmosurvey.org/results/ (Accessed: 3 May 2023).

Morris Hargreaves McIntyre (no date) *Culture Segments*. Available at: https://www.mhminsight.com/culture-segments/ (Accessed: 3 December 2022).

Münster, M. (2021) *I'm Afraid Debbie from Marketing Has Left For the Day*. London: Laurence King Publishing.

Murawski, M. (2020) *A Moment for Accountability, Transformation & Real Questions*. Available at: https://www.museumsarenotneutral.com/learn-more/real-questions-for-transformation (Accessed: 25 January 2023).

Museum Accreditation (2018) *Accreditation Standard*. Available at: https://www.artscouncil.org.uk/supporting-arts-museums-and-libraries/uk-museum-accreditation-scheme/accreditation-how-apply (Accessed: 23 February 2023).

Museums Are Not Neutral (no date) *Join the Movement*. Available at: https://www.museumsarenotneutral.com/ (Accessed: 24 September 2022).

The Museums Association (2020) *Code of Ethics for Museums*. Available at: https://www.museumsassociation.org/app/uploads/2020/06/20012016-code-of-ethics-single-page-8.pdf (Accessed: 25 January 2023).

National Lottery Heritage Fund (no date) *Inclusive Heritage*. Available at: https://www.heritagefund.org.uk/our-work/inclusion (Accessed: 25 September 2022).

Naylor, R., McLean, B., and Griffiths, C. (2016) *Character Matters: Attitudes, Behaviours and Skills in the UK Museum Workforce*. Available at: https://www.artscouncil.org.uk/sites/default/files/download-file/Museums%20Workforce%20ABS%20BOP%20Final%20Report.pdf (Accessed: 8 March 2023).

One Further (2022) *The Cultural Content Report 2022*. Available at: https://onefurther.com/resources/cultural-content-report-2022 (Accessed: 7 April 2023).

Pine, B. J. and Gilmore, J. H. (2020) *The Experience Economy*. Boston: Harvard Business Review Press.

Rentschler, R. (2007) 'Museum marketing: no longer a dirty word', in R. Rentschler & A. Hede (eds.) *Museum Marketing: Competing in the Global Marketplace*, pp. 12–20. Burlington: Routledge.

Rosen, E. (2009) *The Anatomy of Buzz Revisited. Real-life Lessons in Word-of-Mouth Marketing*. New York: Doubleday.

Salonlahti, O. and Salovaara, S. (eds.) (2022) *Accessibility and Diversity Checklist for Museums*. Translated by Heiskanen, S. Culture for All Service / For Culture on Equal Terms and The Finnish National Committee of ICOM. Available at: https://www.kulttuuriakaikille.fi/accessibility_checklists (Accessed: 14 March 2023).

Sargeant, A. and Wymer, W. (2018) *The Routledge Companion to Nonprofit Marketing*. Abingdon: Routledge.

SHARE Museums East (2023) *Annual Museums Survey East of England 2021–22*. Available at: https://infogram.com/1pzm59yvjnwm15i25eevn3ldjmi1dpqnxn7 (Accessed: 2 February 2023).

Simon, N. (2010) *The Participatory Museum*. Santa Cruz: Museum.

Sinek, S. (2019) *Start with Why*. London: Penguin Business.

Smilanksy, S. (2013) *Experiential Marketing. A Practical Guide to Interactive Brand Experiences*. London: Kogan Page.

Smithsonian Institution (2001) *Audience Building: Marketing Art Museums*. Available at: https://www.si.edu/content/opanda/docs/rpts2001/01.10.marketingart.final.pdf (Accessed: 18 April 2023).

Staves, J. (2019) *The Story Behind Stories and Our Journalistic Approach to Digital Content*. Available at: https://stacks.wellcomecollection.org/the-story-behind-stories-

and-our-journalistic-approach-to-digital-content-ad196b8665ab (Accessed: 12 March 2023).

Taking Part (2020) *National Statistics. Museums - Taking Part Survey 2019/20*. Available at: https://www.gov.uk/government/statistics/taking-part-201920-museums/museums-taking-part-survey-201920 (Accessed: 20 September 2022).

UK Evaluation Society (2019) *Guidelines for Good Practice in Evaluation*. Available at: https://www.evaluation.org.uk/app/uploads/2019/04/UK-Evaluation-Society-Guidelines-for-Good-Practice-in-Evaluation.pdf (Accessed: 9 April 2023).

UNESCO (2015) *Recommendation Concerning the Protection and Promotion of Museums and Collections, Their Diversity and their Role in Society*. Available at: https://unesdoc.unesco.org/ark:/48223/pf0000246331 (Accessed: 11 January 2023).

Unlimited (2020) *Accessible Marketing Guide*. Available at: https://weareunlimited.org.uk/resource/accessible-marketing-guide/ (Accessed: 10 January 2023).

Vocal Eyes (2022) *Heritage Access 2022*. Available at: https://vocaleyes.co.uk/research/heritage-access-2022/ (Accessed: 11 January 2023).

Wadeson, I. (2003) *Seminar: Audience Development – Unpacking the Baggage*. Available at: https://www.culturehive.co.uk/wp-content/uploads/2014/01/Audience-Development-Unpacking-the-baggage..Ivan-Wadeson..20031.pdf (Accessed: 21 September 2022).

Walmsley, B., Gilmore, A., O'Brien, D. and Torreggiani, A. (eds.) (2022) *Culture in Crisis*. Available at: https://www.culturehive.co.uk/wp-content/uploads/2022/01/Culture_in_Crisis.pdf (Accessed: 20 September 2022).

What Next? (2021) *#BAMEOver – A Statement for the UK*. Available at: https://www.whatnextculture.co.uk/bameover-a-statement-for-the-uk/ (Accessed: 24 April 2023).

Whitaker, S. (2018) *Hurdles to the Participation Of Children, Families and Young People in Museums: A Literature Review*. Available at: https://kidsinmuseums.org.uk/wp-content/uploads/2018/12/Hurdles-to-Participation.pdf (Accessed: 24 February 2023).

Witkowski, T. H. and Jones, D. G. B. (2016) 'Historical Research in Marketing: Literature, Knowledge, and Disciplinary Status', *Information & Culture*, 51(3), pp. 399–418. Available at: 10.7560/IC51305 (Accessed: 22 February 2023).

World Economic Forum (2022) *The First Alliance to Accelerate Digital Inclusion*. Available at: https://www.weforum.org/impact/digital-inclusion/ (Accessed: 5 January 2023).

Index

4Cs 100
4Ps *see* marketing mix
7Ps 59–60, 100–105, 200

accessible marketing 177–82, 187–8; definition of 177–8; formats 180; language 182; principles of 178–9
action plan 98–105, 128
activism: against and within museums 193; brand 191; by museums 192
advertising 20, 22–3, 160, 163, 165–7; ethics of 23, 197; history of 22; messages 23; public distrust in 174
American Alliance of Museums 8, 15, 192, 197
American Marketing Association 20, 22, 200
American Museum of Natural History, New York 194
analytics 47, 102, 117
Ansoff Matrix 90–2
Apartheid Museum, South Africa 14
Artificial Intelligence (AI) 26, 201
arts marketing 20; definition of 20; overlap with audience development 31
Arts Marketing Association 31, 46, 163
Ashmolean, The, UK 11
Association of Independent Museums (AIM) 79, 149
audience development 20, 46, 76, 162; definition of 30–1; inclusive 182; pricing and 150–1; why undertake 31–2
audience journey 70–1, 164–5, 174
audience research 32–7, 61–3, 66–7, 79, 117
audiences 11, 21, 29–39, 128, 159; children 64, 150; core or traditional 32–3; definition of 29–30; demographics 75–6; disabled 150–1, 177; diversity 149–50; engagement 11, 62, 182; ethnicity 37, 79, 182; existing 75; family 32, 34, 79–80, 99, 150, 160; growth 76; identifying channels to reach 160–2; loyalty 118–19; making decisions about 75–83, 126–7; motivation 33–5, 62; new 37–8, 63, 70, 73, 167; satisfaction 62; target 75–85, 126–7; underrepresented 35–7; what they value 13

Barbican, London 153
Barnsley Museums, UK 39, 130
barriers to engagement 15, 35–7, 169
Beamish Museum, UK 130
benchmarking data 75–6, 99, 163
billboards *132*, 162, 167
Birmingham Museum and Art Gallery, UK 192
Black Lives Matter 12
blockbuster exhibitions 25, 198
BP (British Petroleum) 195
branding 137–44; definition of 138; the importance of 139
brands 137–44; awareness 25, 162, 174; definition of 138; history of 25; museums as 139
British Museum 10, 192
budget 107–12, 129; setting your 107–10; tips 111–12

calls to action (CTA) 173
Chartered Institute of Marketing, The (CIM) 20, 22, 195

Children's Museum of Indianapolis, The, USA 155
climate crisis 11, 24–5, **66**, 198
Climate Museum UK 192
code(s) of conduct 22–3
codes(s) of ethics 195–7
communication 20, 24, 101; internal 48–9; purpose of 169–170
communication channels 128–9, 159–68, 202; deciding on 160; digital 161–2; non-digital 161–2; how to use 163–4
competition 24, 147
competitor analysis 63–5
Cooper Gallery, The, UK 39
consultation 38, 98, 102, 141, 179; *see also* audience research
consumers 22–3, 196–7
content: marketing 111, 163, 167; pillars 102; plan 101–102, 128; warnings 184–5
conversion 74, 104, 120, 191; macro 74; micro 74; rates 72, 74, **129**, 160
Corporate Social Responsibility (CSR) 191
Covid-19 pandemic 156–7, 162, 171, 181, 198; and audiences 38–9; and digital engagement 38–9
culture wars 143
customers 20; *see also* audiences

decolonisation 12, 25, 192
demarketing 197
Denver Museum of Nature & Science, USA 157
Design Museum, London 157
digital: engagement 38–9, 59, 156–7; exclusion 162; marketing 101, 163, 174, 198
disability 36, 79–80, 141, 178–9, 181–2, 185; and pricing 150–1, 153
Disneyfication 12, 19
diversification 76, 94
Dual Bottom Line Matrix 92–4

email marketing **67**, **87**, 110, 128, 167, 173
ethical marketing 24, 27, 190–203, 197–203; frameworks 198–200
ethics 25; approaches to 190–1; definition of 190
evaluation 49, 73, 129; challenges 122; definition of 114; front-end 114, 127; formative 114, 127; methods of 116–21; summative 114; tips 122–3
Experience Economy 12
Extinction Rebellion 193, 195

Facebook 159, 163, 167, 202
features and benefits 171
Floyd, George 24, 183
Food Museum, UK 140–4
fundraising 25, 46, 47, 54, 58, 173, 193–5

German Historical Museum 34
Getty Museum, USA 161
goals 126, 147; definition of 69; examples of 69–70, 72, 73, 98–9
Google 47, 102, 169
Guggenheim Museum: New York 194; Spain 12

Historic Royal Palaces, UK 184
Hong Kong Museum of History 200

Imperial War Museums 201–2
inclusive marketing 177, 182–8; content 183–4; definition of 178; example of 184; language 186–7
income 58, 76, 147; generation 20, 193–4
Instagram 131, 163, 184, 202
International Council of Museums (ICOM) 9, 25, 31, 39, 192, 197
Ipswich Museum, UK 39

Jane Austen's House, UK 83–4

key messages 128, 172–3
Kids in Museums 36–7, 150, 154, 187
Kotler, Philip 22, 197
KPIs (key performance indicators) 129; definition of 72; examples of 72–3

leaflets 25, 37, 47, 162–3, 170, 191
LGBTQ+: LGBT+ History Month 183; people 186; rights 190
Lisser Art Museum, the Netherlands 39
logo *19*, 21, 137, *142–3*
London Transport Museum 154
Louvre: Abu Dhabi, UAE 139; France 9, 139

Manchester Museum, UK 11
market extension 93
market penetration 91

marketer 15, 19, 25–26, 199
marketing: Above the Line 160;
    advocating for 49–50; Below the
    Line 160; budgets 25, 47, 61,
    109–11, 129, 163; cause-related
    196; criticisms of 18–19;
    development of 21–3; definition
    of 18–20; function 31, 45–9,
    103–4, 182, 183; funnel 128–9;
    'good' 26–7; impact of 116;
    inbound 166–7; low-budget 47,
    110–11; outbound 166–7; pull
    166–7; push 166–7; responsibility
    for 45–9, 54, 106–7; social 25, 196;
    values-based 196
marketing campaign 125–33, 174, 201;
    examples of 130–3, 201;
    framework 125
marketing mix 22, 59–60, 100–105, 200
marketing strategy 58; framework 55;
    pitfalls 55; tips 56; why develop
    a 53
measuring: awareness and perceptions
    120; engagement 120–1
memberships 13, 32, 114, 126, 165; and
    pricing 152, 157; and renewal **67**,
    70–1, **73**, **87**, 99, 104, 119
messaging: frequency 174; powerful 173;
    and segmentation 171; timing
    173–4; visual 174–5
Metropolitan Museum of Art, The, New
    York 9
mission 13, 20–1, 58, 138, 142, 147, 201;
    statement 13
monitoring 49, 129; definition of 113; tips
    122–3
Morris Hargreaves McIntyre 81, 127, 171
museum(s): accreditation 27; challenges
    facing 8, 11–12, 15, 25; definition
    of 9–10; evolution of 10–12;
    funding 7, 23, 25, 93, 146–7;
    perceptions of 8–9; purpose of 13,
    15; trust in 8
museum marketing 20–21; development
    of 23–6; definition of 20–21
Museum of Art & Photography (MAP),
    India 131
Museum of Cambridge, The, UK 47, 127
Museum of Contemporary Art, Los
    Angeles 193
Museum of East Anglian Life, UK
    140, 142
Museum of Homelessness, London 192

Museum of Modern Art (MOMA), New
    York 193
Museum of Norwich, England 152
Museum of Old and New Art (Mona),
    Australia 130
Museum of the History of Catalonia,
    The, Spain 34
Museums Aotearoa, New Zealand 192
Museums Are Not Neutral 193
Museums Association, The 11, 192,
    197, 202

National Gallery, The, London 127,
    156, 194
National Historical Museum of Athens,
    The, Greece 34
National Museum of Estonia 34
National Museum of Ireland 34
National Museum of Scotland 34, 102–3
National Portrait Gallery, London 194
Natural History Museum, The, London
    9, 14, 131–2
news release 19, 115, 126, 128
Nordiska Museet, Sweden 34

objectives 126; definition of 71; examples
    of 71–3; SMART 74, 113, 129
Open-Air Museum of Latvia, The 34
organisational culture 48, 183
outcomes 69, 71, 115, 118, 123
outputs 71, 115

Parthenon Marbles 192
People's History Museum, UK 185, 192
personalisation 26, 171–2, 199
PESO Model™ 160, 165–7
PEST *see* STEEPLE
Philadelphia Museum of Art, USA 193
philanthropy 25; toxic 194
positioning 15, 58, 127–8; definition of
    94; map 95–6; strategy 94–5
Postal Museum, The, London 46–7, 187
posters *132*, 162, 167
press release *see* news release
pricing 59, 101, 146–57; audience
    research on 149–51;
    communication of 151;
    concessions 153–4; decisions
    around 146–7, 149–50; digital
    products 156–7; dynamic 154–5;
    elasticity of demand 147–8;
    factors affecting 147–8; free
    admission 149–50; inclusive

150–1; Pay What You Decide/Can 155–6; types of pricing 152–6; variable 154

printed marketing materials 25, 106, 109, 122, 163, 191, 198
process 60, 104, 200
product(s) 12–13, 15, 21, 59, 100; definition of 12–13; development 92; examples of 12–13; strategies 87–94
Product life cycle 89–90
promotion 18, 20, 59–60, 101, 200
publicity 18, 47, 195
public relations 90, 110–11, 126, 193

qualitative evaluation 71; definition of 114–15; examples of 114–15
quantitative evaluation 71; definition of 114; examples of 114–15

Rahmi M. Koç Museum, Turkey 99
repeat visits 101, 118, 146
Return on investment (ROI) 119–20, 160
Rijksmuseum, The, Netherlands 34, 133
Royal Academy of Arts, London 193
Royal Ontario Museum, The, Canada 161

Santa Cruz Museum of Art and History, USA 14
schools marketing **64**, 74, **77**, **88**, 99, 148, 170
Science Museum, London 195
segmentation 19, 24, 61, 76–84, 117–18; behavioural 80–1; choosing a system 82–3; demographic 79–80; geographic 78–9; and messaging 170–1; psychographic 81–2; types of 78–82
SEO, search engine optimisation 161, 167, 180–1
services 20, 59, 88, 100–101, 126; ethics and 191, 197; pricing of 108, 146, 148, 153
situational analysis 57–68, 70, 75, 125–6
social media 26, 47, 115–6, 160–2, 170, 184, 202; policies 184; trolling 184
sponsorship 25, 194
stakeholders 8, 15, 54, 63, 126, 199
STEEPLE analysis 57, 65–6

storytelling 21, 103
strategic marketing *19*, 127; definition of 52; examples of 98–99
suppliers 47–8, 129–30
sustainability 25, 190, 197–8
SWOT analysis 67–8, 70, 86, 93, 126

tactical marketing *19*, 98–105, 128–9; definition of 52; examples of 98–9
target audiences 61, 99, 126, 147
Tate, UK 14
technology 23, 26
TikTok 159
timescales 53–4, 106
tone of voice 95, 130, 138, 175, 187
touchpoints 164–5
tourism 12, 76, 160, 197–8
The Tower of London 154
TOWS analysis 86–7, 93
trademarks 25, 137
Twitter 131

user experience 30, 60, 104
user-generated content 128, 159, 184
USP (Unique Selling Point or Proposition) 65, 94

value for money 148–9
values 25, 58, 142–3, 147, 169, 199–202
the Van Gogh Museum, the Netherlands 200
vanity metrics 72, 116
Victoria and Albert Museum (V&A), London 193–4
vision 13, 58, 138, 142; statement 13–4
visitor surveys 34, 79, 117; *see also* audience research
visitors *see* audiences

website 116–7, 120, 161, 163–4, 166–7, 169, 187
Wellcome Collection, London 164
Western Australian Museum, The 200

Wonderbound, USA 162
York Castle Museum, UK 94
York Museums Trust, UK 131
York's Chocolate Story, UK 94
YouTube 180

For Product Safety Concerns and Information please contact our EU
representative GPSR@taylorandfrancis.com
Taylor & Francis Verlag GmbH, Kaufingerstraße 24, 80331 München, Germany

www.ingramcontent.com/pod-product-compliance
Lightning Source LLC
Chambersburg PA
CBHW051356290426
44108CB00015B/2039